PROMISING PHARMACEUTICALS

Edited by **Purusotam Basnet**

Promising Pharmaceuticals
Edited by Purusotam Basnet

Published by InTech
Janeza Trdine 9, 51000 Rijeka, Croatia

Publishing Process Manager Ana Skalamera

Technical Editor Teodora Smiljanic

Cover Designer InTech Design Team

Additional hard copies can be obtained from orders@intechopen.com

Promising Pharmaceuticals, Edited by Purusotam Basnet
p. cm.
ISBN 978-953-51-0631-9

For EU product safety concerns:
IN TECH d.o.o., Prolaz Marije Krucifikse Kozulić 3, 51000 Rijeka, Croatia,
info@intechopen.com or visit our website at intechopen.com.

Meet the editor

Dr. Purusotam Basnet received his Ph.D. in Pharmaceutical Sciences from Toyama Medical and Pharmaceutical University, Japan (Monbusho Fellowship), did Post-doctoral researches in same university and as Alexander-von-Humboldt Fellow in Heidelberg University and Boehringer Mannheim, Germany. Before joining current position as the Head of IVF Laboratory, Department of Obstetrics and Gyaenocology, University Hospital of North Norway, he served as Visiting Associate Professor in Toyama Medical and Pharmaceutical University and Visiting Professor in Ehime University, Japan. He established new B.Pharm, M.Pharm. and BMLT programs in Pokhara University, Nepal where he served as Professor, Program Director, Dean and members of University apex bodies. Dr. Basnet has been involved in drug discovery-development researches for more than 22 years and published more than 80 original research papers and more than 100 other scientific contributions as patents, reviews, proceeding papers and others.

Contents

Preface

Today, we live almost twice longer than the generations living in the beginning of the last century. Our life expectancy has increased 35-70 years in the last 100 years. There are several factors which are important for our longer and healthier life. One very important factor is a better understanding of the human biology. Scientists are making new breakthroughs every day. Better understanding of human biology also taught us how to improve sanitation, hygiene and fight against diseases. In order to live a longer and healthier life, human body should be maintained in normal physiology without serious interferences with the environmental factors. Food and drugs play very important role in normal physiology. Food is a main source providing all needed components to maintain normal physiological conditions in a healthy body. However, with the chronic and/or acute change of environmental factors such as temperature, radiation, vibrations, magnetic fields and also invasion of microbial or chemical pathogens into the normal body, normal physiological conditions of the body can not remain as such. Often normal physiological conditions will be changed because of the internal factors such as DNA or enzyme induction and functions. Whether the factors are internal or external, the patho-physiologic conditions make our body deviate from normal functions – it is what we call disease condition. In a case of a disease, the special chemicals, care and food are important for the body i.e. the facilitation of biological reactions to bring back the body into the normal physiology by medical treatment.

The knowledge advancement on human biology and development of technical tools in the field of medical treatment led us discover and develop new and advanced drugs. In fact, drugs are pharmacologically active chemical substances specially designed or formulated to be useful to the human body. As opposed to food, drug substance is used for a body system which is not in a normal condition. Therefore, discovery, production, distribution, and the phase of administration of patients' quality assurance has to be controlled with a technological procedure and tight regulations to make the system as effective as possible for the benefit of human health. Our book provides selected but vital information on the sources, tools, technologies and regulations regarding the current status of medicine development. The knowledge which helped drug substance to be used in medicine is tremendously increased in the last hundred years. In spite of this a search for safe and more effective drug/medicine is still an important part of the research. Therefore this book especially provides some selected updates on vital information in the field of pharmaceutical sciences. The information provided in our book cover information on the source, discovery, and regulations of the drugs.

March 3, 2012

Purusotam Basnet
Tromsø,
Norway,

1

Modern Medicine and Pharmaceutics

Purusotam Basnet
*Drug Transport and Delivery Research Group, Department of Pharmacy;
In vitro Fertilization Laboratory, Department of Obstetrics and Gynaecology,
University Hospital of North Norway and Women's Health and Perinatology
Research Group, Department of Clinical Medicine,
University of Tromsø, Tromsø,
Norway*

1. Introduction

There are evidences that people have been using medicine to cure illness from the early civilization in Africa, Asia and Europe. The wide varieties of treatments such as Shamanism, surgery and drug formulations have been practiced. The drug materials from the plants, animals, minerals were used for the medicinal purposes, are referred today as "Crude Drugs". As knowledge on disease and drugs is expanded further and more purified form of the materials were chosen to prepare further effective drugs and medicines. As the development of modern societies immersed in the world, two different philosophical approaches in the field of medicinal treatment came forward. In the Eastern societies such as in China and India, holistic approaches were adopted. In these societies, disease or illness is considered as an integral part of the body and can be corrected with the selected foods or formulation of crude drugs mainly derived from plants and a few from animals or minerals together with the body adoptation. But in contrast, in the Western society, disease is considered as the separate entity from the body and can be eliminated by surgery or using particular chemical substance. Especially in the western medicine, the practice of using purified form or pure chemical substances is developed. The knowledge on chemical sciences especially synthetic chemistry and purification techniques were rigorously developed to fulfil the need of chemical substance. This led to not only the foundation for the development of science and technology but also the concept of industrialization came forward.

In general, pure chemical substance is not administered directly to the disease condition to cure or treat the disease. Depending on the disease condition and chemical nature of the drug substance, several kinds of formulation and route of administration are in practice. Therapeutic effect of the drug substance will only be achieved, if the right chemical substance with sufficient amount be delivered in the targeted tissue sites for the sufficient length of time in the person having pathophysiological condition. Formulations play great roles in distributing drugs in the body. Moreover, according to the type and condition of the disease, same drug substance might provide separate therapeutic effects based on the types of formulation, route and interval of administrations. In general, the term 'drug' represents pharmacologically active chemical substance. Pharmaceutical sciences provide the knowledge and technique to utilize the drug substance for the effective therapy. In recent years, because of the advancement in pharmaceutical sciences, several drug substances are better utilized for the health benefit. Pharmaceutical industries contributed enormously for the advancement of modern medicine together with the development of particular the formulation for desired route of administration in order to obtain optimum therapeutic value of the drugs substance.

2. Historical overview on the development of modern drugs

In fact, many of the drug substances which are used today commercially have certain historical links to the traditional uses. Among them, the history of morphine and acetyl salicylic acid (aspirin) are widely discussed and well documented.

There are evidences of using latex of opium plant (*Papaverum somniferum*) in Chinese traditional medicine, Ayurveda, and Ancient Greek medicine to relieve pain. The desire to obtain more effective and purer drug has always been remained as the deep thrust in human nature. The first report of morphine purification was made by Derosne in 1803 and further detail was published by Seguin in 1814. (Derosne, 1803; Seguin, 1814). A German pharmacist, Sertürner claimed the first purification of active compound from opium latex and published in 1805, later it was found that the isolated compound was not an alkaline narcotic component rather it was identified as meconic acid (Sertürner, 1805; 1806). On continuing, Sertürner extracted the opium poppy latex with hot water and precipitated with ammonia and obtained a pure crystalline compound having narcotic properties of opium (Sertürner, 1817). The compound was named as morphine (**1**) and structure was confirmed later. In 1874, Wright reported heroin (**2**), a diacetyl derivative of morphine (Wright, 1874), and it was commercialised by Bayer AG in 1898. Because of the strong narcotic properties, heroin was banned for the therapeutic use but morphine and codeine (**3**), another derivative of morphine, are still very important commercial drugs today after almost 200 years of their discovery (**Figure 1**).

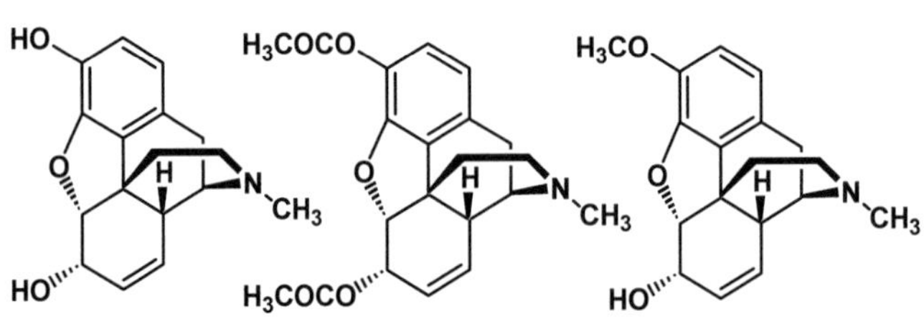

Morphine (1) Heroin (2) Codeine (3)

Fig. 1. Structure of morphine and its derivatives.

After extraction and purification of morphine, the technique was applied to isolate other important alkaloids and they were commercialized immediately. In 1817, Pelletier and co-worker reported emetine (**4**) from *Ipecacuanha* and strychnine (**5**) from *Strychnos* (Pelletier, 1817). In 1820, same group reported the isolation of quinine (**6**) from *Cincona* species (Pelletier, 1820) which was commercialized as the anti-malarial drug. Other important alkaloids such as brucine (**7**) and caffeine (**8**) in 1819, colchecin (**9**) in 1920, codeine (**3**) in 1833, atropine (**10**) in 1848 were isolated (Nicolaou & Montagnon, 2008). The complete structures of many of these compounds were confirmed later. Coniine (**11**) was isolated in

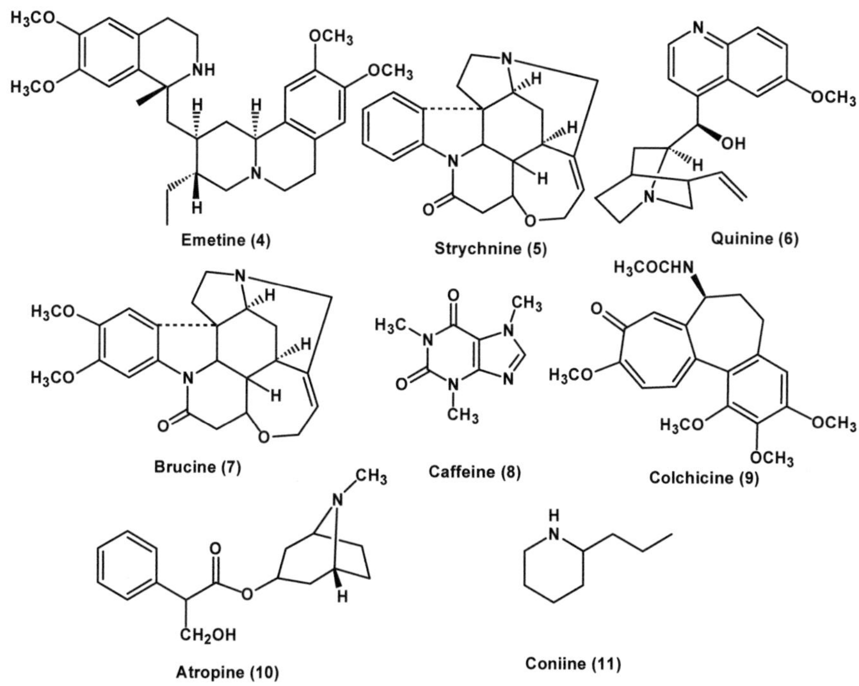

Fig. 2. Structure of alkaloids having therapeutic and commercial uses. Discovery of these alkaloids led to the foundation for the modern medicine and industrialisation.

1826, complete structure was elucidated in 1870 and later synthesized in 1881. All these drugs with almost of 200 years of history are still used in commercial scale (**Figure 2**) (Newman, 2010).

Another important modern drug with long history and widely discussed molecule is acetyl salicylic acid (aspirin) (**13**). In spite of development of several effective antipyretic drugs the importance of aspirin has never been diminished.

Acetylsalicylic acid (**13**), an acetyl-derivative of salicylic acid (**14**), is a mild, non-narcotic analgesic. It is useful in the relief of headache and muscle and joint aches. The drug works by inhibiting prostaglandins production which sensitizes nerve endings to pain. The discovery of aspirin (**13**) is linked to **14**, salicyl aldehyde (**15**) and salicin (**16**), a chemical component derived from the bark of Willow tree.

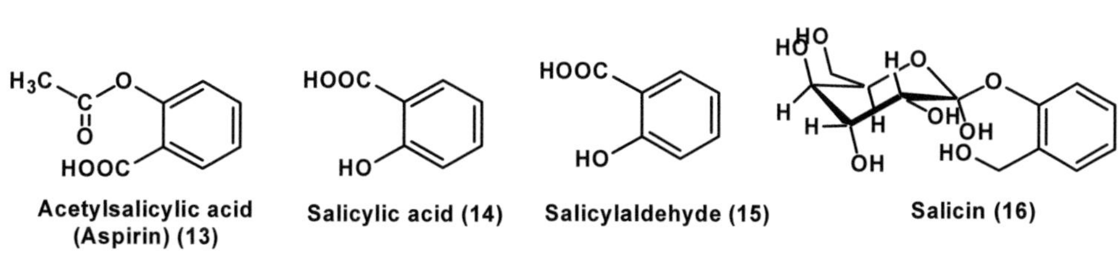

Fig. 3. Structure of aspirin and other related compounds. Salicin, a compound isolated from the bark of Willow tree led to the discovery of aspirin.

Hippocrates (460-377 B.C.), the father of modern medicine, described the prescription of using the powder made from the bark of the willow tree for the treatment of headaches, pains and fevers. By 1829, scientists discovered that the pain relieving compound as salicin (**16**) in willow plants. The active ingredient in willow bark was isolated by Johann Buchner, a tiny amount of bitter tasting yellow, needle-like crystals, which he called salicin. Two Italians, Brugnatelli and Fontana, had in fact already obtained salicin in 1826, but in a highly impure form. In 1829, Henri Leroux had extracted salicin, in crystalline form for the first time, and in 1839, Raffaele Piria succeeded in obtaining the salicylic acid by oxidation (Piria, 1839) (**Figure 3**). Although salicylic acid was found with analgesic and antipyretic properties, its strong side effect of stomach upsetting could not be utilized clinically. A French chemist, Charles Frederic Gerhardt in 1853, neutralized the side effect of salicylic acid by buffering it with sodium hydroxide (sodium salicylate) and acetyl chloride, creating acetylsalicylic acid. Gerhardt's discovery could not be commercialized (Gerhardt, 1853; Nicolaou & Montagnon, 2008).

In 1899, a German chemist, Felix Hoffmann, who worked for Bayer, rediscovered Gerhardt's formula. Felix Hoffmann made the formula for the treatment of his father who was suffering from the pain of arthritis. With good results, Bayer marketed the new wonder drug (Nicolaou & Montagnon, 2008). Aspirin was patented on February 27, 1900. The name Aspirin was given to- 'A' for acetyl, the "spir" for *Spiraea ulmaria* (source of salicylic acid) and 'in' for ending name for medicine.

Year	Drug substance	Therapeutic uses
1806	Morphine	Analgesic, sedative
1875	Salicylic acid	Analgesic, antipyretic
1884	Cocaine	CNS stimulant (serotonin-dopamin-norepinephrine reuptake inhibitor), local anesthetic
1888	Phenacetin	Analgesic, antipyretic
1889	Acetyl salicylic acid	Analgesic, antipyretic (cyclooxygenase inhibitor)
1903	Barbiturate	Sedative
1909	Arsphenamine	Treatment for syphilis and trypanosomiasis
1921	Procain	local anesthetics (sodium channel blocker)
1922	Insulin	Anti-diabetic
1928	Estron	Sex hormone
1928	Penicillin	Anti-biotic
1935	Sulphachrysoidin	Anti-bacterial
1944	Streptomycin	Anti-biotic
1945	Chloroquin	Anti-malarial
1952	Chloropromazin	Anti-psychotic (neuroleptic)
1956	Tolbutamide	Oral anti-diabetic
1960	Chlordiazepoxide	Tranquilizer
1962	Verapamil	Anti-hypertensive (calcium channel blocker)
1963	Propranolol	Beta-blocker (used for hypertension, anxiety and panic)
1964	Furosemide	Diuretics (congestive heart failure and edema)
1971	L-DOPA	Neurotransmitter (Parkinson's disease)
1975	Nifedipine	Calcium channel blocker (anti-hypertensive)
1976	Cimetidine	H_2-blocker (peptic ulcer)
1981	Captopril	Angiotensin-converting enzyme (ACE)-blocker (anti-hypertensive)
1981	Ranitidin	H_2-blocker (peptic ulcer)
1983	Cyclosporin A	Immunosupressive
1984	Enalapril	ACE-blocker (anti-hypertensive)
1985	Mefloquin	Anti-malarial
1986	Fluoxetin	Anti-dipressant (serotonin reuptake inhibitor)
1987	Artemisinin	Anti-malarial
1987	Lovastatin	Hypolipidemic (prevention of cardiovascular disease)
1988	Omeprazole	Proton pump inhibitor (Anti-ulcer)
1990	Ondansetron	5-HT3-Bolcker (anti-emetic)
1991	Sumatriptan	Anti-migraine headaches
1993	Risperidone	Anti-psychotic (Schizophrenia)

The list of drugs in the table was adopted from Böhm et al, 2002 with modification (Böhm et al, 2002).

Table 1. A list of some important modern medicines in chronological order of discovery with therapeutic uses.

In the beginning, aspirin was sold in the powder form but in 1915, the first aspirin tablets were marketed. Aspirin and heroin were once trademarks of Bayer. After Germany lost World War I, Bayer was forced to give up both trademarks as part of the Treaty of Versailles in 1919 (Belis, 2012).

In addition to morphine and aspirin, there are several other chemical substances which initiated the industrialization and changed our social structure due to the development of corporate culture and globalization trends for the discovery of modern medicine. A list of some important drugs with their therapeutic uses and chronological order of discovery are given in **Table 1.**

3. Pharmaceutical Industry

3.1 Development of pharmaceutical industry

Merck in Germany was possibly the earliest company founded in Darmstadt in 1668. In 1827, Heinrich Emanuel Merck began the transition towards an industrial and scientific concern, by manufacturing and selling alkaloids (Merck Group History, 2012). GlaxoSmithKline's origins can be traced back to 1715, it was only in the middle of the 19th century that Beecham became involved in the industrial production of medicine, producing patented medicine from 1842, and the world's first factory for producing only medicines in 1859 (GSK History, 2012).

In the USA, Pfizer was founded in 1849, by two German immigrants, initially as a fine chemicals business. They expanded rapidly during the American civil war as demand for painkillers and antiseptics rocketed (Pfizer History, 2012). Whilst Pfizer was providing the medicines needed for the Union war effort, a young cavalry commander named Colonel Eli Lilly was serving in their army. A trained pharmaceutical chemist, Lilly was an archetype of the dynamic and multi-talented 19th century American industrialist, who set up a pharmaceutical business in 1876 and was a pioneer of new methods in the industry, being one of the first to focus on R&D as well as manufacturing.

Pharmaceutical industries grew rapidly in number and size after the advancement of basic knowledge on the isolation and purification of chemical component from the crude drugs. In the meantime, it encouraged to the development of synthetic chemistry. The pharmacological properties of pure compound obtained either from isolation from natural resources or synthesized in the laboratories were studied. The public and private investments were carried on pharmaceutical industry and drug market expanded rapidly. The pharmaceutical industries established in the early history are still continuing today and their economic impact in the development of country is extremely crucial. Some of the pharmaceutical industries which initiate some important drugs in the early development of modern medicine are listed as in the **Table 2.**

3.2 Economic impact of the pharmaceutical industry

Today, the revenue collection by big pharmaceutical industry is bigger than that of national budge of many small and poor nations. Based on the revenue collection, top ten pharmaceutical industries are listed in **Table 3** (Roth et al., 2010)**.** Because of the huge investment of pharmaceutical industries, it led to open the research and development of

Year	Drug substance	Commercial resource	Producer
1826	Morphine (natural compound)	Plant	Merck
1899	Acetyl salicylic acid Aspirin (synthetic analogue)	Plant	Bayer
1941	Penicillin (natural compound)	Microbe	Merck
1964	Cephalothin (semi synthetic)	Microbe	Eli Lilly
1983	Cyclosporin A (natural compound)	Microbe	Sandoz
1987	Artemisinin (natural compound)	Plant	Baiyushan
1987	Lovastatin (natural compound)	Microbe	Merck
1988	Simvastatin (semi-synthetic)	Microbe	Merck
1989	Pravastatin (semi-synthetic)	Microbe	Snakyo/BMS
1990	Acarbose (natural compound)	Microbe	Bayer
1993	Paclitaxel (natural compound)	Plant	BMS
1993	FK506 (natural compound)	Microbe	Fujisawa
1994	Fluvastatin (synthetic analogue)	Microbe	Sandoz
1995	Docetaxel (semi-synthetic)	Plant	Rhone PR
1996	Topotecan (semi-synthetic)	Plant	SKB,Pharmacia-Upjohn
1996	Miglitol (synthetic analogue)	Plant, Microbes	Bayer

This table is taken from Grabley & Thiericke, 1999 with modification.

Table 2. Chronological order of commercialization of some important modern drugs.

further understanding in human biology and medicine. In the meantime, it is also partly responsible to widen the gap between rich and poor which made unstable and unhappy society. In term of wealth, these top pharmaceutical industries are able to challenge the whole nation and have power to change the social structure.

Top 10 pharmaceutical industries account for 59.40% of total revenue of the top 50 pharmaceutical companies. In the same top 20 pharmaceutical industries accounts for 81.53% of total revenue of the top 50 pharmaceutical companies. Therefore the global drug markets are dominated by a few large pharmaceutical industries. Several small pharmaceutical industries in developing countries are only able to produce generic drugs and their impact in the global market is negligibly small.

	Pharmaceutical Industry	Revenue (Millions USD)
1.	Pfizer	58,523
2.	Novartis	44,420
3.	Merck & Co.	39,811
4.	Sanofi-Aventis	37,403
5.	Glaxo-SmithKline	36,156
6.	AstraZeneca	32,515
7	Johnson & Johnson	22,396
8.	Eli Lilly & Co	21,685
9.	Abbott Laboratories	19,894
10.	Bristrol-Myers Squibb	19,484
11.	Teva	16,121
12	Takeda Pharma	14,829
13.	Bayer Schering	14,485
14.	Boehringer_Ingelheim	12,883
15.	Astellas	11,161
16.	Daiichi-Sankyo	10,794
17.	Eisai	8,542
18.	Otsuka Pharmaceutical	8,440
19.	Gilead Sciences	7,390
20.	Mylan	5,404

Table 3. Top twenty pharmaceutical companies based on 2010 revenues (in million USD).

3.3 The most industrialized drugs

Each year new and more effective drugs come into the market and they replace previous drugs. There is hard completion among the pharmaceutical industries to make more profit for their industry. In addition, some drugs because of unreported side effects, they have to be withdrawn from the market. Therefore it is difficult to stand top selling drug of all the time. According to revenue collection, a list of top ten selling drugs is listed in **Table 4** (Top ten selling drug, 2011). The revenue obtained by selling single drug is much higher than that of a national budget of a small and poor country.

Drug name	Treatment for	Produced by	Sale (billions)
1. Lipitor (Atorvastatin)	Statin i.e., a cholesterol-lowering drug. Lowers LDL cholesterol and triglyceride levels	Pfizer	13.5
2. Plavix (Clopidogrel)	Inhibits blood clots in arteries such as coronary, carotid and peripheral arteries of the limbs and prevents ischemia and thrombosis	Bristol-Myers Squibb & Sanofi-Aventis	7.3
3. Nexium (Esomeprazole)	A proton pump inhibitor (H^+/K^+-ATPase enzyme) which is used in the treatment of dyspepsia, peptic ulcer disease, gastro esophageal reflux disease.	AstraZeneca	7.27
4. Seretide/ Advair (Fluticasone+ salmeterol) -	It is a bronchodilator which relaxes the muscles in the walls of the small air passages in the lungs.	GlaxoSmith Kline	7.1
5. Enbrel (Etanercept)	A tumor necrosis factor (TNF)-blocker, is widely used in immune diseases (rheumatoid arthritis, juvenile idiopathic arthritis, ankylosing spondylitis, psoriatic arthritis, plaque psoriasis) and reduce inflammation.	Amgen and Wyeth	5.3
6. Zyprexa (Olanzapine)	An atypical antipsychotic used in the treatment of schizophrenia, depressive episodes associated with bipolar disorder, acute manic episodes and maintenance treatment in bipolar disorder.	Eli Lilly	5.3
7. Risperdal (Risperidone)	Risperidone is an antipsychotic used to treat schizophrenia including adolescent schizophrenia, the mixed and manic states associated with bipolar disorder, and irritability in children with autism.	Janssen-Cilag	4.9
8. Seroquel (Quetiapine)	An antipsychotic used in the management of schizophrenia and bipolar I disorder, including insomnia and anxiety disorders.	Astra Zeneca	4.6
9. Singulair (Montelukast sodium)	A leukotriene receptor antagonist used in the treatment of asthma and to relieve symptoms of seasonal allergies.	Merck & Co., Inc	4.5
10. Aranesp (Darbepoetin alfa)	A synthetic form of erythropoietin which stimulates erythropoiesis to treat anemia, commonly associated with chronic renal failure and cancer chemotherapy.	Amgen	4.4

Revenue collection is expressed as in 1 year (billion).

Table 4. Top ten pharmaceutical products world wide based on yearly revenue collection.

3.4 Global pharmaceutical market

The global pharmaceutical market grew to $808 billion in 2009, at a compound annual growth rate of 9.3% between 1999 and 2009. Year-on-year growth in the global pharmaceutical market decreased to 4.6% in 2009, largely as a result of cost containment in the US and major European markets and the impact of several blockbuster patent expiried in 2008 and 2009. Almost 125 pharmaceutical drugs generated more than 1 billion USD in global sales. The leading therapy areas by global pharmaceutical sales in 2009 were CNS with a 15.8% market share and cardiovascular with 14.5%. The CNS pharmaceutical market will decrease from $127.8 billion in 2009 to $118.5 billion in 2014. The major five Germany, France, Italy, Spain and the UK, together accounted for over 60% of all European pharmaceutical sales. The global pharmaceutical market is expected to earn over a trillion dollar in revenues by 2012 according to "Global Pharmaceutical Market Forecast to 2012". These include the shift of growth from the developed markets to the emerging ones, increasing focus on biotech-based drugs, fewer new drug approvals, and a strong growth in the prevalence of generics (Global market, 2012).

4. Role of pharmaceutical technology

4.1 Dosage form of modern medicine

In general, drugs are not administered as pure chemical substance alone rather given formulated preparation as medicines. With appropriate additives or excipients in the formulation, drug is administered to human body. The main objective of the using additives to prepare various dosage forms is to obtain the optimum therapeutic action. Dosage forms also contributed for the development of modern pharmaceutical industry. Currently available important dosage forms are shown in **Table 5** (York, 2007).

Route of administration	Dosage forms
Oral	Tablets, capsules, powder, granules, emulsion, suspension, syrup, solution
Topical	Cream, pastes, lotions, ointments, gels, solution, transdermal patches, topical aerosol
Rectal	Ointment, Suppositories, creams, powder, solutions
Parenteral	Injections (solution, suspension emulsion), implant
Inhalation	Aerosols, spray, gases
Nasal	Solution, inhalation, spray
Eye	Solution, ointment, cream
Ear	Solution, suspension, ointment, creams

Table 5. Currently available some important doses form of the modern medicines.

During early development of drugs, most of the drugs given to patient were in the powder form and route of administration was oral. It was difficult to administered right amount. The first aspirin powder was formulated in the tablet form. This gave new direction to the pharmaceutical industries. Today, more and more patient compliance adopted and choice of formulation is based on the patient interest. The flavour was introduced on the drug to make more palatable. Drug compound in the tablet or in the capsules is coated in order to make palatable and slow dissolution to carry the drug substance into the targeted sites.

Same drug can be administered by different route to obtain different therapeutic effects. For example drug substance administered *i.v.* route comes in blood circulation within a few seconds, while it might take minutes to hours if it is taken by oral route depending on the type of formulation. Some coated tablets or capsules deliver the drugs into the blood circulation after several hours. Therefore the design of formulation and selection of route can provide the controlled bioavailability of the drugs. The knowledge of pharmaceutical technology optimized the therapeutic value of the drugs and reduced the side effect. The major routes used for the administration of drugs are shown diagrammatically in **Figure 4**.

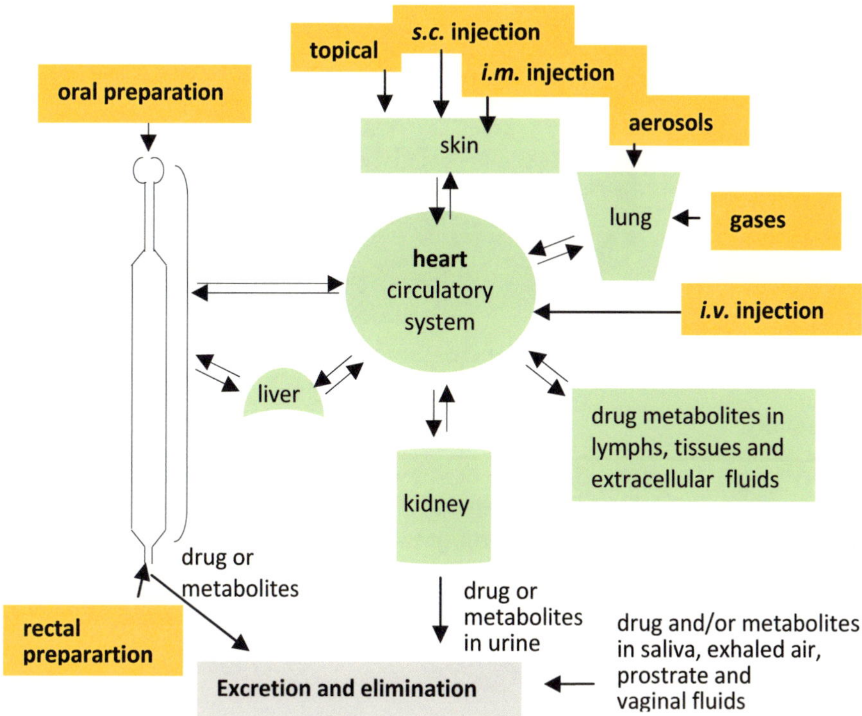

Fig. 4. Schematic diagram showing major routes of administration in the human body and drug metabolism.

4.2 Drug target

In general, drug formulation is administered through one of the routes into the human body. To obtained the therapeutic effect of the drug, all pharmacological properties of the drugs have to be explained. The drug action mechanisms of most of the modern drugs are well explained otherwise it would not be approved by the authority. The stability and activity of the drugs are thoroughly monitored from the point of administeration to the point of elimination. In order to understand the drug action, the action of drugs on particular receptor or enzymes is studied. In spite of growing knowledge on gene analysis and understanding, almost half of the drugs efficacies are targeted to the receptor on the cells. The drugs bind directly or activate certain protein to bind on the receptor molecule which results the cascade of the molecular activity inside the cells to cure disease. Some of the pathophysiological conditions appear because of the excessive or decreased production and activity of certain enzyme. Thus drugs are targeted to particular enzyme activity. Almost close to one third of the drugs available today are targeted to enzymes. Some major targets of the modern drugs for their action are shown in **Figure 5** (Drews, 2000). Understanding on drug target to DNA, nuclear receptor and ion channel are relatively low at present, however, it is expected to increase in the future.

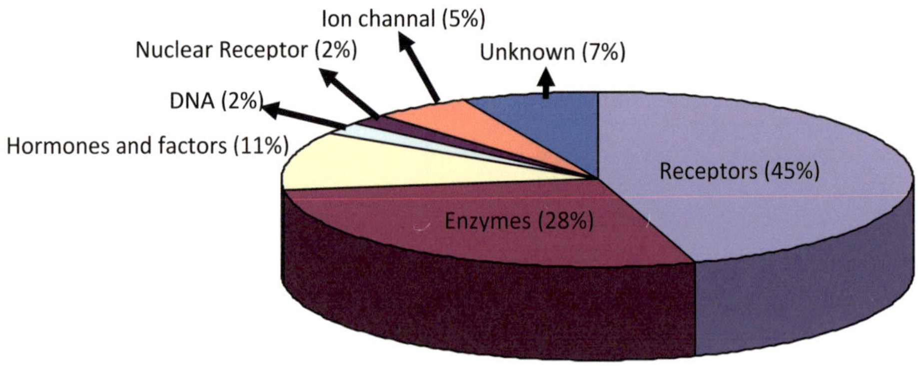

Fig. 5. Biochemical classes of drug targets of current therapies.

4.3 Drug discovery

Drug discovery project is a great challenge of knowledge, human resources and money. In order to make one successful medicine, generally it needs up to 14 years to complete all steps if all the steps remain successful according to our present knowledge. In mean time it might cost up to a total of 800 million US dollar investment. A general outline of drug discovery strategy is presented in **Figure 6**. According to the current trend, a new drug is hardly marketed even after detail analysis of almost 100000 small molecules in initial study.

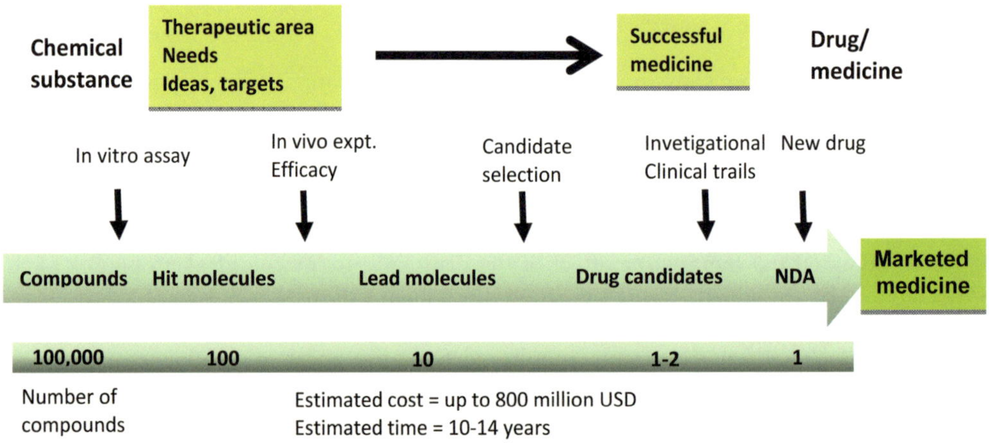

Fig. 6. Schematic diagram of drug discovery strategy.

In spite of huge effort there is still high percentage drug candidates fails to reach as new drug agent (NDA). There are several factors which contribute to the failure of drugs. In general most of the drug candidate showing potent pharmacological property in *in vitro* and animal experiment fails during the translation to human. It is mainly due to difficulty to study the pharmacokinetic properties in human. A general trend of failure rate during the drug discovery is presented in **Table 6.**

Failure rate	Percentage
Poor pharmacokinetic properties in human	39
Clinical efficacy	29
Toxicity and adverse effects	21
Commercial limitations	6

Table 6. Failure rate (%) of drug development process at different stages.

4.4 Preclinical strategy of drug discovery

Almost 70 to 80% of the total budget and two third of the total time period in the drug discovery project are consumed by the clinical trial. Therefore in order to enhance the success rate, preclinical strategy should be strong, effective and logical. A diagrammatic outline for preclinical strategy is given in **figure 7.**

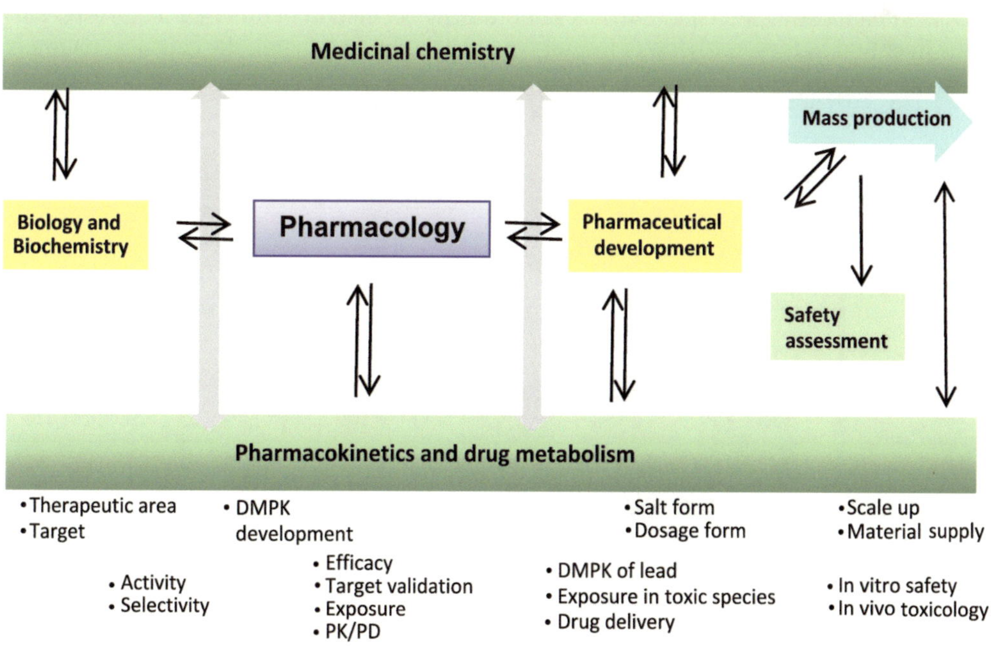

Fig. 7. Diagrammatic representation of preclinical strategy in drug development.

4.5 Evaluation for bioavailability

In addition to technological advancement, most of the drugs are taken from oral route and dosage form is tablet. Even a good drug cannot exert its therapeutic beneficial effects if it is not **reaching its target site** in the body at an **appropriate concentration** for a **sufficient length of time**. Swallowing a pharmacologically active chemical compound in the tablet or any other form by the patient might not be enough to obtain medicinal value.

Several other factors have to be considered:

- In the stomach, the tablet might not be disintegrated, the drug might not be released from the dosage form
- Drug might not be soluble into the gastrointestinal fluids
- If drug is not soluble, in general, it will not be absorbed and will not be able to reach the targeted site passing through the epithelial membranes of gastrointestinal tract
- Some drugs chemically or enzymatically degrade in the stomach or might have gastric irritation
- In some case the drug dissolves very fast and is absorbed very quickly from the gastrointestinal tract, in spite of high plasma concentration peak and fast elimination, such drug type might have short duration of action so drug has to taken very frequently and leading to strong fluctuations in plasma concentration.
- Some drugs can not be delivered by the oral route as they are metabolized in the intestine and/or liver, before reaching to systemic circulation
- Some drugs may have strong side effect profile, which may prohibit efficient treatment.

Drugs administered through the oral route must pass through the intestinal barrier to reach into the circulatory system. Therefore the drugs which are easily absorbed in gastrointestinal track with high permeation and remains stable during circulation in different tissue especially in the liver and kidneys provide optimum bio-availability. In general, the chemical nature of the drugs determines its bioavailability. Bioavailability of the drugs can be predicted mainly by the molecular size and hydrogen bonding capacity (Lipinsky Rule of 5).

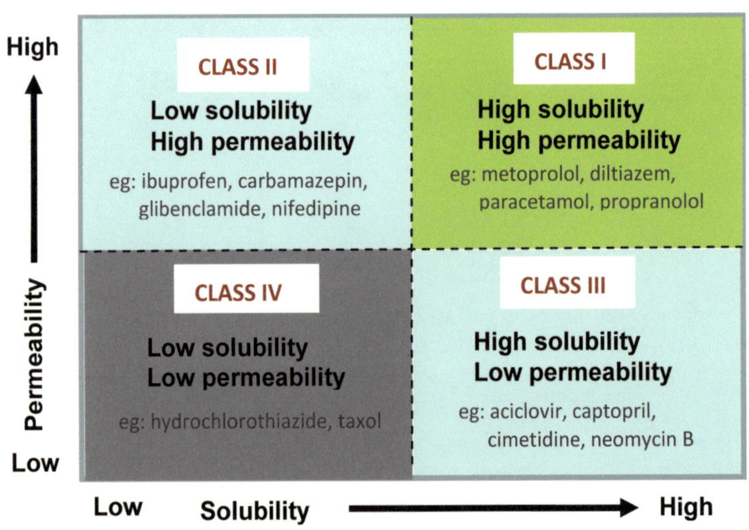

Fig. 8. Classification of drugs based on the solubility and permeability.

Based on the permeability and solubility, the drug substance can be classified into four groups **(Figure 8)**. In case of Class I drugs (high solubility and high permeability) the desired bioavailability can easily be reached and the role of formulation will be minimum. In case of Class IV drugs (low solubility and low permeability), it is very difficult to attain sufficient bioavailability. But in case of Class II or Class III drugs because of the improvement of formulation, bioavailability can be enhanced by increasing solubility or permeability.

For those drug candidates having low solubility or low permeability, by the simple structure modification or use of additives the bioavailability can be increased. A flow chart scheme to enhance the bioavailability is give in **Figure 9.**

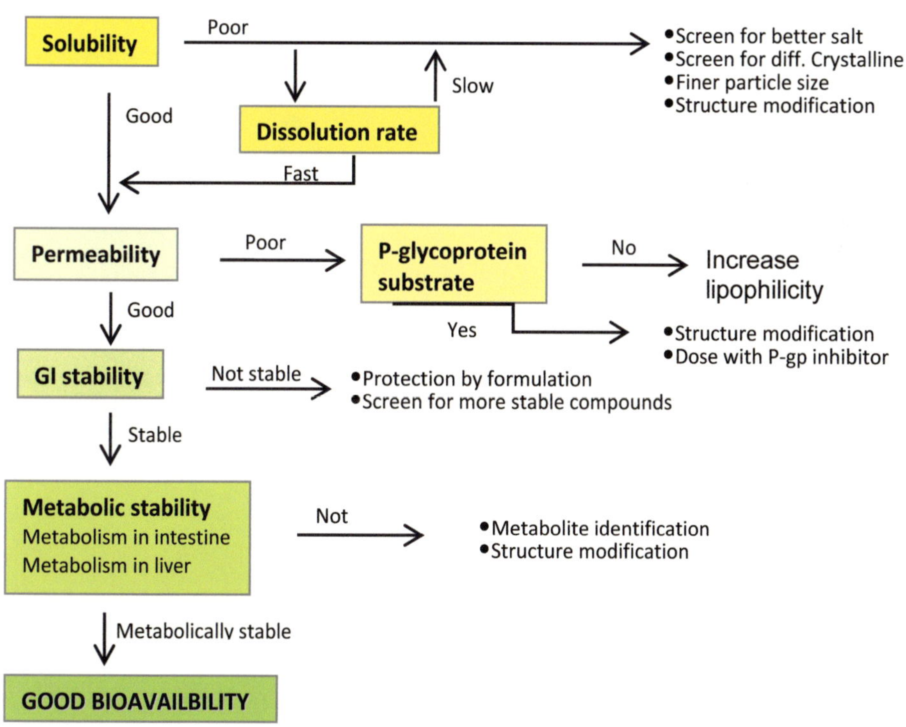

Fig. 9. Flowchart showing to increase the bioavailability.

4.6 Multifunctional pharmaceutical nano-carriers drug delivery

Drug discovery is very expensive and time consuming process. In addition to this, it is not sure that the successful candidate will appear at the end. Therefore the research on development of drug, especially the delivery system to enhance the bioavailability will make more fruitful therapeutic outcome. The development of new drug-delivery technologies also made the existing drug more useful. In the present book, the nano-carrier as delivery system is discussed in brief.

Nano-carrier drug delivery is mainly focused to those drugs which are potent pharmacologically but it could not be utilized fully because of toxicity (side effect) or less efficacy due to low bioavailability. In general, less soluble or less permeable drugs can not reach to optimum concentration in the systemic circulation. Therefore these classes of drugs are easily packed into the lipid nano-particles in the form of liposome or micelle. Because of the drug encapsulation inside the lipid molecule cluster, the physical properties of the drug molecules dominated by the lipid cluster particle and therefore lipid molecule cluster serves as nano-carrier and drug molecule can be delivered to the targeted site. Nano-particle of lipid encapsulated with drug molecules can easily be solubilised and penetrated into the cell.

There are already several drugs based on nano-carrier delivery formulations. A good example of nano-carrier delivery is liposomal formulation of amphoteracin B. Amphoteracin B has a broad spectrum of activity and is a drug of choice for life threatening invasive fungal infections, including disseminated candidiasis, aspergillosis and protozoal infection affecting the internal organ (*Viscerel leishmaniasis*). However, its use is compromised by associated adverse side effects.

But because of nano-carrier delivery liposomal formulation three products such as **AmBisome** (a small unilameller liposomes formulation with the size of 80 nm, composed of hydrogenated soy phosphatidyl choline, cholesterol, disteroyl phosphatidyl glycerol and amphotericin B in a 2:1:0.8:0.4 molar ratio with α-tocopherol), **Abelecet** (composed of amphotericin B, dimyristoyl phosphatidyl choline and dimyristoyl phosphatidyl glycerol in a 1:1 drug-to-lipid molar ratio with sizes is up to 1.6-11 μm) and **Amphotec** (containing amphotericin B in a complex with cholesteryl sulphate at a molar ration (1:1) with the particle size of 100-140 nm) are commercialized. Lipid-based nano-carrier formulations are found to be superior in clinical efficacy.

Based on the lipid type and physical condition, the size of particles, nature of the particles can be designed. In addition one or more desired ligands can me inserted to drug encapsulated nano-particle which allows the drug molecule to be delivered into the targeted sites in controlled manner. The additional ligands might be monoclonal antibody (binds to specific site), polyethylene glycan (remains longer time in circulation), binding with heavy metal (allows to trace the particle), cell penetrating peptide (allows the particle to penetrate into the cells), DNA binding (allows the DNA to be delivered) and magnetic nano-carrier (to trace the particles) (**Figure 10**).

These one or more ligands can be incorporated in the same particles therefore multi-functions of nano-carriers can be achieved together with the delivery of the drugs. Already the first generation of multifunctional nano-carriers is developed. For example, the nano-carrier type (B+C) having immunospecific and PEG ligands, should have ability to carry the drug molecule to the immunospecific cells where ligand binds and deliver the drugs and PEG allows the nano-carrier to remain longer hours in the systemic circulation (**Figure 11**).

The future medicine will be the nano-particles packed with several ligands which will be able to carry the drug molecules to particular targeted cell with monoclonal antibody and penetrated the cell membrane and required drug can easily be delivered without interfering with the circulatory system and other tissues or biomolecules (**Figure 12**). Such smart drug delivery will reduce the side effect and enhance the drug efficacy. This will be the foundation of 'Intelligent Therapeutics' of future drug formulation.

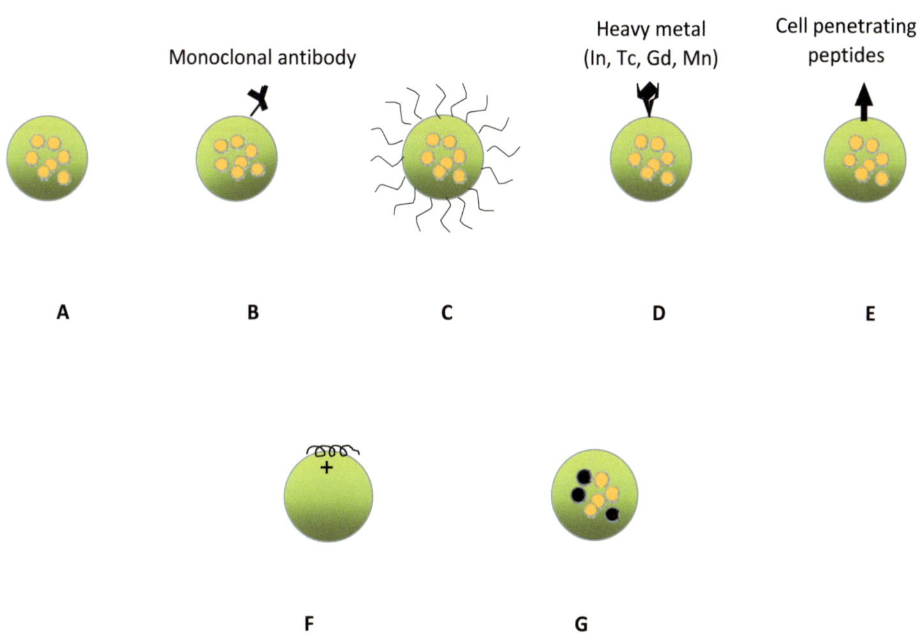

Fig. 10. Diagrammatic representation of nano-carrier designed for the pharmaceutical purpose. **A**: Traditional nano-carrier; **B**: Targeted nano-carrier (Immunospecific); **C**: Long circulating nano-carrier (PEG protected); **D**: Contrast nano-carrier (for imaging); **E**: Cell-penetrating nano-carrier; **F**: DNA-carrying nano-carrier; **G**: Magnetic nano-carrier.

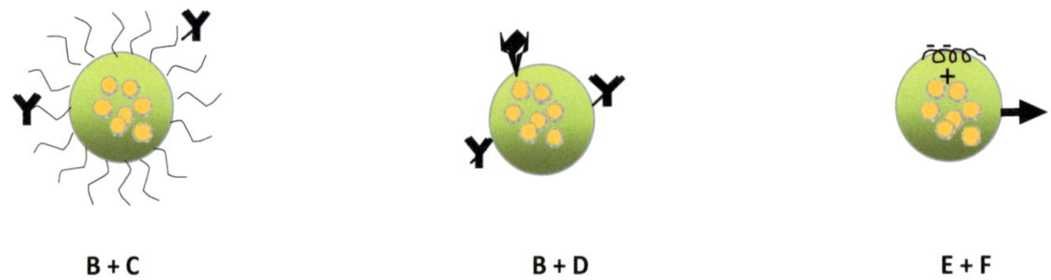

Fig. 11. Diagrammatic representation of first generation multifunctional nano-carriers.

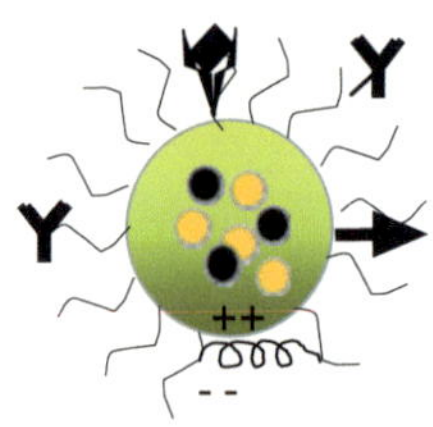

Fig. 12. Dream multifunctional nano-carrier.

5. Conclusion

Happy life, healthier life and long life have been remained as the goal of human life philosophy. Modern medicine, at least in a part, contributed to humanity to become more prosperous and more civilized. In fact, in searching of more effective medicine in the quest of healthier and longer lives, it led to the development of basic chemistry and human biology. The traditional agricultural based human demographical society transformed to industrialisation and pharmaceutical industries have great role for the globalization of the world. Moreover, modern medicine discovery and development not only supported to healthier and longer life but also encouraged to prosper the development of the modern science and technology.

6. References

Belis M. (February 2012). *History of Aspirin,* available from: http://inventors.about.com/library/inventors/blaspirin.htm (accessed on 25.02.2012)

Böhm H. J., Klebe G., Kubinyi H. (2002). *Wirkstoffdesign: Der Weg zum Arzneimittel*, Spektrum Akademischer Verlag, ISBN 3-8274-1353-2, Heidelberg, Germany

Derosne, J. F. (1803). Memoire sur I'opium, *Annalen. Chim.*, Vol.45, pp. 257-285

Drews, J. (2000). Drug Discovery: A Historical Perspective, *Science*, Vol.287, (17 March 2000), pp. 1960-1964, online ISSN 1095-9203

Gerhardt, C. F. (1853) Untersuchungen über die wasserfrei organischen Säuren, *Ann. Chem. Pharm.*, Vol.87, pp. 149-179

Global Market (2012) available from http://www.prlog.org/10124036-global-pharmaceutical-market-forecast-to-2012.html (accessed on 25.02.2012)

Grabley, S. & Thiericke R. (1999). *Drug Discovery from Nature*, Springer-Verlag, ISBN 3-540-64844-5, Heidelberg, Germany

GSK History (February 2012). Available from http://www.gsk.com/about/history.htm . (accessed on 25.02.2012)

McLagan, T. J. (1876) The Treatment of acute Rheumatism with Salicin, *Lancet*, Vol. 1, pp. 342-343 & 383-384.

Merck Group History (February 2012) available from http://www.merck.de/en/company/history/history.html (accessed on 25.02 2012)

Newman, D. J. & Cragg G. M. (2002). Natural Products as Drugs and Leads to Drugs: The Historical Perspective, In: *Natural Product Chemistry for Drug Discovery*, A. D. Buss & M. S. Butler, (Ed.), 3-27, RSC Publishing, ISBN 978-0-85404-193-0, Cambridge, UK

Nicolaou, K. C. & Montagnon, T. (2008). *Molecules that Changed the World*, Wiley-VCH GmbH & Co.KGaA, ISBN 978-3-527-30983-3, Weinheim, Germany

Pelletier, P. J. & Caventou, J. B. (1820). Recherches Chimiques sur les quinquinas, *Annalen Chimiques Physik*, Vol.15, pp. 289-318

Pelletier, P. J. & Magendie, F. (1817) Recherches Chimiques et Physiologique sur I' ipecacuanna, *Annalen Chimiques Physik*, Vol.4, pp. 172-185

Pfizer History (February 2012) available from http://www.pfizer.com/about/history/history.jsp , (accessed on 25.02.2012)

Piria, R. (1839). Recherches sur la Salicine et les produits qui en' de'rivent, *C. R. Acad. Sci*, Vol.8, pp. 479-485

Roth, G. Y., Brookes, K, Lowe, D. B. (2010). *Top 20 Phamra report*, available from http://www.contractpharma.com/issues/2011-07/view_features/the-top-20-pharmaceutical-companies/ (accessed on 25.02.2012)

Seguin, M. A. (1814). Premier Me'moire sur I'opium, *Annalen Chim*, Vol.92, pp. 225-245

Sertürner, F. (1805).Auszuge aus briefen an den Herausgeber (a) Säure im Opium. (b) Ein deres Schreiben von Ebendenselben. Nachtrag zur Charakteristik der Saüre im Opium, *Journal der Pharmazie für Artze, Apotheker und Chemiscten von D. J. B. Trommsdroff*, Vol.13, pp. 29-30

Sertürner, F. (1806). Darstelling der reinen Mohnsäure (Opium säure) nebst einer Chemischen Untersuching des Opium mit vorzüglicher Hinsicht auf einen darin neu entdeckten stoff und die dahin gehörigen Bemerkungen, *Journal der Pharmazie fur Artze, Apotheke*, Vol.14, pp. 47-93

Sertürner, F. (1817). Uber das Morphium, eine neue salzfähige Grundlage, und die Mekonsäure, als Hauptbestandtheile des Opium, *Gilbert's Annalen der Physik*, Vol.25, pp. 56-89

Top Ten Selling of the World (2011) available from http://www.medindia.net/health_statistics/health_facts/top-ten-selling-drugs.htm#ixzz1t8ck78Zv (accessed on 25.02.2012)

Wright C. R. A. (1874) On the Action of Organic Acids and their Anhydrides on the Natural Alkaloids: Part I, *Journal of Chemical Society*, Vol.27, pp. 1031-1042

York, P. (2007). Design of dosage form, In: *Aulton's Pharmaceutics: The Design and manufacture of Medicine, 3rd Ed*, M. E. Aulton, (Ed.), 4-7, Elsevier Limited, ISBN 978-0-443-10108-3, London, UK

2

Drug Designing, Discovery and Development Techniques

Elvis A. Martis[1] and Rakesh R. Somani[2]
[1]*Department of Pharmaceutical Chemistry, Bombay College of Pharmacy, Santacruz [E], Mumbai,*
[2]*Department of Pharmaceutical Chemistry, V.E.S. College of Pharmacy, Chembur [E], Mumbai, India*

1. Introduction

Human body is a complex chemical machinery, with as many as thousands of chemicals, namely proteins, carbohydrates, fats, etc. which exist all together. Every process in the body is some sort of chemical conversion that leads to movements, thought processes, feelings, pain and many more such complex as well as simple processes. The human body has also been provided with all the necessary chemical components or precursors, various enzymes and neurotransmitters for the balanced and proper functioning of all the life sustaining processes. Yet it so happens that some machineries or bioprocesses fail to function due to several exogenous or endogenous factors. Hence providing external aids, which we call "Drugs" or "Medicines", becomes essential to restore the normal functioning. Drugs are nothing but chemical entities of synthetic or natural origin, which only modulate the body functions and have no new action on the body. This explanation however does not fit the chemotherapeutic agents used to treat parasitic infections, as they have no action on the human body, but, are targeted to the invading organism (Richard et al., 2009). The exogenous factors are varied right from parasitic invasion to some chemical entities which tend to disrupt the normal bodily functions. Hence repairing becomes mandatory, if bodily repair mechanism cannot match the rate of damage. The endogenous factor maybe faulty, functioning of organs, any genetic or congenital factor, over or under-production of some precursors which may lead to disorders. The classical examples of disorders due to endogenous factors are the neurodegenerative disorders like Parkinsonism and Alzheimer's disease which arise due to the imbalance of acetylcholine and dopamine in the central nervous systems. Though there is no cure for these disorders but drugs and therapies have been developed to prolong and improve the quality of life. (Moore et al., 2005; Cummings et al., 1998). Hence, drug discovery can also called as patient-oriented science meant for improving the quality of life by developing newer and safer agents.

Drug discovery plays an important role for the growth of any pharmaceutical industry and also to the society, as newer and safe drugs are launched in the market with the view to improve the therapeutic value and safety of the agents. The pharmaceutical industry has consistently shown that it can discover and develop innovative medicines for a wide range of diseases (Ratti & Trist, 2011). The revenue that flows in with the invention of newer agents has always been the motivation for the industry to keep up the pace and keep abreast with the ever increasing demand for medicines.

The advent of molecular biology, along with numerous developments in the screening and synthetic chemistry technologies, has allowed learning both, the knowledge about the receptor and random screening to be used for drug discovery. Today, more or less all pharmaceutical industries follow common techniques for discovering drugs. These include cloning and expressing human receptors and enzymes in formats that allow high-throughput screening and the application of combinatorial chemistry. Thus, random screening can now be done with libraries sufficiently large and diverse to have a relatively high probability to find a novel molecule. These libraries are possible because they can be generated by the techniques of combinatorial chemistry (Black, 2000).

Drug research, as we know it today, began its career when chemistry had reached a degree of maturity that allowed its principles and methods to be applied to the problems outside of chemistry itself and when pharmacology had become a well-defined scientific discipline in its own right. By 1870, some of the essential foundations of chemical theory had been laid. Avogadro's atomic hypothesis had been confirmed and a periodic table of elements established. Chemistry had developed a theory that allowed it to organize the elements according to their atomic weights and valencies. There were set of theories of acids and bases. In 1865, August Kekulé formulated his pioneering theory on the structure of aromatic organic molecules (Drews, 2000a and 1999b). During the first half of the 20th century drug research began shaping up and was developed by several new technologies, which carried the drug discovery process to its best. Biochemistry also had tremendous influence on drug research in many ways. The concept of targeting enzymes as drug targets came in to existence, that led to the designing of enzyme substrates which acted either as inhibitors or showed their action by modifying various feedback mechanisms. (Meidrum & Roughton, 1933).

Table 1 shows some important discoveries in the field of medicine, right from 19th century to 21st century

Sr. no	Year of Discovery	Drug Name	Category
1.	1806	Morphine	Hypnotic agent
2.	1899	Aspirin	Analgesic and Anti-pyretic agent
3.	1922	Insulin	Anti-Diabetic agent
4.	1928	Penicillin	Antibiotic
5.	1960	Chlordiazepoxide	Tranquillizer
6.	1971	L-dopa	Anti-Parkinson agent
7.	1987	Artemisinin	Anti-malarial agent
8.	1998	Sildenafil	Erectile Dysfunctioning treatment
9.	1999	Celecoxib, Rofecoxib	Selective COX-2 inhibitors
10.	1999	Zanamavir, Oseltamivir	Anti-influenza agents
11.	2001	Imatinib	Leukemia treatment

Table 1. Important discoveries in medicine

The present day drug discovery process is a very time consuming process as it takes at least 14-16 years of research for a molecule to completely transform into a drug. There are several 100 basic research projects, before desired molecule is discovered. But, this molecule is not yet ready to be called as a drug. After the pre-clinical establishment and confirmation of its action and toxicity data, the FDA approves the candidate for clinical studies. The Clinical phase of the study takes at least 6-8 years, before the candidate can be launched in to the market. After this stage, the molecule is said to have transformed from a molecule to drug. Even after the launch of the drug in the market, the post-marketing surveillance and pharmacovigilance program is being carried out to find out whether any new adverse reaction or incompatibilities towards other agents, when given as combination therapies. (Congreve, et al., 2005). Figure 1 depicts the entire drug discovery process with the tentative timeline.

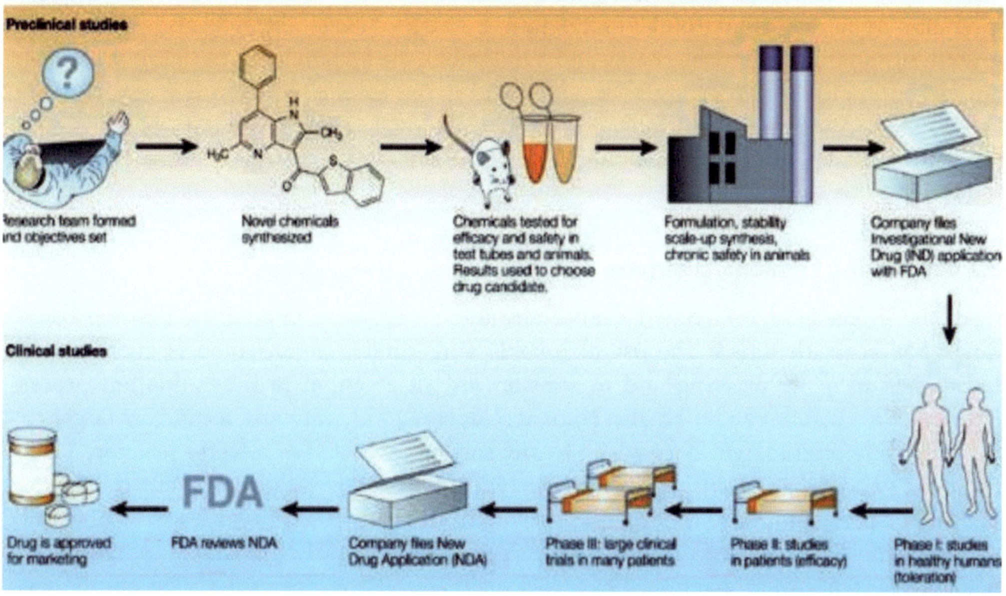

Fig. 1. Drug discovery and development process (Lombardino and Lowe, 2004).

2. Drug discovery process

Drug discovery process basically is a patient oriented science, where researchers strive to improve the existing drugs or invent a totally new chemical entity, which should be ideally more potent than any existing drug of a similar category. If not, then at least it should be safer than those existing. This process is a very time consuming and expensive activity, calling for the expertise of many eminent researchers. It takes nearly 12-14 years of exhaustive research and a huge amount of financial investment for the discovery of a single drug. Right from the chemical synthesis to its clinical development and finally formulating it to a suitable form. Failure at any stage would mean a huge loss for the company. Hence, a lot of planning is required even before the project is underway. Recently, with the use of technology the process is becoming a less risky business, because of the ability of the computers to predict the possible outcomes. This will surely reduce the efforts in fruitless directions (Augen, 2002).

The following paragraphs shall discuss the various stages of drug discovery process.

2.1 Identification of biological targets

The human body functions normally by the virtue of the biochemical process which go on, producing all the necessary chemicals required for numerous functions to undergo smoothly within the body. Many of these processes are regulated by the enzymes and the endogenous effector molecules via their respective receptors. A diseased state, may hence, be identified by, either the abnormal biochemical functioning or, over or underproduction of some of the intermediates. Hence , the most important and most common biological targets for drug discovery are either enzymes regulating the biochemistry or the receptors through which many hormones and endogenous effectors show their response. For example, inhibition of human dihydrofolate reductase, by methotrexate, brought under control the growth of tumour in humans (Borsa and Whitemore, 1969). Similarly, blocking of the beta-adrenoceptors in the cardiac muscles was found to reduce the hypertensive state (Pearson, et al., 1989). Another type of biological targets are nucleic acids. Though they are rarely targeted as compared to those mentioned above, yet they are important targets. (Overington, et al., 2006).

2.2 Validation of biological targets

Once the target is identified, it becomes absolutely necessary to confirm, that the correct target has been identified. The use of reliable and suitable animal models and the latest techniques in gene targeting and expression are all essential to the validation process. (Abuin, et al., 2002). Validation also helps researchers to identify any secondary target that the drug may bind to, which may lead to any sort of unwanted or adverse reaction. Ideally the drug candidate should be such that it binds to a single target only, but this seldom happens. Thus, binding to other targets, apart from the correct target leads to unwanted pharmacological actions. These cannot be completely avoided. It can be minimized to negligible extent. (Marton, et al., 1998). G-protein coupled receptors (GCPRs) are the most common and the major targets where a drug binds. Hence, over 30% of drugs in market are modulators of GPCR. The quantitative polymerase chain reaction (qPCR) analysis is one of the techniques used to measure the mRNA expression on the receptor. (Wise, et al., 2002).

2.3 Lead structure search

A lead compound is the one that has basic structural requirements for exhibiting the desired action. This means that, a lead compound has many structural spaces for further development of the structure, to give a compound with further enhanced action. High-throughput screening is a technique, which helps to identify the lead compound out of the many synthesized compounds or those compounds which are collected from the natural source. Hence, it becomes utmost important to identify the lead compound, as this forms the basis for further development of the molecule(s). (Bleicher, et al., 2003). Figure 2 illustrates the design cycle for lead search. The various other techniques involved in lead identification are virtual screening, informatics, pharmacaphore mapping, High throughput docking, NMR-based screening and chemical genetics. (Xue and Bajorath, 2000).

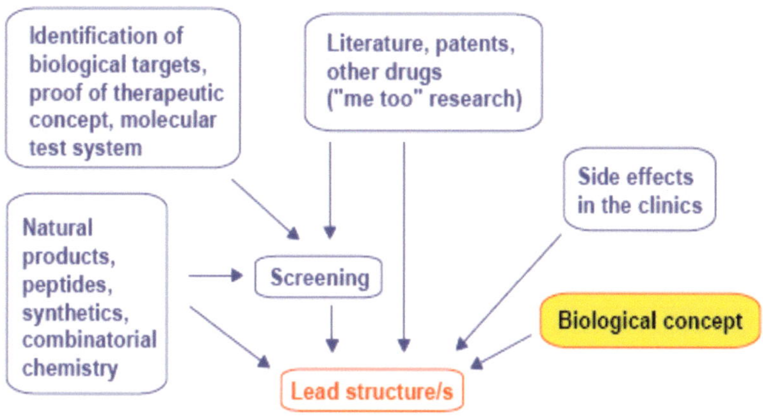

Fig. 2. The Design cycle describes the optimization of a lead structure to one or several development candidates.

2.4 Lead optimization

As soon as the lead structure is identified, the next step is to optimize the same. Here, the chemists in close collaboration with the pharmacologists will carefully study the structure-activity relationship and will synthesize such other derivatives, so as to get a compound with the best possible desired activity. The various other approaches for lead optimization are Structure-Based Drug Design (SBDD), Quantitative Structure-Activity Relationship (QSAR) and Computer-Assisted Drug Design (CADD). All such approaches generate a huge amount of data, so as to assist the chemist in optimizing the lead to the best possible structure, with best possible desired action. These aforementioned approaches shall be dealt in detail in the later part of the chapter. (Joseph-McCarthy, 1999 & Ooms, 2000). Figure 3 represents the design cycle for lead optimization and drug development.

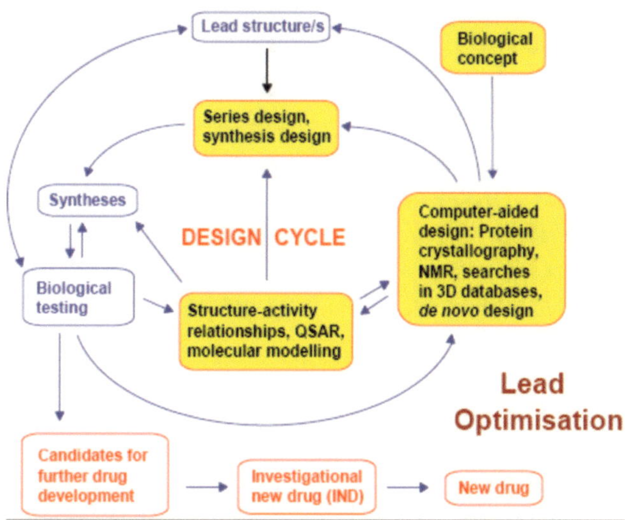

Fig. 3. Design cycle for lead optimization

2.5 Preclinical studies

The main objective of preclinical studies is to ascertain the safety of the newly developed molecule. A newly developed molecule is never permitted to be tested on the human body, unless supported by a confirmed data about the pharmacology and toxicology of the molecule which is, based on animal studies is obtained. This phase, generally deals with elucidating the mode of action the molecule and getting an idea about the pharmacokinetics (PK) and pharmacodynamics (PD) of the molecule. However, the most important is the toxicological data obtained from the animal study, which gives the rough estimate about the possible adverse reactions that may be likely to be seen during the course of the therapy. These are carried out in two stages, in-vitro studies and in-vivo studies. The in-vitro studies make use of different cell-lines and tissue preparations. The in-vivo studies are performed on the live animals and are observed the changes in the animal's behavior. (Caldwell, et al., 2001 & Smith, and van de Waterbeemd, 1999).

2.6 Clinical trials

The next stage after preclinical studies is the clinical studies, actual testing of the molecule in the human volunteers. This phase allows to assess the safety and efficacy of the new molecule. This phase also allows to gather information about the toxicological effects in the human body, as seldom the toxicity shown by animals, cannot be always directly correlated to the humans. Before the start of this stage, the innovator should file an application, namely, "Investigational New Drug (IND)", as the FDA approves based on the preclinical data, the innovator can proceed for clinical studies. This stage consists of three phases, phase 1, phase 2, phase 3 and the phase 4 studies are carried out after the drug has been launched in to the market.

Phase 1 studies are usually carried out on healthy human volunteers and on a small group of people. This phase evaluates the safety, tolerability and PK and PD of the new molecule.

Phase 2 studies are generally carried out on a small population with the target disease. In this phase, the drug's efficacy and safety, metabolism and PK are evaluated in a diseased human body.

Phase 3 studies are extensive and multiple site studies. This phase, covers a large group of individuals with target disease. This phase basically is a therapeutic confirmatory phase, as all the parameters studied in the phase 2 of the study are confirmed in this phase. This phase may take somewhere about 3-6 years to complete. After this phase is successfully completed, the company files the "NEW DRUG APPLICATION (NDA)"to the FDA. Once the FDA issues an approval to the company, based on their data compiled from the clinical trials, the drug can be launched in the market.

Phase 4 (Post-Marketing survilience) studies are carried out, after the drug has been launched into the market. The company continues its monitoring of the drug. The rationale behind this phase is to check for any new adverse or serious reaction which was not detected in the earlier phases and may be observed in this phase. If so happens that some serious adverse reaction is observed, the company may withdraw the drug from the market. (Singh, et al., 2011).

2.7 Formulations for clinical studies

The formulations for clinical studies are usually prepared as capsule dosage form, as it is easy for formulation and also easy for administration. Apart from this advantage, there is another key factor to be considered while formulating a trial batch, as the drug itself has not been tested in humans, any untoward action can be directly ascertained to the drug in the absence of any excipients. Capsules, unlike the tablets can be formulated without any or minimal excipients. Liquid dosage forms may also be formulated, provided the drug is water-soluble, for the ease of preparation and water being the safest medium. Formulations should be properly tested for its stability and must be stable at least for the period the trials are underway. The other reason for choosing simple formulations is to avoid any time lag, as the process of trials itself is lengthy. Any more delay, may further lead to the delay in marketing the drug.

3. Computer-aided drug design

Computers, have found their way in every field of science and technology today. The boon of computers is that a large number of calculations and observations can be done in no time. Drug discovery and designing is no exception to this generalization. Drug designing has received a many fold face-lift by the virtue of computer software dedicated to the designing of ligands and identifying the biological targets. Computer generated structures serve to be good predictive models for the evaluation of biological activity.

A drug exhibits its action when it binds to its biological target, usually receptors. Receptors are nothing but proteins with active sites for the binding of ligands. Hence, in order to design a good ligand, it becomes necessary to know the structure of such receptors and to identify their active sites accurately. The two important aspects involved in predicting molecular-interactions in computer-aided drug design (CADD) are development of pharmacophore-based and molecular docking and scoring techniques. Computerized structure of the known proteins is based on the experimental data present in various literatures and protein data banks. With this, it is possible to deduce the 3D structure of the all the known proteins with the help of sequence homology approach. Hence, these hypothetical proteins behave more or less like the real proteins in their native biological environment (Taft, et al., 2008). Recently, many computer-assisted models are being developed and several thousand candidates are being screened for various activities using these models. The methods of choice for this purpose are computer programs that superimpose molecules by a flexible alignment to derive pharmacophoric patterns and/or quantitative structure-activity relationships, dock molecules to the surface of a protein 3D structure or to a hypothetical pseudoreceptor, or construct new ligands within a predefined binding site (Klebe, 1995 & Kubinyi, 1998a).

Different molecular property fields, such as electrostatic, steric, hydrophobic, hydrogen bond acceptor and donor fields, as well as their weighed combinations, have been used to achieve a fully automated alignment of the molecules. (Mestres, et al., 1997). The process of docking process involves the prediction of ligand conformation and orientation within a targeted binding site. Docking is basically performed for accurate structural modelling and correct prediction of the biological activity. Figure 5 depicts an image witch is generated by docking studies (representational purpose only)

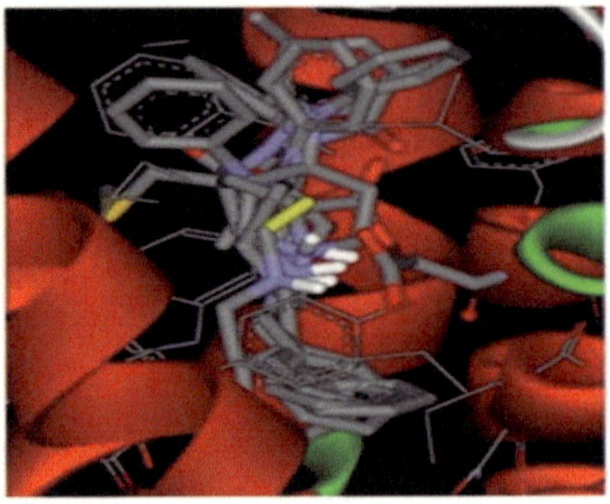

Fig. 5. Representation of molecular docking (Bo, et al., 2010).

Type of study	Software programme	Innovator
Protein-Ligand docking	AUTODOCK	The Scripps Research Institute
	COMBIBUILD	Sandia National Labs
	DOCKVISION	University of Alberta
	FRED	OpenEye
	FLEXIDOCK	Tripos
	FLEXX	BioSolveIT GmbH
	GLIDE	Schrödinger GmbH
	GOLD	CDCC
	HINT!	Virginia Commonwealth University
Protein-Ligand & Protein-Protein docking	DOCK	UCSF Molecular Design Institute
	GRAMM	University of Kansas
	ICM-DOCk	MolSoft LLC

Table 2. lists the various computer programmes used for docking studies. (Structure based drug design and molecular modelling, http://www.imb-jena.de/~rake/Bioinformatics_WEB/dd_tools.html)

4. Molecular modelling and drug design

Theoretical studies of biological molecules permit the study of the relationships between structure, function and dynamics at the atomic level. The entire process is about simulation of the biological processes and quantum mechanical calculation based on the principles of chemistry and physics.

4.1 Molecular mechanics- force field (Potential energy function)

Current generation force fields (or potential energy functions) provide a reasonably good compromise between accuracy and computational efficiency. They are often calibrated to experimental results and quantum mechanical calculations of small model compounds. Their ability to reproduce physical properties measurable by experiment is tested; these properties include structural data obtained from x-ray crystallography and NMR, dynamic data obtained from spectroscopy and inelastic neutron scattering and thermodynamic data. (MacKerell, et al., 1995).

The molecular structures, properties and energies of a molecule are better understood through the use of the mechanical molecular model. This model involves the development of a simple molecular mechanics energy equation representing the sum of various energy interaction terms comprised of bonds, angles, torsions of both bonded and non-bonded atoms. Force fields the model serves as a simple descriptor for vibrations in molecules. The concept of force fields is now widely employed as one of the simplest tools in molecular modeling.

Force fields are fundamentally important in de novo drug design programs, in pharmacophore mapping, and represent the "scoring functions" in many docking programs. As scoring functions, force fields are used to rank "ligand poses" obtained by a docking algorithm, or in de novo ligand design programs to suggest placement of fragments in the sites in the enzyme with the highest binding affinity. In all these applications, force fields are mainly used to compute the interaction energy between the protein and the ligand as pair-wise interaction potentials consisting of van der Waals and electrostatic interactions, in addition to H-bond energy between the ligand and the enzyme. (Pissurlenkar, et al., 2009).

4.2 Energy minimization methods

The goal of energy minimization is to find a route from an initial conformation to the nearest minimum energy conformation using the smallest number of calculations possible. NMR and X-ray crystal structures tend to have high energy interactions like Pauli repulsions. That is because the methods to retrieve molecular structures are not perfect and especially in x-ray-structures there are crystal contacts, which lead to a compaction of the molecules. Moreover, hydrogen atoms are added to relatively arbitrary positions near their neighbors. Thus, there are atoms lying too close together so that the Pauli repulsion outweighs the dispersion attraction and the energy is raised high above natural energy levels. These high energy interactions lead to local distortions which result in an unstable simulation. They can be released by minimizing the energy of the structure before starting a run. The minimization results in a structure with energy near the lowest possible energy the system can have. (Leach, 2001 & Höltje, et al., 2003)

4.3 Conformational analysis

Conformational analysis deals with the computation of minimal energy configurations of deformable molecules and docking involves matching one molecular structure to the receptor site of another molecule and computing the most energetically favorable 3-D conformation. (Go and Scherga, 1970).

4.3.1 Systematic search (Scheraga, et al., 1992)

Due to the convoluted nature of the potential energy surface of molecules, minimization usually leads to the nearest local minimum, and not the global minimum. To scan the potential surface with some surety of completeness, systematic, or grid, search procedures have been developed. The following protocol is used for the same,

1. Rigid geometry approximation
2. Combinatorial nature of the problem
3. Pruning the combinatorial tree
4. Rigid body rotations
5. Exploitation of rings
6. Conformational clustering and families
7. Conformational analysis

4.3.2 Monte Carlo simulation

The Monte Carlo simulation is based on statistical mechanics and generates sufficient different configurations of a system by computer simulation to allow the desired structural, statistical, and thermodynamic properties to be calculated as a weighted average of these properties over these configurations. A useful application has combined Monte Carlo sampling with variable temperatures (simulated annealing) to optimize the docking of ligands into active sites. (Allen, & Tildesley, 1989)

4.3.4 Molecular dynamic simulation

Molecular dynamics is a deterministic process based on the simulation of molecular motion by solving Newton's equations of motion for each atom and incrementing the position and velocity of each atom by use of a small time increment. Molecular dynamics simulations represent another technique to sample configuration space, based on the aforementioned principle. Combined with the use of "reasonable" temperatures (a few hundreds or thousands of degrees), this means that only the local area around the starting point is sampled, and that only relatively small barriers (a few tens of a kJ/mol) can be overcome. Different (local) minima may be generated by selecting configurations at suitable intervals during the simulation and subsequently minimizing these structures. MD methods use the inherent dynamics of the system to search out the low-energy deformation modes and they can be used for sampling the conformational space for large confined systems (Tuckerman, & Martyna, 2000).

4.4 Structure-based and Ligand-based drug design approaches

Structure-based drug design by the use of structural biology remains one of the most logical approaches in drug discovery. It combines information from several fields: X- ray crystallography and/or NMR, molecular modeling, synthetic organic chemistry, QSAR, and biological evaluation (Marrone, et al., 1997). Figure 6 shows the schematic process.

Many of the naturally occurring molecules are found to be very potent, and also the endogenous chemicals give a lot of information for drug designing. The use of such ligands to generate and design newer ligands is called ligand-based drug design. Many a times straightforward design process starts from conformationally restricted natural receptor ligands, such as from polypeptides or proteins. Some of the applications of structure and ligand based drug design are Renin and protease inhibitors, β-lactamase inhibitors, reverse transcriptase inhibitors, angiotensin converting enzyme inhibitors, HIV-1 integrase inhibitors and many more. (Kubinyi, 1998b).

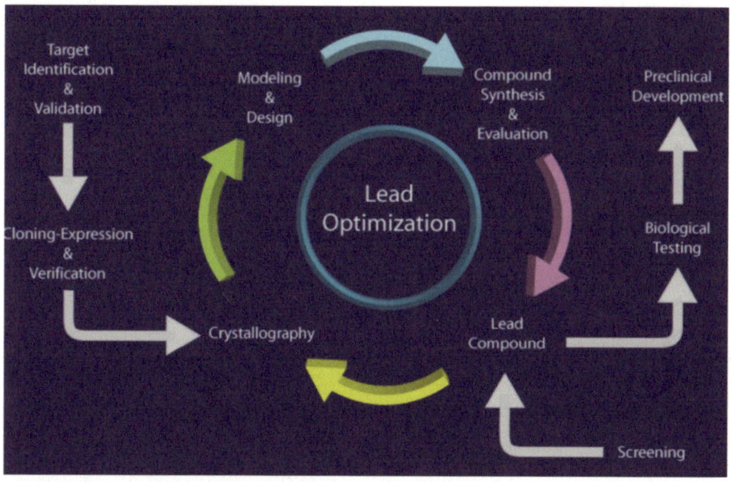

Fig. 6. Representation of structure based drug design.

4.5 3D pharmacophore modeling

Various conformations of a range of ligands that all act at the same receptor site can provide significantly more information than just a single ligand structure. With a sufficiently broad range of ligands, it is often possible to generate a pharmacophore model of the receptor site. The advantage of such a pharmacophore model is that smaller, non-peptide molecules that might have improved stability and bioavailability over their peptide counterparts can be designed, relative easy and certain amount of confidence towards getting successful outcome. (Nielsen, et al., 1999).

4.6 Rational drug design

The Concept of rational drug design simply lies in logical reasoning before designing any therapeutic agents. For example, to prepare any competitive inhibitor of a particular target, the logic of predicting the structure is to simply design an molecule with similar structural features exhibited by the endogenous agent or by closely examining the active binding site. Close examination of the active site gives many hints about the interacting amino acid residues, so it becomes simple to predict the nature and type of substituents and the favorable position in the molecule, which will favor better binding.

4.6.1 Design of enzyme inhibitors

Almost every biochemical process in the human or parasite is catalyzed by various enzymes of diverse function. As a result enzymes have always been the hot target for designing new drugs for various clinical conditions. The most popular example is the inhibition of acetylcholinesterase enzyme in the human brain is one of the most successful targets to treat the symptoms of Alzheimer's disease. The first step in designing an agent to inhibit an enzyme is to study thoroughly the structure and the binding site/pocket of the endogenous substrate. It is always favorable to design the new agent based on the structural requirements into the pocket of the catalytic site of the enzyme based on endogenous substrate or agents already designed for the purpose. The binding of the inhibitor should be more preferred or favourable than the endogenous substrate, in order to develop a successful inhibitor and at the same time care should also be taken so as to not develop an irreversible inhibitor, this may permanently destroy the enzyme. Popular drugs designed in this fashion are the HIV-1 protease inhibitors, thrombin inhibitors, neuraminidase inhibitors and many more. (Prasad, et al., 1996, Kimball, 1995 & Wade, 1997).

4.6.2 De Novo Ligand design

Designing of novel chemical structures that are capable of interacting with a receptor of known structure using methodology that is much more reliable, is what we call De Novo Ligand design. Techniques for the design of novel structures to interact with a known receptor site are becoming more and more available and have shown a lot of promise for the future. The thorough understanding of the various classes of chemicals interacting with the particular receptor, can give a lot of information to design novel agents by replacing the scaffold with another one to have similar sort of interaction and at the same binding site. (Klebe, 2000 & Bohm, and Stahl, 2000).

5. Quantitative Structure Activity Relationship (QSAR)

QSAR correlate, within congeneric series of compounds, affinities of ligands to their binding sites, inhibition constants, rate constants, and other biological activities, either with certain structural features (Free Wilson analysis) or with atomic, group or molecular properties, such as lipophilicity, polarizability, electronic and steric properties. (Kubinyi, 1995).

5.1 Parameters

5.1.2 Hydrophobicity

Molecular recognition depends strongly on hydrophobic interactions between ligands and receptors. Hydrophobicities of solutes can readily be determined by measuring partition coefficients designated as P. Partition coefficients are additive-constitutive, free energy-related properties. Log P represents the overall hydrophobicity of a molecule, which includes the sum of the hydrophobic contributions of the "parent" molecule and its substituent. Whole-molecule approaches use molecular properties or spatial properties to predict log P values. (Taylor, 1990 & Kellogg, et al., 1992).

5.1.3 Electronic

Electronic attributes of molecules are intimately related to their chemical reactivities and biological activities. The extent to which a given reaction responds to electronic perturbation constitutes a measure of the electronic demands of that reaction, which is determined by its mechanism. Hammett employed, as a model reaction, and determined their equilibrium constants K_a, which led to the definition of an operational constant, called the Hammett's constant σ, It is a measure of the size of the electronic effect for a given substituent and represents a measure of electronic charge distribution in the parent nucleus. (Hammett, 1966).

5.1.4 Steric effects

The quantitation of steric effects is complex and challenging in all other situations, particularly at the molecular level. Sterics are of utmost importance in ligand-receptor interactions as well as in transport phenomena in biological systems. The first steric parameter to be quantified was Taft's E_s constant. One of the most widely used steric parameters is molar refraction (MR). MR is generally scaled by 0.1 and used in biological QSAR, where intermolecular effects are of primary importance. The failure of the MR descriptor to adequately address three-dimensional shape issues led to Verloop's development of STERIMOL parameters, which define the steric constraints of a given substituent along several fixed axes. (Taft, 1956, Tute, 1990 & Verloop, 1987).

5.2 Quantitative models

All QSAR analyses are based on the assumption of linear additive contributions of the different structural properties or features of a compound to its biological activity, provided that there are no nonlinear dependences of transport or binding on certain physicochemical properties. (Kubinyi, 1997).

5.2.1 Hansch analysis

The linear free-energy-related Hansch model, also sometimes referred to as the 'extrathermodynamic approach. The model makes use of log P and Hammett constant. The equation of this model is as follows

$$\log 1/C = a(\log P)^2 + b\log P + c\sigma + \ldots + k$$

where P is the partition coefficient, σ is the Hammett electronic parameter, k is a constant term, and a, b, c are the regression coefficient. This equation is built on the concept that the permeation of drug in the cell, and the binding of the drug are function of its lipophilicity, electronic properties and other linear free-energy related properties. (Hansch, and Leo, 1995).

5.2.2 Free Wilson analysis

Free-Wilson approach is truly a structure-activity-based methodology because it incorporates the contributions made by various structural fragments to the overall biological activity. The equation of this model is as follows

$$\mathbf{BA}_i = \sum_j a_j \mathbf{X}_{ij} + \mu$$

Where BA stands for biological activity, X_j is the jth substituent, which carries a value 1 if present and 0 if absent, a_j represents the contribution of the jth substituent to biological activity. (Franke, 1984 & Free, and Wilson, 1964).

5.3 Other QSAR approaches

In this section, we discuss some of the most widely used 3D-QSAR techniques. The review by Evans et al on 3D-QSAR is worth reading for further understanding (Verma, et al., 2010).

5.3.1 Hologram Quantitative Structure Activity relationship (HQSAR)

Hologram QSAR is a unique QSAR method. This method does not require the exact 3D information for the ligands. In this technique, the molecule is hashed to a molecular fingerprint that encodes the frequency of the occurrence of various molecular fragment types. In simpler words, the fragment size controls both the minimum and maximum length of the fragments to be included in the hologram fingerprint. Molecular holograms are produced by generating all the linear and branched fragments, which range in size from 4 to 7 atoms. (Suh, et al., 2002).

5.3.2 Comparative Molecular Field Analysis (CoMFA)

Comparative molecular field analysis (CoMFA) is a promising new approach to structure-activity correlation. Work on CoMFA began in at 70's and is one of the more famous 3D QSAR methods. It provides steric and electrostatic values in addition to ClogP values. ClogP means the hydrophobic parameters of the ligands. (Cramer, et al., 1988 &Wold, et al., 1984).

5.3.3 Comparative Molecular Similarity Indices Analysis (CoMSIA)

Comparative Molecular Similarity Indices Analysis (CoMSIA) is known as one of the newer 3D QSAR methodology. This technique is most commonly used in drug discovery to find the common features that are important in binding to the relevant biological receptor. In this technique, both steric and electrostatic features, hydrogen bond donor, hydrogen bond acceptor and hydrophobic fields are considered. (Malinowski, and Howery, 1980).

6. Combinatorial chemistry and High-Throughput Screening (HTS)

Combinatorial Chemistry is a technology for synthesizing and characterizing collections of compounds and screening them against various diseases. It was primarily used for the synthesis of peptide and oligonucleotide libraries. Many compounds discovered combinatorially have at least entered preclinical or clinical trials. That's some proof of the value of combinatorial chemistry. But the bottom line is that many researchers in academia, industry, and government already recognize it as an integral component of the drug discovery repertoire. (Borman, 2002).

High-Throughput Screening (HTS) a high-tech approach for drug discovery, is more and more gaining popularity among industrial researchers as well as students doing their post-graduate and/or doctorate research projects. It is basically a process of screening and assaying huge number of biological modulators and effectors against selected and specific targets. The principles and methods of HTS find their application for screening of combinatorial chemistry, genomics, protein, and peptide libraries. The main purpose or goal of this technique is to hasten the drug discovery process by screening the large compound libraries with a speed which may exceed a few thousand compounds per day or per week. For any assay or screening by HTS to be successful several steps like target identification, reagent preparation, compound management, assay development and high-throughput library screening should be carried out with utmost care and precision. (Martis, et al., 2011a).

7. Conclusions

Many more approaches like metabolomics, genomics, proteomics also compliment well with the other techniques so that more target specific agents can be discovered with more accuracy. The review on metabolomics shall explain more in detail (Martis, et al., 2011b). Drug discovery is yet more to be explored, even more than that explored till date. The findings of the human genome project has added more understanding to the target identification. Nature has made all the provisions for curing a disease or disorder, human efforts of finding is what is required. Exploring natural sources which is ill-explored should be effective done as nature is source of countless chemicals which could lead to a successful drug candidates.

8. Acknowledgements

The authors would like to acknowledge the efforts of Ms. Rewa R. Badve, from V.E.S. College of Pharmacy, Chembur [E], Mumbai, India, for proofreading the manuscript and rectifying the spelling and grammatical mistakes.

9. References

Abuin, A.; Holt, K.H.; Platt, K.A.; Sands, A.T.; Zambrowicz, B.P. (2002). Full-speed mammalian genetics: in vivo target validation in the drug discovery process. Trends Biotechnol., Vol. 20, no. 1, pp. 36-42.

Allen, M. P.; Tildesley, D. J. (1989). Computer Simulation of Liquids, Oxford Science Publications, Oxford, UK, pp. 385.

Augen, J. (2002). The evolving role of information technology in the drug discovery process. Drug Discovery Today, Vol. 7, No, 5, pp. 315-323.

Black, J.W. (2000) Introduction: Bioassays - past uses and future potentials, In: The *Pharmacology of Functional, Biochemical, and Recombinant Receptor Systems*, Kenakin, T. and Angus, J.A., pp. 1–11, Springer-Verlag, ISBN 3-540-66124-7, Berlin.

Bleicher, K.H.; Bohm, H.J.; Muller, K.; Alanine, A.I. (2003). Hit and Lead generation: Beyond High-Throughput Screening. Nature Reviews Drug Discovery, Vol. 2, pp. 369-378.

Bo, L.; Ming, L.; Wen-Xiang, H. (2010). Molecular Docking and Molecular Dynamics Simulations of Fentanyl Analogs Binding to μ-Opioid Receptors. Acta Physico-Chimica Sinica, Vol. 26 no. 1, pp. 206-214.

Bohm, H.J.; Stahl, M. (2000). Structure-based library design: molecular modeling merges with combinatorial chemistry. Curr. Opin. Chem. Biol., Vol. 4, pp. 283-286.

Borman, S. (2002). Combinatorial Chemistry. Chemical & Enggineering News, vol 80, no 45, pp. 43-57.

Borsa, J.; Whitemore, G.F. (1969). Cell Killing Studies on the Mode of Action of Methotrexate on L-cells in Vitro. Cancer Research, Vol. 29, no. 4, pp. 737-744.

Caldwell, G.W.; Ritchie, D.M.; Masucci, J.A.; Hageman, W.; Yan, Z. (2001). The New Pre-Preclinical Paradigm: Compound Optimization in Early and Late Phase Drug Discovery. Current Topics in Medicinal Chemistry, Vol. 1, No. 5, pp. 353-366.

Congreve, M.; Murray, C.W.; Blundell T.L. (2005). Keynote review: Structural Biology and Drug Discovery. *Drug Discovery Today*, Vol. 10, no. 13, pp. 895-907.

Cramer,R.D; Patterson, D.E.; Bunce, J.D. (1988). Comparative Molecular Field Analysis (CoMFA). 1. Effect of Shape on Binding of Steroids to Carrier Proteins. J. Am. Chem. Soc., Vol. 110, pp. 5959-5967.

Cummings, J.L.; Vinters, H.V.; Cole, G.M.; Khachaturian, Z.S. (1998). Alzheimer's disease Etiologies, pathophysiology, cognitive reserve, and treatment opportunities. *Neurology*, Vol. 51 no. 1, Suppl 1, pp. S2-S17.

Drews, J. (2000a). Drug Discovery: A Historical Perspective. *Science*, Vol. 287, No. 5460, pp. 1960-1964.

Drews, J. (Ed.). (1999b). *In Quest of Tomorrow's Medicines*, Springer-Verlag, ISBN 0-387-95542-9, New York.

Franke, R. (1984). In Nauta, W.Th.; Rekker, R.F., Eds. Theoretical Drug Design Methods, Elsevier, New York, pp. 256.

Free, S.M.; Wilson, J.W. (1964) . A Mathematical contribution to structure-activity studies. J. Med. Chem., Vol. 7, no. 4 pp. 395-399..

Go, N; Scherga, H.A. (1970). Ring closure and local conformational deformations of chain molecules. Macromolecules, Vol. 3, no. 2, pp. 178-187.

Hammett, L.P. (1966). Physical Organic Chemistry in Retrospect. J. Chem. Ed., Vol. 43, no 9, pp. 464-468.

Hansch, C.; Leo, A. (1995) Exploring QSAR. Fundamentals and Applications in Chemist and biology, American Chemical Society.

Höltje, H.D., et al. (2003) Molecular Modeling, 2nd ed., Wiley-VCH.

Joseph-McCarthy, D. (1999). Computational approaches to structure-based ligand design. Pharmacol. Ther., Vol. 84, pp. 179-191.

Kellogg, G.E.; Joshi, G. J.; Abraham, D.J. (1992). New tools for modeling and understanding hydrophobicity and hydrophobic interactions. Med. Chem. Res., Vol. 1, pp. 444-453.

Kimball, S.D.(1995). Thrombin active site inhibitors. Curr Pharm Des, Vol. 1, pp. 441-468.

Klebe, G. (1995). Toward a more efficient handling of conformational flexibility in computer-assisted modeling of drug molecules. Persp Drug Discov Design, Vol. 3, pp. 85-105.

Klebe, G. (2000). Recent developments in structure-based drug design. J. Mol Med, Vol. 78, pp. 269-281.

Kubiny, H. (1997). QSAR and 3D QSAR in drug design Part 1: methodology. Drug Discovery Today, Vol. 2, No. 11, pp. 457-467.

Kubinyi, H. (1995) in Burger's Medicinal Chemistry, (Vol. 1, 5th edn) (Wolff, M.E.. ed.), pp. 497-571, John Wiley & Sons.

Kubinyi, H. (1998a). Combinatorial and computational approaches in structure-based drug design. Current Opinion in Drug Discovery and Development, Vol. 1, No. 1, pp. 16-26.

Kubinyi, H. (1998b). Structure-based design of enzyme inhibitors and receptor ligands. Current Opinion in Drug Discovery and Development, Vol. 1, no 1, pp. 4-15.

Leach A.R. (2001). Molecular Modelling, Pearson Prentice Hall, Harlow, GB.

Lombardino, J.G.; Lowe, J.A. (2004). The role of the medicinal chemist in drug discovery – then and now. Nature Reviews Drug Discovery, Vol. 3, pp. 853-862.

MacKerell, A.D.; Wiórkiewicz-Kuczera, J.; Karplus, M. (1995). An All-Atom Empirical Energy Function for the Simulation of Nucleic Acids, J. Am. Chem. Soc., Vol. 117, pp. 11946-11975.

Malinowski, E.R.; Howery, D.G. (1980). Factor Analysis in Chemistry; Wiley: New York.

Marrone, T.J.; Briggs, J.M.; McCammon, J.A. (1997). Structure-Based Drug Design: Computational Advances. Annu. Rev. Pharmacol. Toxicol, Vol. 37, pp. 71-90.

Martis, E.A.; Ahire D.C.; Singh R.O. (2011b). Metabolomics in Drug Discovery: A Review. International Journal of Pharmacy and Pharmaceutical Science Research, Vol. 1, no. 2, pp. 67-74.

Martis, E.A.; Radhakrishnan, R.; Badve, R.R. (2011a). High-throughput Screening: The Hits and Leads of Drug Discovery- An Overview. Journal of Applied Pharmaceutical Science, Vol. 1, no 1, pp. 2-10.

Marton, M.J.; Derisi, J.L.; Bennett, H.A.; Iyer, V.R.; Meyer, M.R.; et al. (1998). Drug target validation and identification of secondary drug target effects using DNA microarrays. Nature Medicine, Vol. 4, no. 11, pp. 1293-1301.

Meidrum, N.U.; Roughton, F.J.W. (1933). Carbonic Anhydrase. Its Preparation and Properties. Journal of Physiology, Vol. 80, no. 2, pp. 113-142.

Mestres, J,; Rohrer, D.C.; Maggiora G.M. (1997). MIMIC: a molecular- field matching program. Exploiting the applicability of molecular similarity approaches. J Comput Chem, Vol. 18, pp. 934-954.

Moore, D.J.; West, A.B.; Dawson, V.L.; Dawson, T.M. (2005). Molecular Pathophysiology of Parkinson's Disease. Annu. Rev. Neurosci., Vol. 28, pp. 57-87.

Nielsen, K.J.; Adarns, D.; Thomas, L.; Bond, T.; Alewood, P.F.; Craik, D.J.; Lewis, R.J. (1999). Structure-activity relationships of omega-conotoxins MVIIA, MVIIC and 14 loop splice hybrids at N and P/Q-type calcium channels. J. Mol. Biol., vol 289, no. 5, pp. 1405-1421.

Ooms, F. (2000). Molecular modeling and computer aided drug design. Examples of their applications in medicinal chemistry. Curr. Med. Chem., Vol. 7, 141-158.

Overington J.P.; Al-Lazikani, B.; Hopkins, A.L. (2006). How many drug targets are there?. Nature Reviews Drug Discovery, Vol. 5, No. 12, pp. 993-996.

Pearson, A.A.; Gaffney, T.E.; Privitera P.J. (1989). A stereoselective central hypotensive action of atenolol. The Journal of Pharmacology and experimental Therapeutics, Vol. 250, No. 3,pp. 759-763.

Pissurlenkar, R.R.S.; Shaikh, M.S.; Iyer, R.P.; Coutinho, E.C. (2009). Molecular Mechanics Force Fields and their Applications in Drug Design. Anti-Infective Agents in Medicinal Chemistry, Vol. 8, no. 2, pp. 128-150.

Prasad, J.V.N.V.; Lunney, E.A.; Para, K.S.; Tummino, P.J.; Ferguson, D.; et al. (1996). Nonpeptidic potent HIV-1 protease inhibitors. Drug Design Discov, Vol 13, pp.15-28.

Ratti, E.; Trist, D. (2011). Continuing evolution of the drug discovery process in the pharmaceutical industry. Pure Appl. Chem., Vol. 73, No. 1, pp. 67–75.

Richard, F.; Clark, M.A.; Cubeddu, L.X. (Eds.). (2009). *Lippincott's Illustrated Reviews: Pharmacology*, Lippincott Williams & Wilkins, ISBN 978-0-7817-7155-9, pp. 348-358, Baltimore.

Scheraga, H. A. In Lipkowitz, K. B.; Boyd, D. B. Eds. (1992) Revisions in Computational Chemistry, VCH, New York, pp. 73-142.

Singh, R.; Nagori, B.P.; Soni, B.; Singh, J.V. (2011). A Review: Clinical Trial and Data Management. Pharmacophore, Vol. 2, no. 3, pp. 200-209

Smith, D.A.; van de Waterbeemd, H. (1999). Pharmacokinetics and metabolism in early drug discovery. Curr. Opin. Chem. Biol., Vol. 3, pp. 373-378.

Structure based drug design and molecular modelling. Available from http://www.imb-jena.de/~rake/Bioinformatics_WEB/dd_tools.html

Structure-Based Drug-Design. Available online: http://www.proxychem.com/sbdd.html

Suh, M.; Park, S.; Jee, H. (2002). Comparison of QSAR Methods (CoMFA, CoMSIA, HQSAR) of Anticancer 1-N-Substituted Imidazoquinoline-4,9-dione Derivatives. Bull. Korean Chem. Soc., Vol. 23, no. 3, pp. 417-422.

Taft, C.A.; Da Silva, V.B.; Da Silva, C.H.T.D. (2008). Current Topics in Computer-Assisted Drug Design. Journal of Pharmaceutical sciences, Vol. 97, no. 3, pp. 1089-1098.

Taft, R.W.(1956). In Newrnan, M.S. Ed., Steric Effects in Organic Chemistry, John Wiley & Sons, NY, p. 556.

Taylor, P. J. (1990). In Ramsden, C.A. Ed., Comprehensive Medicinal Chemistry. The Rational Design, Mechanistic Study and Therapeutic Application of Chemical Compounds, Vol. 4, Quantitative Drug Design, Pergamon, Elmsford, NY, p. 241.

Tuckerman, M. E.; Martyna, G. J. (2000). Understanding Modern Molecular Dynamics: Techniques and Applications. J. Phys. Chem. B, Vol. 104, pp. 159-178.

Tute, M.S. (1990). In Ramsden, C.A., Ed., Comprehensive Medicinal Chemistry. The Rational Design, Mechanistic Study and Therapeutic Application of Chemical Compounds, Vol. 4, Quantitative Drug Design, Pergamon, Elmsford, NY, p. 18.

Verloop, A. (1987) The STERIMOL Approach to Drug Design, Marcel Dekker, New York.

Verma, J.; Khedkar, V.M.; Coutinho, E.C. (2010). 3D-QSAR in drug design-a review. Curr Top Med Chem., Vol. 10, no. 1, pp. 95-115.

Wade, R.C. (1997). 'Flu' and structure-based drug design. Structure, Vol. 5, pp. 1139-1145.

Wise, A.; Gearing, K.; Rees, S. (2002). Target validation of G-protein coupled receptors. Drug Discovery Today, Vol. 7, no. 4, pp. 235-246.

Wold, S.; Ruhe, A.; Wold, H.; Dunn, W.J. (1984). The collinearity problem in linear regression. The partial least squares approach to generalized inverse. SIAM J. Sci. Stat. Comput., Vol. 5, pp. 735-743.

Xue, L.; Bajorath, J. (2000). Molecular descriptors in chemoinformatics, computational combinatorial chemistry, and virtual screening. Comb. Chem. High Throughput Screen., Vol. 3, pp.363-372.

3

Pharmacognostic Methods for Analysis of Herbal Drugs, According to European Pharmacopoeia

Duțu Ligia Elena
University of Medicine and Pharmacy
„Carol Davila" Bucharest,
Faculty of Pharmacy,
Romania

1. Introduction

Plants had been used for medical purpose long before recorded history.

At the present time, according with the WHO reports, about 80 % of the world's population use herbal medicines for some aspects of their primary health care. This phenomena is in relationship with a rapidly expanding of the phytopharmaceutical industry and market, especialy for dietary supplements. Unfortunately, these supplements are insufficiently studied and have a low quality. For this reason, today, the tendency is to militate for to decrease the number of supplements and to increase the number of herbal medicinal products, which are more rigorously analyzed before marketing authorization and after that, according to European Medicines Agency guidelines.

European Pharmacopoeia is the official book about the quality of medicines, recognized in Europe. It was inaugurated in 1964 through the Convention on the elaboration of a European pharmacopoeia, under the auspices of Council of Europe. The current seventh edition became effective on the 1st January 2011.

This chapter presents the quality specification and specific methods (pharmacognostic methods) for analysis of herbal drugs, according to European Pharmacopoeia.

2. Herbal drug: Definition, nomenclature, types (classification)

2.1 Definition

According to European Pharmacopoeia (EP), a herbal drug is mainly a whole, fragmented, or a cut plant, part of a plant, algae, fungi or lichen, in an unprocessed state, usually in dried form but sometimes fresh. Certain exudates that have not been subjected to a specific treatment are also considered to be herbal drugs.

The herbal drug may be used in therapy, due to its content of active principle. Active principle means an organic compound or a mixture of organic compounds, which are present in a herbal drug and has a specific pharmacological activity.

2.2 Nomenclature

Herbal drugs are defined by the botanical scientific name, according to the binominal system. The first word defines genus and/or species and / or variety, but sometimes organoleptic characteristics, processing status s.a. The second word defines the type of vegetal drug (botanical organ). Some examples are included in table 1.

Herbal drug	Botanical origin
Althaeae folium	*Althaea officinalis* L.
Belladonnae folium	*Atropa belladonna* L.
Echinaceae angustifoliae radix Echinaceae pallidae radix	*Echinacea angustifolia* D.C. *Echinacea pallida* Nutt.
Foeniculi dulcis fructus	*Foeniculum vulgare* Miller sp. *vulgare* var. *dulce*
Myrtilli fructus recens Myrtilli fructus siccum	*Vaccinium myrtillus* L.

Table 1. Nomenclature for herbal drugs.

2.3 Types of herbal drugs

European Pharmacopoeia contains more than 120 specific monographs about herbal drugs.

A vegetal drug which have a plant origin may consist of subteran organs (radix, rhizoma, tubera, bulbus), bark (cortex) or aerial organs (folium, flos, fructus, pseudofructus, pericarpium, semen, seminis tegumentum, herba). List of monographs is included in table 2.

This chapter discusses only about these „classic" vegetal drugs. Other herbal drugs (like lichens, algae, resins, volatile oils s.a) are not discussed in this chapter.

The grade of fragmentation point of view in pharmacognostic analysis are used the following types of herbal drugs: in toto, concissum, pulveratum. The grade of pulverisation is defined in EP chapter 2.1.4.

3. Pharmacognostic analysis

An adequate methodology must be used for to analyse a vegetal raw material. We will call this methodology as „pharmacognostic analysis".

Herbal drug	Herbal drug	Herbal drug
Agni casti fructus	Frangulae cortex	Polygalae radix
Agrimoniae herba	Fraxini folium	Polygoni avicularis herba
Alchemillae herba	Fumariae herba	Pruni africanae cortex
Althaeae folium	Gentianae radix	Psylli semen
Altaeae radix	Ginkgonis folium	Quercus cortex
Angelicae radix	Ginseng radix	Ratanhiae radix
Anisi fructus	Graminis rhizoma	Rhamni purshianae cortex
Anisi stelati fructus	Hamamelidis folium	Rhei rhizoma
Arnicae flos	Harpagophyti radix	Rosae pseudo-fructus

Herbal drug	Herbal drug	Herbal drug
Astragali mongholici radix	Hederae folium	Rosmarini folium
Auranti amari epicarpium et mesocarpium	Hibisci sabdarifae flos	Rusci rhizoma
Aurantii amari flos	Hydrastidis rhizoma	Sabalis serrulatae fructus
Ballotae nigrae herba	Hyperici herba	Salicis cortex
Belladonnae folium	Ipecacuanhae radix	Salviae officinalis folium
Betulae folium	Iuniperi pseudo-fructus	Salviae trilobae folium
Bistortae rhizoma	Lavandulae flos	Sambuci flos
Boldi folium	Leonuri cardiacae herba	Sanguisorbae radix
Calendulae flos	Levistici radix	Schizandrae chinensis fructus
Capsici fructus	Lini semen	Scutellariae baicalensis radix
Carthami flos	Liquiritiae radix	Sennae folium
Centauri herba	Lupuli flos	Sennae acutifoliae fructus
Centellae asiaticae herba	Lythri herba	Sennae angustifoliae fructus
Chamomillae romanicae flos	Malvae silvestris flos	Serpylli herba
Chelidonii herba	Malvae folium	Silybi mariani fructus
Cinchonae cortex	Marrubii herba	Stephaniae tetrandrae radix
Cinnamomi cortex	Matricariae flos	Stramonii folium
Colae semen	Meliloti herba	Tanaceti parthenii herba
Crataegi fructus	Menthae piperitae folium	Thymi herba
Crataegi folium cum flos	Menyanthidis trifoliatae folium	Tiliae flos
Curcumae xanthorrhizae rhizoma	Millefolii herba	Tormentillae rhizoma
Cynarae folium	Myrtilli fructus recens	Trigonellae foenugreci semen
Echinaceae angustifoliae radix	Myrtilli fructus siccum	Urticae folium
Echinaceae pallidae radix	Notoginseng radix	Uvae ursi folium
Echinaceae purpureae herba	Oleae folium	Valerianae radix
Echinaceae purpureae radix	Ononidis radix	Valerianae radix minutata
Eleuterococci radix	Orthosiphonis folium	Verbasci flos
Equiseti herba	Passiflorae herba	Verbenae citriodoratae folium
Ephedrae herba	Pelargonii radix	Verbenae herba
Eucapypti folium	Plantaginis lanceolatae folium	Violae herba cum flore
Fagopyri herba	Plantaginis ovatae semen	Zingiberis rhozoma
Filipendulae ulmariae herba	Plantaginis ovatae seminis tegumentum	Polygalae radix

Table 2. List of EP monographs (for „classic" vegetal drugs)

It comprises qualitative and quantitative tests in order to verify or to establish the identity, purity and quality of a herbal drug.

Identity parameters: macroscopic examination; microscopic examination; qualitative chemical analysis; chromatographic analysis.

Purity parameters: foreign matter.

Quality parameters: loss on drying; soluble-substances; total ash and ash insoluble in hydrochloric acid; heavy metals; swelling index; bitter value; assay of active principles; microbiological examination (bacteria, yeasts and moulds, specified microorganisms); pesticide residues; aflatoxines; ochratoxines.

3.1 Macroscopic examination

This test have in view to determ the morphological characteristics. It gives details concerning the drug aspect, size, colour, odour and taste.

3.1.1 Methodology

Morphological characters and the colour may be examination with the naked eye or by using a magnifyed glass.

The size can be determ by using a ruler or a caliper.

The odour can be determ by shattering the drug between two fingers and smell, or using an extractive solution.

The taste can be determ by putting a piece of drug or an extractive solution in the mouth.

3.1.2 Evaluation of results

There are not general recomandations in EP in order to the macroscopical examination.

The main characteristics which are frequently analyse are included in table 3.

3.1.3 Limits

The morphologic characteristics vary in large limits, due to the vegetal drug.

Organoleptic characteristics may inform about chemical composition: coloured in yellow conduct to flavones, xanthones, carotenoids; coloured in red for anthocyanins; bitter taste for antracenic-derivatives, alkaloids, cardiotonic glycosides.

3.2 Microscopic examination

This test have in view to determ the anatomic characteristics.

3.2.1 Methodology

According to EP chapter 2.8.23. , the microscopic examination of herbal drugs is carried out on the powdered drug (355). Chloral hydrate is the most commonly prescribed reagent.

Herbal drug	Aspect	Size	Colour	Odour	Taste
Radix, rhizoma, tubera, bulbus	- striated / smooth - shape - decorticated / nondecorticated - harsh / soft - fracture - consistency - tissues' ratio	- length - diameter	external, internal	- present / absent - non-specific/ specific	- present / absent - non-specific/ specific
Cauli	- branched / unbranched - striated / smooth - hollow or not / pubescent / glabrous	- length - diameter	external surface	- present / absent - non-specific/ specific	- present / absent - non-specific/ specific
Folium	- pubescent / glabrous - sessile / petiolate - thin / thick / coriaceous - the shape of lamina - the margin, the base, and the top of lamina - venation	- length of petiole and lamina - width of lamina	upper and lower surfaces	- present / absent - non-specific/ specific	- present / absent - non-specific/ specific
Flos	- isolated flower / inflorescence (type) - bud / mature flower - complete / incomplete - flower formula (description)	- length, width of each component	especially for corola	- present / absent - non-specific/ specific	- present / absent - non-specific/ specific
Fructus	- type - freshy / dry - shape - epicarp characteristics	- length - width - diameter	- internal and external surfaces	- present / absent - non-specific/ specific	- present / absent - non-specific/ specific
Semen	- shape - hylum, rafee - ratio between tegument, endosperme and embryo	- length - width - diameter	external surface	- present / absent - non-specific/ specific	- present / absent - non-specific/ specific
Herba	- the position of leaves and flowers on the stem - aspect of stem, leaves and flowers (*see cauli, folium, flos*)	*see cauli, folium, flos*	*see cauli, folium, flos*	*see cauli, folium, flos*	*see cauli, folium, flos*
Cortex	- shape - thin / thick - outer surface (i.e. lenticels, lichens) - striated / smooth - fracture	- length - width	internal and external surfaces	- present / absent - non-specific/ specific	- present / absent - non-specific/ specific

Table 3. Macroscopic characteristics

Other reagents are: lactic reagent, alcoholic solution of phloroglucinol and hydrochloric acid, ruthenium red solution, glycerol.

3.2.2 Evaluation of results

Phloroglucinol is used to identify the presence of lignin, ruthenium red solution is used to show the presence of mucilage, glycerol is used to show the presence of starch and inulin.

In the case of Plantaginis ovatae semen and Plantaginis ovatae semen tegmentum, lactic reagent makes it possible to visualize lignified cells, cutinized membranes and starch.

Common anatomic elements (which are used for to confirm the organ) and specific elements (which are used for to identify the herbal drug) are analyzed (see table 4).

Herbal drug	Common elements	Specific elements
Radix, rhizoma, tubera, bulbus	large xylem vessels, parenchyma, coak	fibres (celulozic, lignified), starch, calcium oxalate (prisms, cluster-crystals, raphides), sclereids, medullary rays
Cauli	xylem vessels, parenchyma, coak	fibres (celulozic, lignified), starch, calcium oxalate (prisms, cluster-crystals, raphides), sclereids, covering trichomes
Folium	chlorophylian tissue, spiral and annular vessels, stomata	type of stomata, covering- and glandular trichomes, calcium oxalate (prisms, cluster-crystals, raphides), fibres, secretory cells
Flos	papillose cells, pollen grains, endothecium, spiral and annular vessels,	description of pollen grain (size, shape, number of pores, exine aspect), covering- and glandular trichomes, calcium oxalate (prisms, cluster-crystals, raphides), fibres
Fructus	fragments of epicarp, spiral and annular vessels	sclereids, secretory cells, fragment of mesocarp with volatile oil, fatty oil or pigments, fibres, calcium oxalate, covering trichomes
Semen	fragments of endosperma and cotiledone	pigmentary tissue, fibres, starch, mucilaginous cells, aleurone grains, globules of fixed oil
Herba	*see cauli, folium, flos*	*see cauli, folium, flos*
Cortex	parenchyma, coak; xylem vessels are absent	phloem fibres (celulozic, lignified), calcium oxalate (prisms, cluster-crystals, raphides), sclereids, medullary rays

Table 4. Microscopic examination

In EP, a special chapter is named „Stomata and Stomatal index" (chapter 2.8.3.).

The Stomatal index is the ratio (expressed as „%") of the number of stomata in a given area of leaf and the number of total epidermal cells (including stomata, trichomes) in the same area of leaf.

3.2.3 Limits

Using stomatal index, it may distinguish *Cassia acutifolia* (stomatal index 10-12.5-15) from *Cassia angustifolia* (stomatal index 14-17.5-20).

3.3 Qualitative chemical analysis

For unknown vegetal product, this test may establish the chemical composition, and for known herbal drugs this test may confirm the presence of a chemical compound (which may be not the main active principle).

3.3.1 Methodology

Because EP is a reference used for the control of herbal drugs, only reactions in an extractive solution apply.

3.3.2 Evaluation of results

EP examples are included in table 5.

Compound	Herbal drug	Reagent	Result - colour
Antracenic derivatives	Frangulae cortex, Rhei rhizoma, Rhamni purshianae cortex, Sennae fructus	Dilute ammonia	a red colour
Tannins	Quercus cortex	vanillin in hydrochloric acid	a red colour
Tropan alkaloids	Belladonnae folium, Stramonii folium	fuming nitric acid + 30 g/L solution of potassium hydroxide in ethanol 96%	a violet colour
Iridoids	Verbasci flos	hydrochloric acid	a greenish-blue color, and after a few minutes, cloudiness and then a blackish precipitate
Sesquiterpens	Millefolii herba	dimethylaminobenzaldehyde	blue or greenish-blue
Cardenolic glycosides	Digitalis purpureae folium	dinitrobenzoic acid + 1M sodium hydroxide	reddish-violet colour

Table 5. Reactions in an extractive solution.

3.4 Qualitative chromatography

Chromatography is a method of separation based on adsorbtion, repartition, ion exchange. It brings supplementary informations about chemical composition.

Chromatographic techniques: TLC, HPLC, GC

3.4.1 Thin Layer Chromatography (TLC)

3.4.1.1 Methodology

Experimental conditions differ depending of chemical compound have to identify. Examples of mobile phases, references substances and reagents used for some active principles and some herbal drugs are included in tabel 6.

Herbal drug	Active principle	Mobile phase	Reference solution	Reagent, examination
Salicis cortex	salicin	water: methanol: ethyl acetate (7.5:10:75, v/v/v)	salicin, chlorogenic acid	R1, daylight
Agrimoniae herba	Flavones (quercitroside, isoquercitroside,hyperoside, rutin)	anhydrous formic acid: water: ethyl acetate (10:10:80, v/v/v)	isoquercitroside, rutin	R2, UV (365 nm)
Carthami flores	yellow and red pigments (including flavones)	acetic acid: anhydrous formic acid: water: ethyl acetate (11:11:27:100, v/v/v/v).	rutin, quercetin	daylight; R2, UV (365 nm)
Malvae silvestris flos	anthocyanins (6"-malonyl malvin, malvin)	acetic acid: water: butanol (15:30:60, v/v/v).	quinaldine red	daylight
Malvae folium	fluorescent compounds (including flavones)	anhydrous formic acid: anhydrous acetic acid: water: ethyl formate: 3-pentanone (4:11:14:20: 50, v/v/v/v/v).	rutin, hyperoside	R2, UV (365 nm)
Althaeae folium	fluorescent compounds (including flavones and polyphenol-carboxylic acids)	acetic acid: anhydrous formic acid: water: ethyl acetate (11:11:27:100, v/v/v/v).	chlorogenic acid, quercitrin	R2, UV (365 nm)
Ephedrae herba	alkaloids (ephedrine)	concentrated ammonia: methanol: methylene chloride (0.5:5:20, v/v/v).	ephedrine, 2-indanamine	R3, daylight
Sennae folium, Sennae fructus (acutifoliae, angustifoliae)	antracenic derivatives (including sennosides)	glacial acetic acid: water: ethyl acetate: propanol (1:30:40:40, v/v/v/v)	senna extract	R4, daylight

Legend: R1 - sulphuric acid; R2- diphenylboric acid aminoethyl ester + macrogol 400; R3 – ninhydrin; R4 - nitric acid + potassium hydroxide.

Table 6. TLC experimental conditions

3.4.1.2 Evaluation of results

Each compound has a characteristic spot, with a definit Rf-value, colour and / or fluorescence.

3.4.1.3 Limits

Most of pharmacopoeia's monographs include TLC as an identification test. Exceptions: Althaeae radix, Graminis rhizoma, Lini semen, Psylli semen.

In some cases, using this technique it may distinguish vegetal sources / herbal drugs, like *Panax sp.; Panax ginseng* C. A. Meyer is the vegetal source for Ginseng radix, and *Panax pseudoginseng* Wall. var. *notoginseng* (Burk.) Hoo et Tseng is the source for Notoginseng radix.

TLC may be used as a purity test, too (see section 2.5. Foreign matter).

3.4.2 High Pressure Liquid Chromatography (HPLC)

This technique is used both for identification and for assay.

For example, HPLC technique is used as an identification test in the case of the following herbal drugs: Echinaceae angustifoliae radix, E. pallidae radix, E. purpureae folium, E. purpureae herba.

3.4.3 Gas-chromatography (GC)

This technique is used both for identification and for assay.

Identification by using GC technique is mentioned for the following herbal drugs: Thymi herba, Lavandulae flos, and Sabalis serrulatae fructus.

3.5 Foreign matter

According to EP chapter 2.8.2., foreign matter is material consisting of foreign organs (matter coming from the source plant but not defined as the drug) and / or foreign elements (matter not coming from the source plant and either of vegetable or mineral origin).

3.5.1 Methodology

A macroscopic examination, microscopic examination, reactions or chromatography are used for to identify foreign matters.

A quantitative evaluation may be applied, too.

3.5.2 Evaluation of results

Organoleptic, morphologic, anatomic and chemical characteristics for the sample are compared with the ones are known for „pure" herbal drug.

The content of foreign matter is expressed as „%, m/m".

3.5.3 Limits

The EP recommendation (monograph „Herbal drugs") is that the content of foreign matter is not more than 2%, unless otherwise prescribed or justified and authorized.

Some impurities are limited, and others are excluded. Some examples are included in table 7.

Herbal drug (active principle)	Foreign matter (active principle)	Test
Papaveris rhoeados flos	maximum 2% of capsules and maximum 1% of other foreign matter	general quantitative evaluation
Sambuci flos	maximum 8%of fragments of coarse pedicels and other foreign matter and maximum 15% of discolored, brown flowers	general quantitative evaluation
Malvae folium	maximum 5% of foreign organs (flowers, fruits and parts of the stem), maximum 5% of leaves with blisters of spores of Puccinia malvacearum and maximum 2% of foreign elements	general quantitative evaluation; microscopic examination of spores
Tiliae flos, from *Tilia cordata* Miller, *Tilia platyphyllos* Scop., *Tilia×vulgaris* Heyne (essential oil - sedative)	*Tilia tomentosa* Moench. (essential oil in a lower content)	macroscopic examination
Thymi herba (essential oil)	*Thymus serpyllum* (essential oil; lower content, and different fingerprint)	macroscopic examination
Digitalis purpureae folium (cardenolic glycosides - purpurea glycosides)	Digitalis lanatae folium (cardenolic glycosides - lanatosides; the pharmacokinetic profile is different)	microscopic examination
Bistortae rhizoma (tannins)	*Paris polyphylla* or *Paris quadrifolia* (steroidal saponins; toxic)	microscopic examination
Graminis rhizoma (inulin, triticin)	*Cynodon dactilon, Imperata cylindrica* (starch)	microscopic examination, using iodine solution
Plantaginis lanceolatae folium (mucilages)	*Digitalis lanata* L. (cardenolic glycosides)	TLC
Primulae radix (triterpenic saponins - expectorant)	*Vincetoxicum hirundinaria medicus* (vincetoxine - toxic)	TLC
Stephaniae tetrandrae radix (bisbenzylisoquinoline alkaloids)	*Aristolochia fangchi* (aristolochic acids - toxic)	Test for aristolochic acids in herbal drugs - method A (TLC)

Table 7. Foreign matter

3.6 Loss on drying

This parameter is stricken by the humidity of the environment. On the other hand, it may affect the quality of the herbal drugs among the storage. A high content of water may favor the growth of microorganisms (fungi which produce mycotoxins), or may activate enzymatic systems which will generate compounds with a less activity (specific hydrolases may degrade primary cardenolic glycosides to secondary cardenolic glycosides, which have less activity).

3.6.1 Methodology

Usually, the powdered drug is dried in an oven at 105 ^{0}C for 2 h.

When the content of essential oil is high (Carvi fructus, Eucalypti folium, Foeniculi fructus, Iuniperi pseudo-fructus, Menthae piperitae folium, Zingiberis rhizoma, Thymi herba), EP recommendation is to determ the content of water (according to cap 2.2.13) and the content of essential oils (chapter 2.8.12).

3.6.2 Evaluation of results

The result is expressed as „%, m/m" or „mL/kg".

3.6.3 Limits

Usually, the limits are about 10 - 12% (100 - 120 mL/kg).

Unusual limits (for example maximum 6% for Digitalis purpureae folium, maximum 8% for Lini semen and Syllibi mariani fructus, max. 80 mL/kg for Foeniculi amari fructus and Foeniculi dulcis fructus, and maximum 70 mL/kg for Anisi fructus) are exceptions. These lower limits are in relationship with the stability of the active compounds - cardenolic glycosides (Digitalis purpureae folium), lipids and mucilages (Lini semen), only lipids (the other upper-mentioned vegetal drugs).

In the case of Lini semen, mucilages may favor the growth of microorganisms (fungi which produce mycotoxins), if the content of water is higher.

In Digitalis purpureae folium, water may activate enzymatic systems (specific hydrolases) and so, primary cardenolic glycosides degrade to secondary cardenolic glycosides, which have less activity.

If the vegetal drug with a high content of lipids is stored in a light, hot and wet place, unsaturated fatty acids degrade (peroxidation, polymerization); the lipids are ranciding.

3.7 Soluble substances

This parameter refers to all vegetal compounds which can be extracted with a certain solvent, in certain experimental conditions. When the solvent is water, the parameter calls „water-soluble extractive". When another solvent is used, it calls „extractable matter".

3.7.1 Methodology

Any general EP method exists. Generally, the powdered drug is extracted with the solvent (definite quantity) under the conditions specified in monograph, the solvent is evaporated, the residue is dried up to fixed mass and finally weighed.

Experimental protocols are included in table 8.

3.7.2 Evaluation of results

The result is expressed as „%, m/m".

3.7.3 Limits

The limits vary, due to the vegetal drug (table 8).

Herbal drug	Sieve (µm)	Solvent	Method	Vegetal drug:solvent ratio	Limits
Aurantii amari epicarpium et mesocarpium	250	a mixture of water and ethanol (3:7)	shake, 2 h	1:5	min. 6%
Gentianae radix	710	boiling water	shake, 10 min.	1:40	min. 33%
Graminis rhizoma	355	boiling water	shake, 10 min.	1:40	min. 25%
Lupuli flos	355	ethanol 70 %	heat on a water-bath under a reflux condenser, 10 min.	1:30	min. 25%
Pruni africanae cortex	250	methylene chloride	continuous extraction apparatus (Soxhlet type), 4h	-	min. 0.5%

Table 8. Soluble substances

For a medicinal product development, the results obtained by using a vegetal raw material and different solvents and different experimental parameters help to evaluate the efficiency of the extraction, to establish the proper solvent and the optimum working technology.

3.8 Total ash and ash insoluble in hydrochloric acid

These parameters express the content of metallic ions (mineral compounds) of a vegetal drug, and they are in relationship with the pedoclimatic conditions.

3.8.1 Methodology

Essentially, according to EP general monograph (chapter 2.4.16), for to determ the total ash, the vegetal drug is ignited to constant mass in a muffle furnace at about 600 °C.

According to EP general monograph (chapter 2.8.1.), for to determ the ash insoluble in hydrochloric acid, the following method apply: the residue from the determination of total ash is boiled with dilute hydrochloric acid, and the solution is filtered through a ashless filter; the filter is dried, is ignited, allow to cool in a desiccator and finally is weighed.

3.8.2 Evaluation of results

The result is expressed as „%, m/m".

3.8.3 Limits

Parameter „Total ash" is included in all monographs.

Parameter „Ash insoluble in hydrochloric acid" is included in most of monographs; exceptions are the following: Agni casti fructus, Agrimoniae herba, Alchemillae herba,

Althaeae radix, Anisi stellati fructus, Arnicae flos, Aurantii amari epicarpium et mesocarpium, Aurantii amari flos, Ballotae nigrae herba, Betulae folium, Boldi folium, Calendulae flos, Capsici fructus,Caryophylli flos, Carvi fructus, Centaurii herba, Centellae asiaticae herba, Chamomillae romanae flos, Chelidonii herba, Cinchonae cortex, Cinnamomi cortex, Coriandri fructus, Crataegi fructus, Crataegi folium cum flore, Cynarae folium, Colae semen, Curcumae xanthorrhizae rhizoma, Echinaceae purpureae herba, Eleutherococci radix, Ephedrae herba, Eucalypti folium, Fagopyri herba, Filipendulae ulmariae herba, Foeniculi amari fructus, Foeniculi dulcis fructus, Frangulae cortex, Fraxini folium, Fumariae herba, Gentianae radix, Ginkgonis folium, Harpagophyti radix, Hederae folium, Hibisci sabdariffae flos, Hyperici herba, Iuniperi pseudo-fructus, Lavandulae flos, Leonuri cardiacae herba, Lini semen, Lythri herba, Lupuli flos, Matricariae flos, Meliloti herba, Melissae folium, Menyanthidis trifoliatae folium, Myrtilli fructus siccus, Myrtilli fructus recens, Oleae folium, Ononidis radix, Orthosiphonis folium, Papaveris rhoeados flos, Passiflorae herba, Plantaginis lanceolatae folium, Plantaginis ovatae semen, Plantaginis ovatae seminis tegumentum, Polygoni avicularis herba, Pruni africanae cortex, Psyllii semen, Quercus cortex, Ratanhiae radix, Rhamni purshianae cortex, Rosae pseudo-fructus, Rosmarini folium, Sabalis serrulatae fructus, Salicis cortex, Salviae officinalis folium, Salviae trilobae folium, Sambuci flos, Schisandrae chinensis fructus, Silybi mariani fructus, Solidaginis virgaureae herba, Tanaceti parthenii herba, Tiliae folium, Tormentillae rhizoma, Trigonellae foenugraeci semen, Uvae ursi folium, Violae herba cum flore, Zingiberis rhizoma.

The limits vary, due to the vegetal drug (for examples see table 9).

Herbal drug	Total ash	Ash insoluble in hydrochloric acid
Anisi fructus	max. 12%	max. 2.5%
Belladonnae folium	max. 16%	max. 4%
Bistortae rhizoma	max. 9%	max.1%
Carthami flos	max. 10%	max. 3%
Echinaceae angustifoliae radix	max. 9%	max. 3%
Echinaceae pallidae radix	max. 7%	max. 2%
Echinaceae purpureae herba	max. 12%	-
Echinaceae purpureae radix	max. 9%	max. 2%
Ephedrae herba	max. 9%	max. 3%
Equiseti herba	12 - 27%	3 - 15%
Malvae folium	max. 17%	max. 3%
Rhei radix	max. 12%	max. 2%
Urticae folium	max. 20%	max. 4%
Verbasci flos	max. 6%	max. 2%

Table 9. Total ash and ash insoluble in hydrochloric acid (examples)

3.9 Heavy metals

This parameter espress the pollution.

3.9.1 Methodology

Atomic absorption spectrometry is used. This is described in EP general chapter 2.4.27.

3.9.2 Evaluation of results

The limits of suitability are given as a maximum value expressed as units ppm.

3.9.3 Limits

In monograph „Herbal drugs", the following limits are mentioned: cadmium - max. 1.0 ppm; lead - max. 5.0 ppm; mercury - max. 0.1 ppm.

Other limits for cadmium are mentioned in monographs for Fumariae herba (max. 1.5 ppm), Lini semen (max. 0.5 ppm), Salicis cortex (max. 2.0 ppm) and Tormentillae rhizoma (max. 2.0 ppm).

3.10 Swelling index

The swelling index is the volume (expressed in milliliters) occupied by 1 gram of an herbal drug and the adhering mucilage, after it has swollen in an aqueous liquid.

It expressed a high content of mucilage in an herbal drug.

3.10.1 Methodology

A general EP method is described in chapter 2.8.4. Generally, 1 gram of herbal drug (the degree of comminution prescribed in the monograph) is placed in a 25 mL ground-glass stoppered cylinder graduated and then is moistened with alcohol. Add 25 mL water, close the cylinder and shake it for 1 h, with a standard frequency. Allow to stand 3 h. Finally, note the volume occupied by the drug and the adhering mucilage.

3.10.2 Evaluation of results

The result is given by the mean of the 3 tests.

3.10.3 Limits

The limits vary, due to the vegetal drug (table 10).

Herbal drug	**Swelling index**
Althaeae radix	Min. 10
Althaeae folium	Min. 12
Malvae folium	Min. 7
Malvae sylvestris flos	Min. 15
Verbasci flos	Min. 9
Violae herba cum flores	Min. 9
Lini semen	Min. 4
Plantaginis ovatae semen	Min. 9
Plantaginis ovatae seminis tegumentum	Min. 40
Psyllii semen	Min. 10
Trigonellae foenugraeci semen	Min. 6

Table 10. Swelling index

3.11 Bitterness value

The bitterness value is the reciprocal of the maximum dilution of a vegetal drug that still has a bitter taste. It is determined by comparison with quinine hydrochloride, the bitterness value of which is set at 200000.

It expressed a high content of bitter-compounds in an herbal drug, active principles which are used to stimulate the appetite. But, attention: not all vegetal substances with bitter taste are used to stimulate the appetite (e.g. cardenolic glycosides, antracenic derivatives and alkaloids).

3.11.1 Evaluation of results

Depending to the dilutions of the reference substance (quinine hydrochloride) and of the test solution, expressions for correction factor and for bitterness value are described in the monograph.

The result is given by the mean of all 6 tests.

3.11.2 Limits

The acceptance limits vary, due to the vegetal drug (table 11).

Herbal drug	Bitterness value
Centauri herba	min. 2000
Gentianae radix	min. 10000
Menyanthidis trifoliatae folium	min. 3000

Table 11. Bitterness value

3.12 Colouring intensity

This parameter expresses the content of pigments (yellow and /or red pigments).

3.12.1 Methodology

Spectral methods apply. These methods consist of the measuring the absorbance at a specific wavelength for a solution having a definit concentration.

3.12.2 Evaluation of results

The absorbance is recorded using a suitable spectrophotometer.

3.12.3 Limits

Specific limits of admisibility are mentioned in monographs. The details are mentioned in tabel 12.

3.13 Assay

In the case of herbal drugs with constituents of known therapeutic activity or with active markers, assays of their content are applied. When the constituents responsible for the therapeutic activity are unknown assays of analytical markers are required.

Herbal drug	Protocol	Limits (absorbance)
Carthami flos	Yellow pigment: macerate 0.1 g of the powdered drug (355) in 150 mL of water, stir for 1 h, filter through a sintered-glass filter (40) and dilute to 500.0 mL; record the absorbance at 401 nm.	min. 0.40
	Red pigment: to 0.25 g of the powdered drug (355) add 50 mL of a mixture of 20 volumes of water and 80 volumes of acetone; heat on a water-bath at 50 °C for 90 min.; allow to cool, filter through a sintered-glass filter (40) and dilute to 100.0 mL; record the absorbance at 518 nm.	min. 0.40
Hibisci sabdariffae flos	To 1.0 g of the powdered drug (355) add 25 mL of boiling water and heat for 15 min on a water-bath with frequent shaking. Filter the hot mixture into a 50 mL graduated flask; after cooling, dilute to 50 mL with water. Dilute 5 mL of this solution to 50 mL with water. Record the absorbance at 520 nm using water as the compensation liquid.	min. 0.350 for the whole drug; min. 0.250 for the cut drug.
Papaveris rhoeados flos	To 1.0 g of the powdered drug (355) add 100 mL of ethanol 30% (V/V) and macerate for 4 h with frequent stirring; filter and discard the first 10 mL; to 10 mL of the filtrate add 2 mL of hydrochloric acid and dilute to 100 mL with ethanol 30%; allow to stand for 10 min. record the absorbance at 523 nm using ethanol 30% as the compensation liquid	min. 0.6

Table 12. Colouring intensity

Titrimetric, spectrofotometric or chromatographic methods are described in EP monographs.

3.13.1 Titrimetric methods

Titrimetry consists in determining the number of moles of reagent (titrant), required to react quantitatively with the substance being determined.

3.13.1.1 Methodology

The standard technique involves the addition of a controlled volume of a reagent-solution (titrant) to a known volume of a sample solution. In some cases, an exces of reagent is added and the excess is measured by back titration.

Various methods are available for end-point determination: spectrophotometry, potentiometry, amperometry, conductometry etc. The potentiometric end-point determination is the most widely used. In this method, the end-point of the titration is determined by following the variation of the potential difference between two electrodes immersed in a sample solution as function of the quantity of the titrant solution added.

Other times, visual indicators may be used, too.

3.13.1.2 Evaluation of results

The content of active or analitycal marker is calculated by having in view the stoechiometry of the titration reaction.

3.13.1.3 Limits

Specific limits of admisibility are mentioned in monographs. The details are mentioned in tabel 13.

Herbal drug	Protocol	Limits
Belladonnae folium	Back titration: 0.01M sulfuric acid + 0.02M sodium hydroxide; end-point-methyl red	min. 0.30% of total alkaloids, expressed as hyoscyamine
Stramonii folium		min. 0.25% of total alkaloids, expressed as hyoscyamine
Fumariae herba	standard titration: 0.02M perchloric acid; potentiometric end-point determination	min. 0.40% of total alkaloids, expressed as protopine
Hibisci sabdariffae flos	standard titration: 0.1M sodium hydroxide; potentiometric end-point determination	min.13.5% of acids, expressed as citric acid

Table 13. Assay - titrimetric methods

3.13.2 Spectrophotometric methods

Spectrophotometric analysis is based on the measurement of radiation intensity as a function of wavelength.

These methods may be used because the active / analytical marker or its derivatives has a definite UV or VIS spectrum.

3.13.2.1 Methodology

Specific spectrophotometric methods are described in monographs. Usually, the following parameters vary: the degree of comminution of the herbal drug, solvent for extraction, methodology for obtaining the sample and the reference solutions, coloring reagent, wavelength for detection. Some details are mentioned in tabel 14.

A general method for determination of tannins in herbal drugs is described in EP chapter 2.8.14. This method consists of the following steps: the herbal drug is extracted with water on a water-bath; total polyphenols are determined in this solution, using a spectrophotometric method; shake the solution with hide powder, filter and assay the polyphenols not adsorbed by the hide powder in the filtrate, using the same spectrophotometric method.

Herbal drug	Reagent	Detection (wavelength)	Evaluation of results
Cinchonae cortex	-	316 nm and 348 nm	alkaloids, expressed as quinine-type alkaloids; comparing with reference solutions (quinine, cinchonine)
Millefolii herba	-	608 nm	proazulenes, expressed as chamazulene; A= 23.8
Hyperici herba	-	590 nm	total hypericins, expressed as hypericin; A = 870
Myrtilli fructus recens	-	528 nm	anthocyanins, expressed as cyanidin 3-O-glucoside chloride (chrysanthemin); A = 718
Rosmarini folium	hydrochloric acid + (sodium nitrite + sodium molybdate) + sodium hydroxide	505 nm	total hydroxycinnamic derivatives, expressed as rosmarinic acid; A = 400
Ballotae nigrae herba, Plantaginis lanceolatae folium		525 nm	total ortho-dihydroxycinnamic acid derivatives, expressed as acteoside; A = 185
Fraxini folium		525 nm	total hydroxycinnamic acid derivatives, expressed as chlorogenic acid; A = 188
Passiflorae herba	boric acid + oxalic acid	401 nm	total flavonoids, expressed as vitexin; A = 628
Violae herba cum flore		405 nm	flavonoids, expressed as violanthin; A = 400
Crataegi folium cum flore		410 nm	total flavonoids, expressed as hyperoside; A = 405
Curcumae xanthorrhizae rhizoma		530 nm	dicinnamoyl methane derivatives, expressed as curcumin; A = 2350
Carthami flos	aluminium chloride	420 nm	total flavonoids, expressed as hyperoside; A = 400
Betulae folium, Calendulae flos, Leonuri cardiacae herba, Polygoni avicularis herba, Solidaginis herba, Solidaginis virgaureae herba	aluminium chloride + sodium acetate	425 nm	total flavonoids, expressed as hyperoside; A = 500
Equiseti herba, Sambuci flos		425 nm	flavonoids, expressed as isoquercitroside; A = 500
Auranti amari flos	magnesium + hydrochloric acid	530 nm	total flavonoids, expressed as naringin; A = 52
Crataegi fructus	hydrochloric acid	545 nm	procyanidins, expressed as cyanidin chloride; A = 75
Frangulae cortex	magnesium acetate	515 nm	glucofrangulins, expressed as glucofrangulin; A = 204
Rhamni purshianae cortex			hydroxyanthracene glycosides, expressed as cascaroside A; A = 180
Rhei rhizoma			hydroxyanthracene derivatives,

Herbal drug	Reagent	Detection (wavelength)	Evaluation of results
			expressed as rhein; A = 468
Sennae folium, Sennae fructus acutifoliae, Sennae fructus angustifoliae			hydroxyanthracene glycosides, expressed as sennoside B; A = 240
Digitalis purpureae folium	dinitrobenzoic acid + sodium hydroxide	540 nm	cardenolic glycosides, expressed as digitoxin; comparing with reference solution (digitoxin)
Chelidoni herba	chromotropic acid, sodium salt	570 nm	total alkaloids, expressed as chelidonine; A = 933
Rosae pseudo-fructus	dinitrophenylhydrazine + sulfuric acid	520 nm	ascorbic acid; comparing with reference solution (ascorbic acid)
Agrimoniae herba, Bistortae rhizoma, Hammamelidis folium, Lythri herba, Quercus cortex, Ratanhiae radix, Sanguisorbae radix, Tormentillae rhizoma	phosphomolybdotungstic reagent + sodium carbonate (general method, chapter 2.8.14)	760 nm	tannins, expressed as pyrogallol; comparing with reference solution (pyrogallol)

Table 14. Assay - spectrophotometric methods

3.13.2.2 Evaluation of results

The content of active or analitycal marker is calculated by using the specific absorbance or by comparing with the reference solution.

In the case of the method described in chapter 2.8.14., the formula for the content of tannins have in view the diference between the value for total polyphenols and the value for polyphenols not adsorbed by the hide powder.

3.13.2.3 Limits

Specific acceptance limits are mentioned in monographs.

3.13.3 High-Performance Liquid Chromatography (HPLC)

Is a chromatographic technique that is used to separate, identify, quantify and purify the individual components of the mixture, due to a different migration of the compounds through the column (solid stationary phase).

In the case of herbal drugs, the separations are based upon partition mechanisms using chemically modified silica as the stationary phase and polar solvents as the mobile phase.

3.13.3.1 Methodology

The apparatus consists of a pumping system (which must deliver the mobile phase at a constant flow rate), an injector (which can operate at high pressure and is capable to release an exact volume of solutions), a proper chromatographic column (eventually having a temperature controller), a detector (commonly a ultraviolet / visible spectrophotometer) and a data aquisition system.

Usually, the following parameters vary: column characteristics (type, dimensions, particle size), qualitative and quantitative composition of the mobile phase, method of separation (isocratic flow / gradient elution), the gradient, characteristics of the sample and reference solutions, using an external or an internal standard, flow rate, injection volumes, run time, wavelength for detection. Some details are mentioned in tabel 15.

3.13.3.2 Evaluation of results

When an extern standard is used, the content of active or analitycal marker is calculated by comparing the response of the sample with the response of the reference.

Herbal drug	**Marker**	**Method of separation**	**Type of standard**
Uvae ursi folium	arbutin	isocratic flow	external standard (arbutin)
Salicis cortex	total salicylic derivatives, expressed as salicin	isocratic flow	external standard (salicin + picein)
Cynarae folium	Chlorogenic acid	gradient elution	external standard (chlorogenic acid)
Urticae folium	caffeoylmalic acid + chlorogenic acid, expressed as chlorogenic acid	gradient elution	external standard (chlorogenic acid)
Echinaceae purpureae herba, Echinaceae purpureae radix	caftaric acid + cichoric acid	gradient elution	external standard (chlorogenic acid + caffeic acid)
Echinaceae palidae radix, Echinaceae angustifoliae radix	echinacoside	gradient elution	external standard (chlorogenic acid + caffeic acid)
Meliloti herba	coumarin	isocratic flow	external standard (coumarin)
Fagopyri herba	rutin	gradient elution	external standard (rutin)
Ginko folium	flavonoids, expressed as flavone glycosides	gradient elution	external standard (quercetol)
Matricariae flos	apigenin-7-glucozide	isocratic flow	external standard (apigenin-7-glucoside)
Scutellariae baicalensis radix	baicalin	gradient elution	external standard (baicalin + methyl parahydroxybenzoat)
Silybi mariani fructus	silymarin, expressed as silibinin	gradient elution	external standard (milk thistle standardised dry extract)
Harpagophyti radix	harpagoside	isocratic flow	external standard (harpagoside)
Marrubii herba	marubin	gradient elution	external standard (marubin)
Oleae folium	oleuropein	gradient elution	external standard (oleuropein)
Agnus casti fructus	casticin	gradient elution	external standard (casticin)
Valerianae radix	sesquiterpenic acids, expressed as valerenic	gradient elution	external standard (valerian dry extract)

Herbal drug	Marker	Method of separation	Type of standard
	acid		
Arnicae flores	total sesquiterpene lactones, expressed as dihydrohelenalin tiglate	gradient elution	internal standard (santonin)
Tanaceti parthenii herba	parthenolide	isocratic flow	external standard (parthenolide)
Rusci rhizoma	sapogenins, expressed as ruscogenins	gradient elution	external standard (ruscogenins)
Centelae asiaticae herba	total triterpenoid derivatives, expressed as asiaticoside	gradient elution	external standard asiaticoside
Hederae folium	hederacoside	gradient elution	external standard (ivy leaf standardized tincture)
Liquiritiae radix	glycyrrhizic acid	isocratic flow	external standard (monoammonium glycyrrhizate)
Ginseng radix	ginsenoside Rg1 + ginsenoside Rb1	gradient elution	external standard (ginsenoside Rg1 + ginsenoside Rb1 + ginsenoside Re+ ginsenoside Rf)
Notoginseng radix	ginsenoside Rg1 + ginsenoside Rb1	gradient elution	external standard (ginsenoside Rg1 + ginsenoside Rb1 + ginsenoside Rf)
Eleutheroccoci radix	eleutheroside B + eleutheroside E	isocratic flow	external standard (ferulic acid)
Astragali mongholici radix	astragaloside IV	gradient elution	external standard (astragaloside IV)
Boldi folium	total alkaloids, expressed as boldine	isocratic flow	external standard (boldine)
Hydrastidis rhizoma	hydrastine, berberine	isocratic flow	external standard (hydrastine hydrochloride + berberine chloride)
Stephaniae tetrandrae radix	tetrandrine + fangchinoline, expressed as tetrandrine	isocratic flow	external standard (tetrandrine)
Colae semen	caffeine	isocratic flow	external standard (caffeine + theobromine)
Ephedrae herba	ephedrine	isocratic flow	external standard (ephedrine hydrochloride + terbutaline sulfate)
Capsici fructus	total capsaicinoids, expressed as capsaicin	isocratic flow	external standard (capsaicin + nonivamide)
Orthosiphonis folium	sinensetin	isocratic flow	external standard (sinensetin)
Schisandrae chinensis fructus	schisandrin	gradient elution	external standard (schisandrin)

Table 15. Assay - HPLC methods

When an internal standard is used, the content of this standard must have in view.

3.13.3.3 Limits

Specific limits of admisibility are mentioned in monographs.

3.13.4 Gas Chromatography (GC)

Is a chromatographic technique that is used to separate, identify, quantify and purify the volatile components (or volatile derivatives of the components) of the mixture, due to a different migration of the species through a solid or a liquid stationary phase.

3.13.4.1 Methodology

The apparatus consists of an injector, a chromatographic column (which is included in an oven), a detector (commonly a flame-ionisation detector) and a data acquisition system.

Usually, the following parameters vary: the type and the characteristics of the stationary phase, the carrier gas, method of separation (normalisation / derivatisation), temperature (for column, injection port, detector), characteristics of the sample and reference solutions, flow rate, injection volumes, split ratio, run time. Some details are mentioned in tabel 16.

3.13.4.2 Evaluation of results

The content of active or analitycal marker is calculated by comparing the response of the sample with the response of the reference. The results is expressed as a minim value (%) in the essential oil.

3.13.4.3 Limits

Specific limits of admisibility are mentioned in monographs.

Herbal drug	Marker	Method of separation	Type of standard
Anisi stelati fructus	Trans-anethole	normalisation procedure	external standard (estragole + α-terpineol + anethole)
Foeniculi amari fructus	Anethole, fenchone	normalisation procedure	external standard (anethole + fenchone)
Foeniculi dulcis fructus	Anethole	normalisation procedure	external standard (anethole)
Thymi herba, Origani herba	Thymol + carvacrol	normalisation procedure	external standard (thymol + carvacrol)
Sabalis serrulatae fructus	Total fatty acids	derivatisation procedure, using trimethylsulfonium hydroxide	internal standard (methyl margarate + methyl pelargonate)

Table 16. Assay - GC methods

3.13.5 Determination of essential oils in herbal drugs

A general method for extraction and assay of essential oils in herbal drugs is described in EP chapter 2.8.12.

3.13.5.1 Methodology

Essentially, the determination is carried out by steam distilation in a special apparatus in the conditions described in chapter 2.8.12. The distilate is collected in the graduated tube, using (usually) xylene to take up the essential oil, and the aquueous phase is automatically returned to the distillation flask. The mass of herbal drug used for extraction, the type and the volume of solvent, distilation rate and distilation time vary, and so that these parameters are mentioned in specific monographs.

3.13.5.2 Evaluation of results

The volume of liquid collected in the graduated tube is readed, the volume of xylene is substracted and so the volume of essential oil is obtained. The result is expressed as „mL/ kg".

3.13.5.3 Limits

Specific limits of admisibility are mentioned in monographs.

The content of essential oil is mentioned in the following monographs: Angelicae radix, Anisi fructus, Anisi stelati fructus, Auranti amari epicarpium et mesocarpium, Aurantii amari flos, Carvi fructus, Caryophylli flos, Chamomillae romanicae flos, Cinnamomi cortex, Coriandri fructus, Curcumae xanthorrhizae rhizoma, Eucapypti folium, Filipendulae ulmariae herba, Foeniculi amari fructus, Foeniculi dulcis fructus, Iuniperi pseudo-fructus, Lavandulae flos, Levistici radix, Matricariae flos, Menthae piperitae folium, Millefolii herba, Origani herba, Rosmarini folium, Salviae officinalis folium, Salviae trilobae folium, Serpylli herba, Thymi herba, Valerianae radix, Valerianae radix minutata, Verbenae citriodoratae folium, Verbenae herba, Zingiberis rhizoma.

3.14 Pesticide residues

According to EP, chapter 2.8.13, a pesticide is any substance or mixture of substances intended for preventing, destroying or controlling any pest, unwanted species of plants or animals causing harm during or otherwise interfering with the production, processing, storage, transport or marketing of herbal drugs. The item includes substances intended for use as growth-regulators, defoliants or desiccants and any substance applied to crops, either before or after harvest, to protect the commodity from deterioration during storage and transport.

EP chapter refers especially to the organochlorine, organophosphorus and pyrethroid insecticides.

3.14.1 Methodology

A general procedure is described in EP, but this is only for information.

It consists of the following three steps: extraction the pesticides; purification (using size-exclusion chromatography); quantitative analysis (examine by gas-chromatography, using carbophenothion as the internal standard).

3.14.2 Evaluation of results

The content of an insecticide is calculated from the peak area and the concentrations of the solutions. Lists of relative retention times for main organophosphorus insecticides, and the organochlorine and pyrethroid insecticides respectively, are attached in the monograph.

3.14.3 Limits

The limits are expressed as „mg/ kg". A list containing 69 pesticides is presented in the EP chapter. For other substances, the limits are calculated using an expression which have in view acceptable daily intake, body mass and daily dose of the herbal drug.

3.15 Microbial contamination

The presence of micro-organisms may reduce or inactivate the therapeutic activity of the herbal drug, and implicitly of the pharmaceutical product.

This parameter refers to the total aerobic microbial count (TAMC), total combined yeasts / moulds count (TYMC) and specific micro-organisms (e.g. Escherichia coli).

According to monograph „Herbal drugs", it is a compulsory test.

3.15.1 Methodology

Microbial analysis is performed according to specific microbiologic methods. The following methods are discussed in EP (chapters 2.6.12.) for TAMC and TYMC: membrane filtration method and plate-count methods (including pour-plate method, surface-spread method and most-probable-number method).

In chapter 2.6.13. are described tests which allow determination of the absence or limited occurrence of specified micro-organisms (Escherichia coli, Staphylococcus aureus, Pseudomonas aeruginosa, Salmonella sp., Candida albicans, Clostridia, Bile-tolerant gram-negative bacteria).

3.15.2 Evaluation of results

The limits of suitability are given as a maximum value of units CFU.

3.15.3 Limits

The general chapters 5.1.4 „Microbiological quality of non-sterile pharmaceutical preparations and substances for pharmaceutical use" and 5.1.8 „Microbiological quality of herbal medicinal products for oral use" not include limits for herbal substances. So, acceptance limits should be set in relation to the specific herbal substance and subsequent processing. Reduction of the microbial count at level of herbal substance (e.g. geographical origin, appropriate harvest/collection and drying procedures, treatment with water vapour) should be taken into account when setting the limits.

For herbal medicinal products for oral use, containing herbal drugs, intended for the preparation of infusions and decoctions using boiling water (e.g. herbal teas) the limits are: TAMC - max. 10^7CFU/g; TYMC - max. 10^5 CFU/g; Escherichia coli - max. 10^5 CFU/g; Salmonella sp.- absence/25g.

3.16 Determination of aflatoxins

Aflatoxins are naturally occurring mycotoxins that are produced by many species of Aspergillus (a fungus). Aflatoxins are toxic and among the most carcinogenic substances known. Aflatoxin-producing members of Aspergillus are common and widespread in nature. They can colonize and contaminate grain before harvest or during storage. Host crops are particularly susceptible to infection by Aspergillus following prolonged exposure to a high humidity environment, or damage from stressful conditions such as drought, a condition which lowers the barrier to entry. The native habitat of Aspergillus is in soil, decaying vegetation, hay and grains undergoing microbiological deterioration and it invades all types of organic substrates whenever conditions are favorable for its growth. Favorable conditions include high moisture content (at least 7%) and high temperature. The toxin can also be found in the milk of animals which are fed contaminated feed.

3.16.1 Methodology

A specific liquid chromatographic method, using an isocratic flow, fluorescence detection and post-column derivatisations apply. An immunoaffinity column containing antibodies against aflatoxin B_1 is used for to obtain the test solution. The method is described in EP general chapter 2.8.18. It is cited as an example of a method that has been shown to be suitable for devil's claw root, ginger and senna pods.

3.16.2 Evaluation of results

The limits of suitability are given as a maximum value expressed as „ng/g", or „ µg/kg" .

3.16.3 Limits

The EP requires a limit of not more than 2 µg/kg of aflatoxin B_1 and a limit of 4 µg/kg for the sum of aflatoxins B_1, B_2, G_1 and G_2.

3.17 Determination of ochratoxin A

Ochratoxins are a group of mycotoxins produced by some Aspergillus species and Penicillium species including Aspergillus ochraceus and Penicillium viridicatum. Ochratoxin A is the most prevalent and relevant fungal toxin of this group, while ochratoxins B and C are of lesser importance. Ochratoxin A is known to occur in commodities such as cereals, coffee, dried fruit and red wine. It is nephrotoxic and nephrocarcinogenic.

3.17.1 Methodology

A specific liquid chromatographic method, using a gradient elution and a fluorescence detection apply. An immunoaffinity column containing antibodies against aflatoxin B_1 is used for to obtain the test solution. The method is described in EP general chapter 2.8.22. It is suitable for Liquiritiae radix. The EP recommendation is that the suitability of this method for other herbal drugs must be demonstrated or another validated method used.

3.17.2 Evaluation of results

The limits of suitability are given as a maximum value expressed as ng/g.

3.17.3 Limits

In the case of Liquiritiae radix, the acceptance limit of maximum 20 μg/kg is required.

4. Conclusion

A herbal drug is a particular and a complex raw material. Its analysis involves specific pharmacognostic methods, which can be undertaken from European Pharmacopoeia or must be developed by the scientist.

Owing to the complexity of all above-mentioned aspects in studying the medicinal plants (herbal drugs), pharmacists, biologists, chemists and biochemists must co-operate.

5. References

Gîrd, C., E. (2010). *Curs de farmacognozie fitochimie fitoterapie,* volumul 1, Editura Curtea Veche, ISBN 978-973-1983-32-5, Bucharest, Romania

Gîrd, C., E., Duţu, L., E., Popescu, M., L., Iordache A., T., Tudor, I. & Costea, T. . (2010). *Bazale teoretice şi practice ale analizei farmacognostice,* volumul 1 (ediţia a 2-a), Editura Curtea Veche, ISBN 978-973-1983-44-8, Bucharest, Romania

Kealey, D. & Haines, P., J.,. (2002). *Instant notes. Analytical chemistry,* Bios Scientific Publishers Ltd, ISBN 1 85996 4, Oxford, United Kingdom

No author (2011). *European Pharmacopoeia* (7th edition), Council of Europe, Strasbourg, France

No author (2011). *European Pharmacopoeia* (7th edition supplement 1), Council of Europe, Strasbourg, France

4

Biological Products: Manufacturing, Handling, Packaging and Storage

Nahla S. Barakat
King Saud University,
College of Pharmacy,
Dept. of Pharmaceutics,
Saudi Arabia

1. Introduction

A biological product is defined as "a virus, therapeutic serum, toxin, antitoxin, vaccine, blood, blood component or derivative, allergenic product, or analogous product, or any other trivalent organic arsenic compound, applicable to the prevention, treatment or cure of a disease or condition of human beings". Throughout the 20th century, the world witnessed great discoveries in the biological sciences. One of the earliest biological products introduced to the U.S. marketplace was a blood protein called Factor VIII first sold in 1966. The earliest FDA approval for a modern biotech product designed for human therapeutic use was given to human insulin in 1982, approval was given in 1985 to a human growth hormone (HGH) for the treatment of dwarfism. In the 1990s FDA granted approvals for vaccines against rabies, tetanum toxoids, and pertussis. The manufacturing process for a biological product usually different from the process for drugs. The manufacture of biological medicinal products involves certain specific considerations arising from the nature of the products and the processes. Persons responsible for production and quality control should have an adequate background in relevant scientific disciplines, such as bacteriology, biology, biometry, chemistry, medicine, pharmacy, pharmacology, virology, immunology and veterinary medicine. The degree of environmental control of particulate and microbial contamination of the production premises should be adapted to the product and the production step. Animals are used for the manufacture of a number of biological products, in addition, animals may also be used in the quality control of most sera, antibiotics and vaccines. All biological products should be clearly identified by labels which should be approved by the national control authority. The evaluation of stability may necessitate complex analytical methodologies. Assays for biological activity, where applicable, should be part of the pivotal stability studies.

Throughout the 20th century, the world witnessed great discoveries in the biological sciences, many of which led to the prevention or eradication of diseases that have devastated populations in the past. For 100 years, what is now known as FDA's Center for Biologics Evaluation and Research or "CBER," has played a significant role in ensuring the safety and efficacy of the fruits of these scientific discoveries. CBER is responsible for the regulation of "biologics," which are medical products such as vaccines, blood and blood derivatives, allergenic patch tests and extracts, HIV and hepatitis tests, gene therapy products, cells and tissues for transplantation, and new treatments for cancers, arthritis, and other serious diseases. CBER reviewed the first vaccines to immunize persons against infectious diseases, such as polio, pertussis ("whooping cough"), and German measles. CBER research led to important discoveries to safely collect, prepare, and transfuse blood and blood plasma.

2. Biological products, industry history [1]

Biological products were created with biotechnology, the scientific and engineering procedures involved in manipulating organisms or biological components at the cellular, subcellular, or molecular level. These manipulations were carried out to make or modify plants and animals or other biological substances with desired traits. Although examples of primitive biotech processes dated back to ancient times (such as the use of fermentation in brewing and leavening agents in baking), their use in medical and pharmaceutical applications was an innovation of the latter decades of the twentieth century. Some analysts compared the biotech industry's impact on global medical care with the computer industry's impact on communication.

Biotech researchers produced products in essentially three ways: by developing ways to achieve commercial production of naturally occurring substances; by genetically altering naturally occurring substances; and by creating entirely new substances. Some of the tools used by biotech researchers included recombinant DNA and monoclonal antibodies. Recombinant DNA involved the ability to take the deoxyribonucleic acid (DNA) from one organism and combine it with the DNA from another organism thereby creating new products and processes. By using recombinant DNA techniques researchers were able to select specific genes and introduce them into other cells or living organisms to create products with specific attributes. Monoclonal antibodies were developed from cultures of single cells using cloning techniques. They were designed for use in attacking toxins, viruses, and cancer cells. Because the biological products presented for approval often involved new technologies or innovative therapies for diseases that had not been previously treated successfully, the approval process frequently proved to be long and costly. Many companies struggled financially through the 1980s waiting for an FDA determination. One of the earliest biological products introduced to the U.S. marketplace was a blood protein first sold in 1966. The blood protein, called Factor VIII, was used by patients with hemophilia A to control bleeding episodes. Factor VIII, the blood factor responsible for normal clotting action, was manufactured from human blood received from donors. It was followed by the development of Factor IX for patients with hemophilia B.

During the early 1980s, problems arose as a result of AIDS contamination in the blood supply used to produce blood clotting factors. In 1984 manufacturers began using a heat treatment process to guard against future contamination, but, according to a report in the *Wall Street Journal,* approximately half of the nation's 20,000 hemophiliacs contracted AIDS, primarily through the use of Factors VIII and IX. [2]

The earliest FDA approval for a modern biotech product designed for human therapeutic use was given to human insulin in 1982. Human insulin was used for treating patients with diabetes. In 1984 the FDA approved an agricultural vaccine against colibacillosis (a disease commonly called scours, which causes diarrhea or dysentery in newborn animals). Approval was given in 1985 to a human growth hormone (HGH) for the treatment of dwarfism.

The first genetically engineered vaccine approved for use in the United States was a vaccine against hepatitis-B. It received approval in 1986. The vaccine had been created by inserting part of a hepatitis-B virus into yeast cells. Although the portion of the hepatitis-B virus used was not infectious, it caused an immune reaction against infection from the entire hepatitis-B virus.

Other firsts occurring in 1986 included the approval of therapeutic monoclonal antibodies (MABs) and alpha interferon. MABs were approved for use along with immunosuppressive drugs to help prevent kidney rejection in transplant patients. Alpha interferon's first approved use was in the treatment of hairy cell leukemia. Other approved uses for alpha interferon followed: for Kaposi's sarcoma in 1988, venereal warts in 1988, non-A/non-B hepatitis in 1991, and hepatitis-B in 1992. A product to dissolve blood clots in patients with acute myocardial infarction (heart attack) was approved in 1987. An agricultural vaccine to protect against pseudorabies won FDA approval the same year.

Erythropoietin (EPO), which was to become the largest single biotech product, received its first FDA approval in 1989. EPO, a protein that stimulates production of red blood cells, won initial approval for use with anemia associated with kidney disease. In the same year, the Health Care Financing Administration agreed to pay for EPO given to dialysis patients under the Medicare program. Within a few years, EPO was being used by approximately 82,000 dialysis patients in the United States. In 1991 the FDA gave additional approval for its use in treating AIDS-related anemia.

Advances continued during the 1990s. As the industry matured, cooperation between product developers and government regulators improved. The steps in the approval process became more predictable, and a shift in technology was also noted. The primary products of the 1980s had involved the use of recombinant DNA proteins without further alterations. During the early 1990s, researchers turned their attention to products requiring more extensive genetic modification and to more obscure applications.

In the 1990s FDA granted approvals for vaccines against rabies, tetanum toxoids, and pertussis. According to government statements, vaccines were one of the most effective and cheapest ways to eradicate some diseases. Accordingly, the National Institute of Health's Office of Financial Management reported that funding for vaccine research and development rose 65 percent from 1993 to 1999. Concern about health care costs during the early 1990s focused the national spotlight on the pharmaceutical industry and questions were raised about the high cost of biological products (3).

2.1 Definition

The definition of a biologic has changed over time. In the U.S., a biological product is defined as "a virus, therapeutic serum, toxin, antitoxin, vaccine, blood, blood component or derivative, allergenic product, or analogous product, or arsphenanaine, or derivative of arsphenamine) or any other trivalent organic arsenic compound), applicable to the prevention, treatment or cure of a disease or condition of human beings" (Public Health

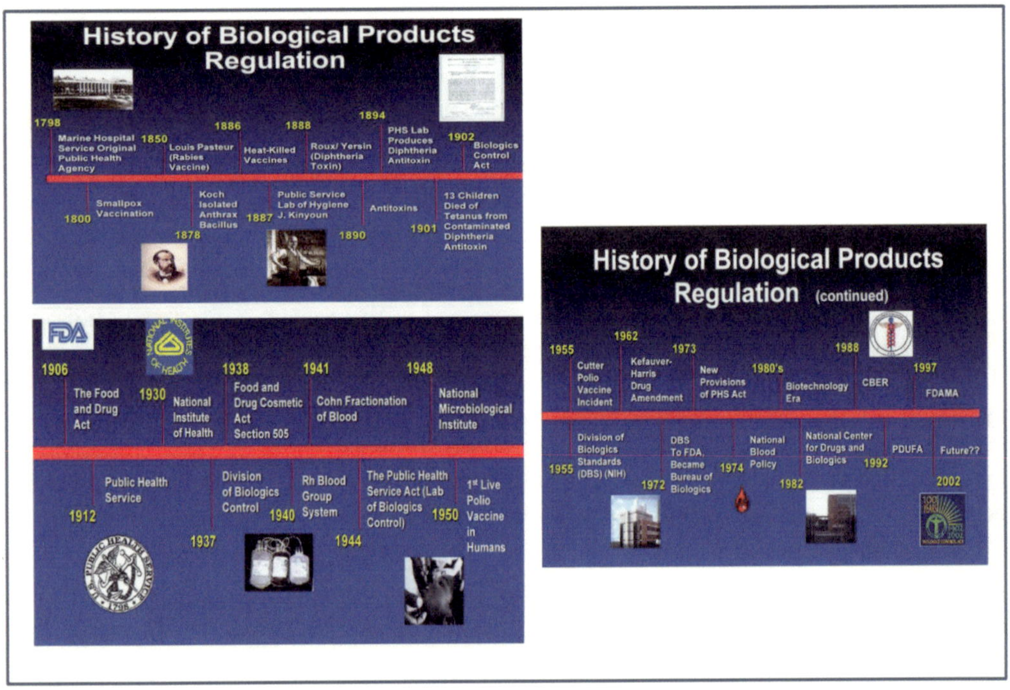

Chart 1. History of biological products regulation

Drug	Indication	Approval Date	2003 Sales $ (million)
Humulin (human insulin)	Diabetes	October 1982	1,060
Intron A (interferon alfa-2b)	Cancer, infection	June 1986	1,851
Humatrope (somatropin)	Growth failure	March 1987	371
Infanrix (diphtheria-tetanus-pertussis vaccine)	Immunization against diphtheria, pertussis, and tetanus	March 1987	551
Epogen (epoetin alfa)	Anemia	June 1989	2,435
Engerix-B (hepatitis B vaccine)	Immunization against hepatitis B	August 1989	684
Botox (botulinum toxin type A)	Cervical dystonia	December 1989	564
Epogin (epoetin beta)	Anemia	April 1990	551
Procrit (epoetin alfa)	Anemia	December 1990	3,984
Neupogen (filgrastim)	Neutropenia	January 1991	1,267
Cerezyme (imiglucerase)	Gaucher's disease	April 1991	739
NovoSeven (recombinant factor VII)	Hemophilia	April 1992	589

* The patents on these products expire after 20 years; most patents are applied for during the drug-development stage. Data are from *MedAdNews*, "Top 200 World's Best Selling Medicines" (2004;23(5):60-4).

Table 1. Top selling Biopharmaceuticals approved before 1993

Services Act 42 U.S.C. § 262(i)). By statute, biological products include viruses, therapeutic sera, toxins and antitoxins, vaccines, blood, blood components or derivatives, allergenic products, any analogous products, and arsphenamines used for treating disease. The statue does not offer a definition of "biologic,"but is fairly broad. The inclusion of the term "analogous products" makes the definition particularly broad since the basis for determining analogous products is not provided by the statue.

1. A virus is interpreted to be a product containing the minute living cause of an infectious disease and includes but is not limited to filterable viruses, bacteria, rickettsia, fungi, and protozoa.
2. A therapeutic serum is a product obtained from blood by removing the clot or clot components and the blood cells.
3. A toxin is a product containing a soluble substance poisonous to laboratory animals or to man in doses of 1 milliliter or less (or equivalent in weight) of the product, and having the property, following the injection of non-fatal doses into an animal, of causing to be produced therein another soluble substance which specifically neutralizes the poisonous substance and which is demonstrable in the serum of the animal thus immunized.
4. An antitoxin is a product containing the soluble substance in serum or other body fluid of an immunized animal which specifically neutralizes the toxin against which the animal is immune.

Biological products, like other drugs, are used for the treatment, prevention or cure of disease in humans. In contrast to chemically synthesized small molecular weight drugs, which have a well-defined structure and can be thoroughly characterized, biological products are generally derived from living material--human, animal, or microorganism- are complex in structure, and thus are usually not fully characterized.

Biological products can be composed of sugars, proteins, or nucleic acids, or a combination of these substances. They may also be living entities, such as cells and tissues. Biologics are made from a variety of natural resources-human, animal, and microorganism-and may be produced by biotechnology methods. Most biologics, however, are complex mixtures that are not easily identified or characterized. Biological products differ from conventional drugs in that they tend to be heat-sensitive and susceptible to microbial contamination. This requires sterile processes to be applied from initial manufacturing steps.

The categories of therapeutic biological products regulated by Center for Drug Evaluation and Research (CDER) (under the Federal Food Drug and Cosmetics Act (FDCA) and/or the Public Health Service Act (PHSA), as appropriate include the following:

- Monoclonal antibodies for in vivo use.
- Most proteins intended for therapeutic use, including cytokines (e.g., interferons), enzymes (e.g. thrombolytics), and other novel proteins, except for those that are specifically assigned to the Center for Biologics Evaluation and Research (CBER) (e.g., vaccines and blood products). This category includes therapeutic proteins derived from plants, animals, humans, or microorganisms, and recombinant versions of these products. Exceptions to this rule are coagulation factors (both recombinant and human-plasma derived).
- Immunomodulators (non-vaccine and non-allergenic products intended to treat disease by inhibiting or down-regulating a pre-existing, pathological immune response).

- Growth factors, cytokines, and monoclonal antibodies intended to mobilize, stimulate, decrease or otherwise alter the production of hematopoietic cells in vivo.

3. Good manufacturing practices for biological products [3, 4]

The manufacturing process for a biological product usually different from the process for drugs because, in many cases, there is limited ability to identify the identity of the clinically active component(s) of a complex biological product, such products are often defined by their manufacturing processes. Changes in the manufacturing process, equipment or facilities could result in changes in the biological product itself and sometimes require additional clinical studies to demonstrate the product's safety, identity, purity and potency. Traditional drug products usually consist of pure chemical substances that are easily analyzed after manufacture. Since there is a significant difference in how biological products are made, the production is monitored by the agency from the early stages to make sure the final product turns out as expected. For this reason, in the manufacture of biological products full adherence to GMP is necessary for all production steps, beginning with those from which the active ingredients are produced.

4. Manufacture of biological medicinal products for human use

4.1 Principle

The manufacture of biological medicinal products involves certain specific considerations arising from the nature of the products and the processes. The ways in which therapeutic biological products are produced, controlled and administered make some particular precautions necessary.

Unlike conventional medicinal products, which are reproduced using chemical and physical techniques capable of a high degree of consistency, the production of therapeutic biological products involves biological processes and materials, such as cultivation of cells or extraction of substances from living organisms, including human, animal and plant tissues. Propagation of microorganisms in embryos or animals, growth of strains of microorganism and eukaryotic cells, hybridoma techniques are also involved. These biological processes may display inherent variability, so that the range and nature of by-products are variable. Moreover, the materials used in these cultivation processes provide good substrates for growth of microbial contaminants.

Control of therapeutic biological products usually involves biological analytical techniques which have a greater variability than physico-chemical determinations. In-process controls therefore take on a great importance in the manufacture of therapeutic biological products.

Therapeutic biological products manufactured by these methods include: vaccines, immune sera, immunoglobulins (including monoclonal antibodies), antigens, hormones, cytokines, allergens, enzymes and other products of fermentation (including products derived from r-DNA).

4.2 Personnel

All personnel (including those concerned with cleaning, maintenance or quality control) employed in areas where biological medicinal products are manufactured should receive additional training specific to the products manufactured and to their work. Personnel should be given relevant information and training in hygiene and microbiology.

Persons responsible for production and quality control should have an adequate background in relevant scientific disciplines, such as bacteriology, biology, biometry, chemistry, medicine, pharmacy, pharmacology, virology, immunology and veterinary medicine, together with sufficient practical experience to enable them to exercise their management function for the process concerned.

The immunological status of personnel may have to be taken into consideration for product safety. All personnel engaged in production, maintenance, testing and animal care (and inspectors) should be vaccinated where necessary with appropriate specific vaccines and have regular health checks. Apart from the obvious problem of exposure of staff to infectious agents, potent toxins or allergens, it is necessary to avoid the risk of contamination of a production batch with infectious agents. Visitors should generally be excluded from production areas.

Any changes in the immunological status of personnel which could adversely affect the quality of the product should preclude work in the production area.

Production of BCG vaccine and tuberculin products should be restricted to staff who are carefully monitored by regular checks of immunological status or chest X-ray. In the case of manufacture of products derived from human blood or plasma, vaccination of workers against hepatitis B is recommended.

During the working day, personnel should not pass from areas where exposure to live organisms or animals is possible to areas where other products or different organisms are handled. If such passage is unavoidable, clearly defined decontamination measures, including change of clothing and shoes and, where necessary, showering should be followed by staff involved in any such production.

The names and qualifications of those responsible for approving lot processing records (protocols) should be registered with the national control authority

4.3 Premises and equipment [5]

The degree of environmental control of particulate and microbial contamination of the production premises should be adapted to the product and the production step, bearing in mind the level of contamination of the starting materials and the risk to the finished product.

The risk of cross-contamination between biological medicinal products, especially during those stages of the manufacturing process in which live organisms are used, may require additional precautions with respect to facilities and equipment, such as the use of dedicated facilities and equipment, production on a campaign basis and the use of closed systems. The nature of the product as well as the equipment used will determine the level of segregation needed to avoid cross-contamination.

In principle, dedicated facilities should be used for the production of BCG vaccine and for the handling of live organisms used in production of tuberculin products. Dedicated facilities should be used for the handling of Bacillus anthracis, of Clostridium botulinum and of Clostridium tetani until the inactivation process is accomplished.

Production on a campaign basis may be acceptable for other spore forming organisms provided that the facilities are dedicated to this group of products and not more than one product is processed at any one time.

Simultaneous production in the same area using closed systems of biofermenters may be acceptable for products such as monoclonal antibodies and products prepared by DNA techniques.

Processing steps after harvesting may be carried out simultaneously in the same production area provided that adequate precautions are taken to prevent cross contamination. For killed vaccines and toxoids, such parallel processing should only be performed after inactivation of the culture or after detoxification.

Positive pressure areas should be used to process sterile products but negative pressure in specific areas at point of exposure of pathogens is acceptable for containment reasons. Where negative pressure areas or safety cabinets are used for aseptic processing of pathogens, they should be surrounded by a positive pressure sterile zone.

Air filtration units should be specific to the processing area concerned and recirculation of air should not occur from areas handling live pathogenic organisms.

The layout and design of production areas and equipment should permit effective cleaning and decontamination (e.g. by fumigation). The adequacy of cleaning and decontamination procedures should be validated.

Equipment used during handling of live organisms should be designed to maintain cultures in a pure state and uncontaminated by external sources during processing. Pipework systems, valves and vent filters should be properly designed to facilitate cleaning and sterilization. The use of 'clean in place' and 'sterilize in place' systems should be encouraged. Valves on fermentation vessels should be completely steam sterilizable. Air vent filters should be hydrophobic and validated for their scheduled life span.

Primary containment should be designed and tested to demonstrate freedom from leakage risk.

Effluents which may contain pathogenic micro-organisms should be effectively decontaminated.

Due to the variability of biological products or processes, some additives or ingredients have to be measured or weighed during the production process (e.g. buffers). In these cases, small stocks of these substances may be kept in the production area.

Seed lots and cell banks used for the production of biological products should be stored separately from other materials. Access should be restricted to authorized personnel.

4.4 Animal cell substrates for biological products

The selection of an appropriate cell substrate for use in the production of biological products has been a recurring focus of attention and anxiety for at least the past 50 years. The reasons for that are not difficult to understand because the central issue has always been "Is the product manufactured in a given cell substrate going to be safe to use in humans?"

4.4.1 Phenotypic characteristics of animal cells grown in vitro

A large number of phenotypic characteristics of animal cells have been described in the literature. Of those, three characteristics have been particularly important in the assessment of cells grown in vitro that might be considered as substrates for the production of biological products. These include: (1) life potential; (2) tumorigenic potential; and (3) chromosomal complement.

With regard to life potential, cells grown in vitro may be divided into two large general classes: those with a finite life potential such as human diploid cells; and those with an apparent infinite life potential such as cells derived from tumor tissue.

When cells grown in vitro are assessed for their ability to produce tumors in animal test systems, they again may be divided into two general classes: those that have the ability to produce tumors; and those that do not display the characteristic.

However, it is important to note that the results of any tumorigenicity assay depend very heavily on the sensitivity of the assay system itself. A variety of such assays have been developed over the past 50 years, and a number of the more recent systems are able to detect the tumorigenic potential of inoculated cells that had been scored as negative in earlier systems. The chromosomal complement of cells grown in vitro also may be divided into two general classes: diploid cells and heteroploid cells. Diploid cells of those that contain the normal number of chromosomes for the species from which the cells were derived; whereas heteroploid cells contain an abnormal number of chromosomes that also usually have numerous structural abnormalities.

4.4.2 Animal quarters and care [6]

Animals are used for the manufacture of a number of biological products (Table 2), for example polio vaccine (monkeys), snake antivenoms (horses and goats), rabies vaccine (rabbits, mice and hamsters) and serum gonadotropin (horses). In addition, animals may also be used in the quality control of most sera and vaccines, e.g. pertussis vaccine (mice), pyrogenicity (rabbits), BCG vaccine (guinea-pigs). Antibodies are often generated using animals as hosts for an antigen towards which an antibody is needed. There are, however, ways of generating antibodies or molecules showing similar properties but using fewer and sometimes no live animals. These include phage, yeast and ribosomal display methods and using egg yolk IgY instead of animal-derived IgG or IgM antibodies.

Other biological products include botulinum toxin, insulin and other hormones and vaccines. Each of these products are produced in batches and some products are still produced in animals.

General requirements for animal quarters, care and quarantine are laid down in Directive 86/609/EEC2. Quarters for animals used in production and control of biological products should be separated from production and control areas. The health status of animals from which some starting materials are derived and of those used for quality control and safety testing should be monitored and recorded. Staff employed in such areas must be provided with special clothing and changing facilities. Where monkeys are used for the production or quality control of biological medicinal products, special consideration is required as laid down in the current WHO Requirements for Biological Substances n° 7

Animal	vaccine
Hamster	SPF Chicken Embryo Measles Vaccine, Live
Rabbit	Attenuated Rubella Vaccine, Live
Monkey	Attenuated Poliomyelitis Vaccine, Live
Gerbil	Attenuated Hemorrhagic Fever with Renal Syndrome Vaccine, Live
Specific-pathogen -free (SPF) Chicken Embryo	Measles Vaccine

Table 2. Animals used in vaccine preparation

5. Documentation

Specifications for biological starting materials may need additional documentation on the source, origin, method of manufacture and controls applied particularly microbiological controls. Specifications are routinely required for intermediate and bulk biological medicinal products.

6. Production

Standard operating procedures should be available and maintained up to date for all manufacturing operations.

The source of cells (laboratory or culture collection) from which the cell substrate was derived should be stated, and relevant references from the scientific literature should be cited. Information obtained directly from the source laboratory is preferred. When this is not available, literature references may be utilized.

6.1 Starting materials

The source, origin and suitability of starting materials for biological products should be clearly defined. Where the necessary tests take a long time, it may be permissible to process starting materials before the results of the tests are available. In such cases, release of a finished product is conditional on satisfactory results of these tests.

Where sterilization of starting materials is required, it should be carried out where possible by heat. Where necessary, other appropriate methods may also be used for inactivation of biological materials (e.g. irradiation).

6.2 Seed lot and cell bank system

In order to prevent the unwanted drift of properties which might ensue from repeated subcultures or multiple generations, the production of biological medicinal products obtained by microbial culture, cell culture or propagation in embryos and animals should be based on a system of master and working seed lots and/or cell banks (Chart. 2).

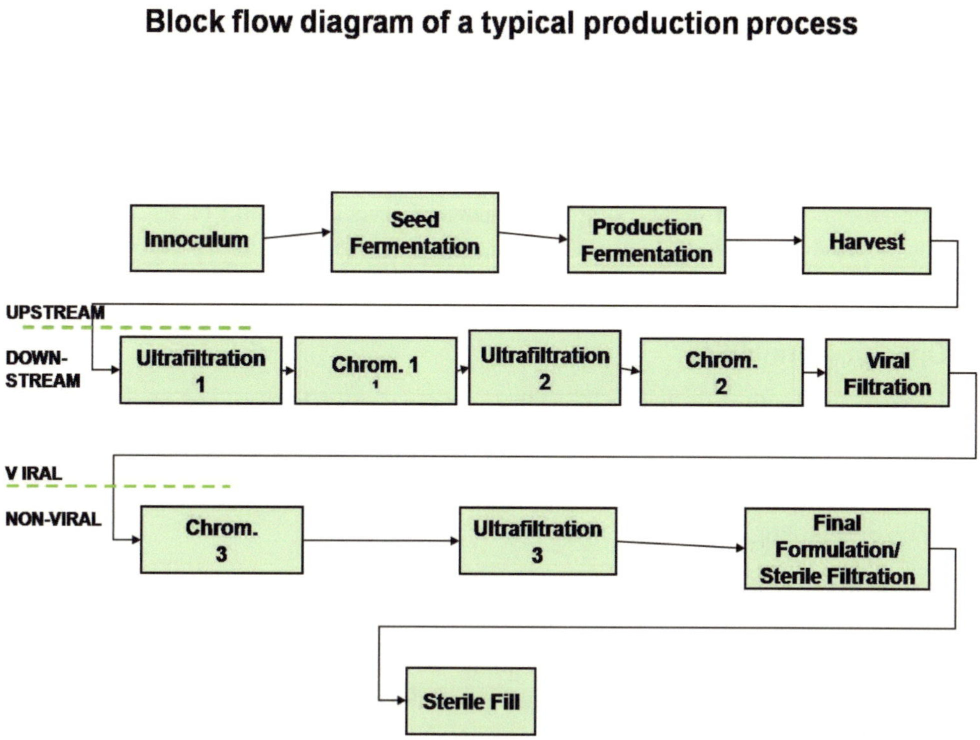

Chart 2. Block flow diagram of a typical production process

The number of generations (doublings, passages) between the seed lot or cell bank and the finished product should be consistent with the marketing authorization dossier. Scaling up of the process should not change this fundamental relationship.

Seed lots and cell banks should be adequately characterized and tested for contaminants. Their suitability for use should be further demonstrated by the consistency of the characteristics and quality of the successive batches of product. Seed lots and cell banks should be established, stored and used in such a way as to minimize the risks of contamination or alteration.

Establishment of the seed lot and cell bank should be performed in a suitably controlled environment to protect the seed lot and the cell bank and, if applicable, the personnel handling it.

During the establishment of the seed lot and cell bank, no other living or infectious material (e.g. virus, cell lines or cell strains) should be handled simultaneously in the same area or by the same persons.

Evidence of the stability and recovery of the seeds and banks should be documented. Storage containers should be hermetically sealed, clearly labelled and kept at an appropriate temperature. An inventory should be meticulously kept. Storage temperature should be recorded continuously for freezers and properly monitored for liquid nitrogen. Any deviation from set limits and any corrective action taken should be recorded.

Only authorized personnel should be allowed to handle the material and this handling should be done under the supervision of a responsible person. Access to stored material should be controlled. Different seed lots or cell banks should be stored in such a way to avoid confusion or cross-contamination. It is desirable to split the seed lots and cell banks and to store the parts at different locations so as to minimize the risks of total loss.

All containers of master or working cell banks and seed lots should be treated identically during storage. Once removed from storage, the containers should not be returned to the stock.

7. Operating principles

The growth promoting properties of culture media should be demonstrated. Addition of materials or cultures to fermenters and other vessels and the taking of samples should be carried out under carefully controlled conditions to ensure that absence of contamination is maintained. Care should be taken to ensure that vessels are correctly connected when addition or sampling take place.

Centrifugation and blending of products can lead to aerosol formation, and containment of such activities to prevent transfer of live micro-organisms is necessary.

If possible, media should be sterilized in situ. In-line sterilising filters for routine addition of gases, media, acids or alkalis, defoaming agents etc. to fermenters should be used where possible.

Careful consideration should be given to the validation of any necessary virus removal or inactivation undertaken. In cases where a virus inactivation or removal process is performed during manufacture, measures should be taken to avoid the risk of recontamination of treated products by nontreated products.

A wide variety of equipment is used for chromatography, and in general such equipment should be dedicated to the purification of one product and should be sterilized or sanitised between batches. The use of the same equipment at different stages of processing should be discouraged. Acceptance criteria, life span and sanitation or sterilization method of columns should be defined.

8. Antibiotics as preservatives [7]

Antibiotics are authorized for use as preservatives for biological products if used within the limitations as to kinds and amounts prescribed in this section.

When an antibiotic or combination of antibiotics, with or without a fungistat is to be used in the preparation of a biological product, the kind(s) and amount(s) of each shall be specified in the outline for such product in such a way that the concentration in the final product may be calculated. Except as may be approved by the Administrator, only those individual antibiotics or combinations of antibiotics listed this section shall be used.

8.1 Permitted individual antibiotics

a. The antibiotic level of a specified individual antibiotic in one ml. of a biological product, when prepared as recommended for use, shall not exceed the amounts listed in this paragraph: *Provided,* That in the case a desiccated biological product is to be used with an indefinite quantity of water or other menstruum, the determination shall be based on 30 ml. per 1,000 dose vial or equivalent.
b. When only one antibiotic be used as a preservative in a biological product, the kind and maximum amount per ml. of such antibiotic shall be restricted to: Ampotericin B 2.5 μg; Nystatin 30 units; Mycostatin 30μg; Penicillin 30 units; Streptomycin 30 μg; polymixin 30μg ; neomycin 30 μg; Gentamycin 30 μg

8.2 Permitted combinations

1. Penicillin and streptomycin.
2. Either amphotericin B or nystatin, but not both, may be used with one of the other antibiotics listed in paragraph (b) of this section, or with a combination of penicillin and streptomycin, or with a combination of polymyxin B and neomycin.
3. The maximum amount of each antibiotic in a combination shall be the amount prescribed for such antibiotic in paragraph (b) of this section.

c. Antibiotics used in virus seed stock purification are not restricted as to kind or amounts provided carryover into the final product is controlled and specified in outlines of production.

9. Labeling

All biological products should be clearly identified by labels. The labels used must remain permanently attached to the containers under all storage conditions and an area of the container should be left uncovered to allow inspection of the contents. If the final container is not suitable for labeling (for example a capillary tube), it should be in a labeled package.

The information given on the label on the container and the label on the package should be approved by the national control authority.

The label on the container should show:

- the name of the drug product
- a list of active ingredients and the amount of each present
- the batch or final lot number assigned by the manufacturer
- the expiration date
- recommended storage conditions
- direction for use and warning and precautions that may be necessary
- the name and address of the manufacturer or the company

The label on the package should show at least the nature and amount of any preservative or additive in the product. The leaflet in the package should provide instructions for the use of the product, and mention and contraindications or potential adverse reactions.

10. Storage and handling

Biological products at licensed establishments should be protected at all times against improper storage and handling. Completed product should be kept under refrigeration at 35 °to 45 °F. (2 °to 7 °C.) unless the inherent nature of the product makes storage at a different temperature advisable, in which case, the proper storage temperature shall be specified in the filed Outline of Production. All biological products to be shipped or delivered should be securely packed.

11. Expiration date determination

Unless otherwise provided for in a Standard Requirement of filed Outline of Production, the expiration date for each product shall be computed from the date of the initiation of the potency test. Prior to licensure, stability of each fraction shall be determined by methods acceptable to Animal and Plant Health Inspection Service. Expiration dates based on this stability data shall be confirmed as follows:

a. *Products consisting of viable organisms.* Each serial shall be tested for potency at release and at the approximate expiration date until a statistically valid stability record has been established.
b. *Nonviable biological products.* Each serial presented in support of licensure shall be tested for potency at release and at or after the dating requested.
c. Subsequent changes in the dating period for a product may be granted, based on statistically valid data submitted to support a revision of the Outline of Production.

12. Quality of biotechnological products [8]

12.1 Stability testing of biotechnological products

The evaluation of stability may necessitate complex analytical methodologies. Assays for biological activity, where applicable, should be part of the pivotal stability studies.

Appropriate physico-chemical, biochemical and immunochemical methods for the analysis of the molecular entity and the quantitative detection of degradation products should also be part of the stability program whenever purity and molecular characteristics of the product permit use of these methodologies.

During manufacture of biotechnological/biological products, the quality and control of certain intermediates may be critical to the production of the final product. In general, the manufacturer should identify intermediates and generate in-house data and process limits that assure their stability within the bounds of the developed process. While the use of pilot plant-scale data is permissible, the manufacturer should establish the suitability of such data using the manufacturing-scale process.

Stability information should be provided on at least three batches of final container product representative of that which will be used at manufacturing scale. Where possible, batches of final container product included in stability testing should be derived from different batches of bulk material. A minimum of six months data at the time of submission should be submitted in cases where storage periods greater than six months are requested. For medicinal products with storage periods of less than six months, the minimum amount of stability data in the initial submission should be determined on a case by case basis.

On the whole, there is no single stability-indicating assay or parameter that profiles the stability characteristics of a biotechnological/biological product. Consequently, the manufacturer should propose a stability-indicating profile that provides assurance that changes in the identity, purity and potency of the product will be detected.

At the time of submission, applicants should have validated the methods that comprise the stability-indicating profile and the data should be available for review.

When the intended use of a product is linked to a definable and measurable biological activity, testing for potency should be part of the stability studies. For the purpose of stability testing of the products described in this guideline, potency is the specific ability or capacity of a product to achieve its intended effect. It is based on the measurement of some attribute of the product and is determined by a suitable quantitative method.

In some biotechnological/biological products, potency is dependent upon the conjugation of the active substance(s) to a second moiety or binding to an adjuvant. Dissociation of the active substance(s) from the carrier used in conjugates or adjuvants should be examined in real-time/real-temperature studies (including conditions encountered during shipment).

The following product characteristics, though not specifically relating to biotechnological/biological products, should be monitored and reported for the medicinal product in its final container:

- Visual appearance of the product (colour and opacity for solutions/suspensions; colour, texture and dissolution time for powders), visible particulates in solutions or after the reconstitution of powders or lyophilised cakes, pH, and moisture level of powders and lyophilised products.
- Sterility testing or alternatives (e.g. container/closure integrity testing) should be performed at a minimum initially and at the end of the proposed shelf life.
- Additives (e.g. stabilisers, preservatives) or excipients may degrade during the dating period of the medicinal product. If there is any indication during preliminary stability studies that reaction or degradation of such materials adversely affect the quality of the medicinal product, these items may need to be monitored during the stability program.
- The container/closure has the potential to adversely affect the product and should be carefully evaluated.

12.2 FDA's role regarding biological products

FDA's regulatory authority for the approval of biologics resides in the Public Health Service Act (PHSA). However, biologics are also subject to regulation under the Federal Food, Drug, and Cosmetic Act (FD&C Act) because most biological products also meet the definition of "drugs" cited within this Act.

Similarly, some medical devices used to produce biologics are regulated by Center for Biologics Evaluation and Research (CBER) under the FD&C Act's Medical Device Amendments of 1976.

FDA also

- reviews new biological products and new indications and usage for already approved products in order to get biological products on the market for the treatment of known diseases
- helps protect against threats of emerging infectious diseases
- helps provide the public with information to promote the safe and appropriate use of biological products
- conducts inspections of plants that manufacture biologics before product approval is granted, and thereafter, on a regular basis
- monitors the safety of biological products after they are marketed

The PHS Act also

- allows FDA to approve biological products and immediately suspend licenses where there exists a danger to public health
- allows the agency to prepare or procure products in the event of shortages and critical public health needs
- enforces regulations to prevent the introduction or spread of communicable diseases within the country and between states

13. The responsibilities of a licensed biologics manufacturer

The PHS Act requires individuals or companies who manufacture biologics for introduction into interstate commerce to hold a license for the products. These licenses are issued by FDA

Responsibilities of a licensed biologics manufacturer include

- complying with the appropriate laws and regulations relevant to their biologics license and identifying any changes needed to help ensure product quality
- reporting certain problems to FDA's Biological Product Deviation Reporting System
- reporting and correcting product problems within established timeframes
- recalling or stopping the manufacture of a product if a significant problem is detected

13.1 Regulation and licensing of biological products

The licensing of a vaccine or other biological product requires the issue of licenses for both the manufacturing establishment and the product. The approval or licensing of a manufacturing establishment for the production of biological products should be granted only if the manufacture complies with the relevant international or equivalent national standards for good manufacturing practice.

The normal procedure for the issue of a product licence consists of the following three stages:

a. the manufacturing establishment and product licence applications are received from the manufacturer, screened for completeness, and then reviewed for evidence of compliance with good manufacturing practices and for safety, quality and efficacy by the authority's technical staff;

b. the authority may perform laboratory tests, review reports of or perform pre-licensing inspections, and seek the advice of external experts on specific technical questions when deciding whether or not to authorize the marketing of the product;
c. the formal administrative action to grant or refuse a licence is then taken by the designated authorized person.

The assessment of the product must be based on its safety, quality and efficacy when used as intended. However, the availability of the product may be dictated by national policy considerations, such as the national need for comparative efficacy and /or safety, or cost-effectiveness.

13.2 Renewal and variation of licences [9]

The precise circumstances under which licence-holders are required to apply for a renewal or variation in a product licence differ from country to country and should be clearly defined by the national authority. In general, if a manufacturer wishes to vary the conditions of the approved licence to any significant extent, the variations must be submitted to the authority for approval. Significant changes might include changes in aspects of the manufacturing procedures or the facility, or in the product specifications, dosage forms or labeling. In many countries, re-registration, but not licence renewal, is required annually. In others, licences must be renewed every 5 or 7 years.

13.3 Post-licensing monitoring

13.3.1 Product release

At the time a product is approved, the national control authority should decide what controls are to be applied to the release of batches of the product. This decision will be influenced by the nature of the product and the resources available for laboratory testing. Controls will usually be imposed on complex products, e.g. vaccines, and on those obtained by complex manufacturing procedures.

The *testing of samples of intermediate,* bulk or final product should confirm compliance with the requirements and agreed specifications. The nature and frequency of the tests to be carried out are decided by the national control authority.

The *evaluation of the manufacturer's protocols* for the manufacture and control of each batch will be undertaken by the national control authority. The critical review of batch protocols by the authority is a most important part of the control of biological products. The information provided should make it possible to review the manufacture and testing of each batch of a particular product, including all required in-process control tests on final products to confirm compliance with the approved specifications.

13.3.2 Inspections

Periodic inspection of the manufacturing facility should be carried out on behalf of the national control authority to assure continued compliance with good manufacturing practices and with the specifications established for the product at the time of approval. Records of complaints and reports of adverse reactions should be examined.

13.3.3 Post-licensing surveillance

Countries should establish a national system for post-licensing surveillance of biological products. Clinicians and other health workers should be encouraged to report to national control authorities and manufacturers any unexpected adverse events occurring after the administration of biological products.

14. Existing legal basis for approval of biologics

Two U.S. statutes apply to the regulation of biological products, the Federal Food, Drug, and Cosmetic Act (21 U.S.C. § 301 *et* seq) (FFDCA), and the Public Health Services Act (42 U.S.C. § 262) (PHSA). The U.S. regulations charge the FDA with the protection of public health in part by ensuring that human drugs and biological products are safe and effective. The FDA administers the FFDCA and PHSA (among other statues). FFDCA applies to all drugs and medical devices, and PHSA applies to "biological products." Marketing approval under the FFDCA is by means of a New Drug Application (NDA) while approval under the PHSA is by means of a Biologics License Application (BLA). Both drugs and biologics are subject to Investigational New Drug Application (INDA) regulations. Pre-clinical research on new compounds is carried out in a laboratory, using a wide variety of techniques. Promising candidates are then studied in animals, and, subsequently, various clinical studies in humans are carried out following strict guidelines:

Phase I: A small number of healthy volunteers is given the compound to determine mainly that the drug is safe for human use.

Phase II: A small number of patients is given the medicine to assess its efficacy and safety and to ensure that there are no unacceptable side-effects.

Phase III: A large number of patients, usually thousands, take the medicine under supervision over a defined period of time, with the results used to establish efficacy.

If the results show the drug to be efficacious and safe, the data are presented to the FDA. The FDA reviews the data, and if the data is acceptable, a marketing authorization is issued. Alternatively, the FDA may request additional studies or reject the application.

Following the grant of marketing authorization, the drug product is studied in large numbers of patients in hospitals and clinics to further assess its clinical effectiveness. This stage is called Phase IV or post-marketing study. Safety Assessment of Marketed Medicines (SAMM) studies help identify any unforeseen side effects.

In order to be marketed, a biologic requires only proper labeling and an approved BLA that indicates the product has been determined safe, pure, and potent, and that the manufacturing facilities meet the requirements to ensure safety, purity, and potency. Though biologics have traditionally been subject to much more scrutiny in manufacturing than drugs, those differences are being eroded.

Biologics have been approved under FFDCA and PHSA, thus, both NDA and BLA applications have been submitted for biologics. The exceptions are glucagon and follistim that were approved under § 505(b)(2), and insulin, which was approved under its own statute for a time. The default approval pathway for biologics now is a BLA, unless the product is a hormone, in which case §505(b) is used.

15. Challenges for the coming years

Biological products often represent the cutting edge of medical science and research. Also known as biologics, these products replicate natural substances such as enzymes, antibodies, or hormones in our bodies.

Biologics are made from a variety of natural resources-human, animal, and microorganism-and may be produced by biotechnology methods.

Gene-based and cellular biologics, at the forefront of biomedical research today, may make it possible to treat a variety of medical conditions, including illnesses for which no other treatments are available. Research continues to develop more biologics that will help treat medical conditions or add to existing treatment options.

New therapies such as xenotransplantation (the transplantation of animal cells, tissues or organs into a human) offer hope for an added source of organs. "One of the challenges in using animal tissues or organs is how do you test for what's infectious? Our biggest challenge over the next century or maybe even less than a century is going to really be to understand this, and how can we make sure that when we repair, replace, restore, regenerate, that it's done in a safe manner?"

With continued advancements in medical research and medical technology, CBER will face new challenges - not just scientific and regulatory, but legal and ethical. In the 21st Century, CBER will continue its rich tradition of melding strong scientific research with innovative regulations that ensure timely access to safe and effective biological products.

CBER's major challenge for the 21st Century is to expedite approval of biological products for use by the public while, at the same time, maintain high levels of safety and quality. CBER's careful risk management of approved products already in the market also plays an important and essential role in protecting the public health.

16. References

[1] "1999 Washington Biotechnology and Medical Technology Annual Report: Carl Feldbaum CEO Interview." *Washington Biotechnology and Medical Technology Online,* April 1999. Available from:http://www.wabio.com/ind/annrpt/ceo_feldbaum.htm .

[2] Burton, Thomas M. "Hemophiliacs Sue Firms, Foundation Over AIDS in '80s." *Wall Street Journal,* 1 October 1993.

[3] Folkers, Gregory, and Anthony S. Fauci. "The Role of U.S. Government Agencies in Vaccine Research and Development." *Nature Medicine Vaccine Supplement,* May 1999.

[4] Good manufacturing practices for pharmaceutical products. In: WHO Expert Committee on specifications for pharmaceutical preparations. Thirty –Second

Report. Geneva, World Health Organization, 1992 (WHO Technical Report Series, No. 823), Annex 1.

[5] Laboratory biosafety manual, 2nd ed. Geneva, World Health Organization, 1993.

[6] WHO Expert Committee on Biological Standardization, Fortieth Report, Geneva, World Health organization, 1990 (WHO Technical Report Series, No, 800).

[7] Quality management for chemical safety testing. Geneva, World Health Organization, 1992 (Environmental Health Criteria, No 141).

[8] http://www.ema.europa.ed/docs/en/GB/document/library/scientific/guideline/2009/09/WC.

[9] Narinder Banait , Ph. D. (650.335.7818, nbanait@fenwick.com), www.fenwick.com. 2005.

5

Apparent Solubility and Dissolution Profile at Non-Sink Conditions as Quality Improvement Tools

Stefania Petralito[1,*], Iacopo Zanardi[2,*], Adriana Memoli[1],
M. Cristina Annesini[3], Vincenzo Millucci[4] and Valter Travagli[2]
[1]Dipartimento di Chimica e Tecnologie del Farmaco,
Sapienza - Università di Roma,
[2]Dipartimento Farmaco Chimico Tecnologico,
Università degli Studi di Siena,
[3]Dipartimento di Ingegneria Chimica Materiali Ambiente,
Sapienza - Università di Roma,
[4]Dipartimento di Fisica,
Università degli Studi di Siena,
Italy

1. Introduction

The excipients used during manufacturing as well as the quality of the pharmaceutical product development and preparation are of great importance to dosage form performance. A continuous know-how improvement of both formulation and production process parameters with respect to drug release profiles is a basic aspect of the quality framework for pharmaceutical products. Drug release/dissolution studies from solid dosage forms can be considered among as the most investigated topics in pharmaceutical research (De Castro et al., 2006; Macheras & Iliadis, 2006; Siepmann & Siepmann, 2008). Such a background becomes of paramount relevance in the case of insoluble or poorly soluble drugs, where dissolution represents the most critical factor affecting the rate of systemic absorption, especially in the presence of polymorphism (Snider et al., 2004). Moreover, apart from representing an important element in development and quality control in drug research, dissolution test is proposed to be a surrogate for drug bioavailability evaluation. In fact, *in vivo-in vitro* relationship represents a useful tool to answer the question about the interchangeability of generic and branded products by revealing differences in dissolution kinetics (Dressmann & Reppas, 2010; Hlinak et al., 2006). In order to increase predictability of these results, several attempts to make *in vitro* test conditions closer to the physiological ones have been made, for example by adjusting pH or by adding surfactants. However, the so-called "sink conditions" (based on bulk drug solubility i.e. in a system where the solute is present for more than 15% of its maximum solubility have been studied), obtained by using

[*] Both the authors equally contributed to this work

a high concentration of a surfactant in the dissolution medium, may not be a proper approach in developing a bio-relevant dissolution method for a poorly water-soluble drugs (Sirisuth et al. 2002; Tang et al., 2001; Jamzad & Fassihi, 2006). "Non-sink conditions" represented a very discriminating dissolution conditions, acting as a sort of magnifier lens for an in-depth evaluation of the dissolution phenomenology, and dissolution tests under non-sink conditions can be a predictive tool during formulation development as well as for batch-to-batch quality control (Siewert et al., 2003).

2. Dissolution testing in pharmacopeia

The methods of *in vitro* dissolution testing can be traced to two general categories: "stirrer beaker method" and "flow through procedure".

From a regulatory standpoint, the legally-binding documents to carry out the dissolution tests are reported in the 7th edition of European Pharmacopoeia (EP), the 34 United States Pharmacopoeia (USP), and the 15th edition of Japanese Pharmacopoeia (JP). The World Health Organization (WHO) provides in the 4th edition of International Pharmacopoeia (IntPh) a more global coverage of issues and strives towards harmonisation among world pharmacopoeia guidance and source material.

The various texts are comparable to the general notions, but differ in the apparatuses described: EP with "Dissolution test for solid dosage forms" (Council of Europe, 2011) and USP with "Dissolution" (United States Convention, 2011a) show four apparatuses: 1 (for Basket method); 2 (for paddle method), 3 (Reciprocating cylinder) and 4 (Flow-through cell), the latter being lacking in the JP "Dissolution test" (Society of Japanese Pharmacopoeia, 2007) monograph. On the other hand, in the IntPh "Dissolution test for solid oral dosage forms" section (World Health Organization, 2011), only the first two devices are indicated. In Table 1, the relation between the dimensions for the first three devices is shown: all the measures are equivalent, and any differences can be noticed only by IntPh, mainly in terms of the significant digits.

Even the choice of the dissolution medium is almost completely overlapped between EP and USP, with a variety of buffers at various pH (e.g. phosphate, acetate, TRIS). Besides, the JP refers to the monographs of specific formulations, but ranging over various possibilities, from pure water to the various buffers. On the other hand, the IntPh indicates eight different points for different pHs of the dissolution media, including simulated gastric fluid (SGF, pH 1.2) and simulated intestinal fluid (SIF); worthy of note is the pH differences of the latter: 7.5 for IntPh *vs.* 6.8 for both EP and USP.

Moreover, in the latest edition of the EP, as well as in the USP section "The dissolution procedure: development and validation" (United States Convention, 2011b), a chapter entitled "Recommendations on methods for dosage forms testing" (Council of Europe, 2010a) is given, suggesting the use of sink-condition. Sink conditions normally occur in a volume of dissolution medium that is at least 5-10 times the saturation volume, usually by adding surfactants. However, such an approach may be inappropriate in developing a bio-relevant dissolution method for a poorly water-soluble drug (Sirisuth et al. 2002; Tang et al., 2001; Jamzad & Fassihi, 2006).

Item	EP 7th	USP 34	JP 15th	IntPh 3rd
Vessel				
Height	160-210	160-210	160-210	168±8
Internal diameter	98-106	98-106	98-106	102±4
Basket				
Shaft Diameter	6.4±0.1 or 9.75±0.35	6.3-6.5 or 9.4-10.1	6.3-6.5 or 9.4-10.1	6.4±0.1 or 9.75±0.35
Screen				
Wire thickness	0.22-0.31	0.25-0.31	0.25-0.31	0.254
Openings	0.36-0.44	0.36-0.44	0.36-0.44	0.381
Height of screen	27.0±1	27.0±1.0	27.0±1	27.0±1
Total height of basket	37±3	37.0±3.0	37±3	36.8±3
Internal diam. of basket	20.2±1	20.2±1.0	20.2±1	20.2±1
External diam. of basket	22.2±1	22.2±1.0	22.2±1	22.2±1
External diam. of ring	25.0±3	25.0±3.0	25.0±3	25.4±3
Vent hole diameter	2.0±0.5	2.0±0.5	2.0±0.5	2
Height of coupling disk	5.1±0.5	5.1±0.5	5.1±0.5	5.1±0.5
Position of the stirring device				
Distance from the bottom	25±2	25±2	25±2	25±2
Distance between shaft axis and vertical axis of the vessel	≤2	≤2	≤2	≤2
Stirring characteristics	Smoothly without significant wobble	Smoothly without significant wobble	Smoothly without significant wobble	Ensure there is no significant wobble on any rotating shaft
Paddle				
Shaft Diameter	9.4-10.1	9.4-10.1	9.4-10.1	9.75±0.35
Blade				
Upper chord	74.5±0.5	74.0-75.0	74.0-75.0	74.5±0.35
Lower chord	42	42.0	42.0	42.0±1
Height	19.0±0.5	19.0±0.5	19.0±0.5	19.0±1
Radius (disk)	41.5	41.5	41.5	41.5
Radius (upper corners)	1.2±0.2	1.2±0.2	1.2±0.2	-
Thickness	4.0±1.0	4.0±1.0	4.0±1.0	4.0±1
Position of the stirring device				
Distance from the bottom	25±2	25±2	25±2	25±2
Distance between shaft axis and vertical axis of the vessel	≤2	≤2	≤2	≤2
Stirring characteristics	Smoothly without significant wobble	Smoothly without significant wobble	Smoothly without significant wobble	Ensure there is no significant wobble on any rotating shaft

Table 1. Dissolution Apparatuses. Dimensions (mm) of the vessel, basket and paddle.

3. Nimesulide

Nimesulide (NIM) is a non-steroidal anti-inflammatory drug, selective COX-2 inhibitor with analgesic and antipyretic properties (Martindale, 2009). IUPAC nomenclature is N-(4-Nitro-2-phenoxyphenyl)methanesulfonamide, with empirical formula $C_{13}H_{12}N_2O_5S$ (MW=308.31) and CAS number 51803-78-2 (Scheme 1). NIM monograph is present only in the EP (Council of Europe, 2010b).

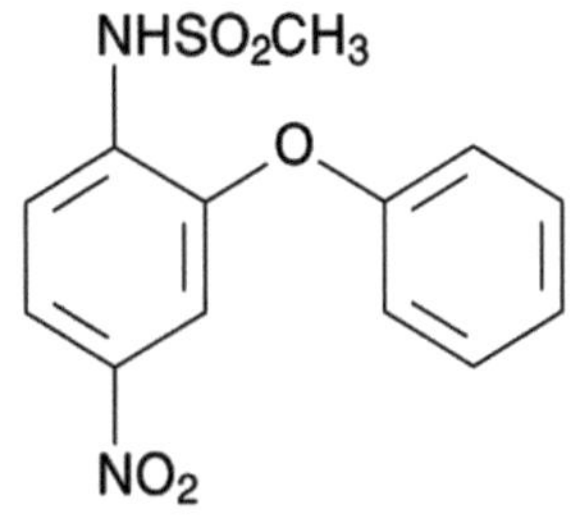

Scheme 1. Chemical structure of NIM

Its approved indications are the treatment of acute pain, the symptomatic treatment of osteoarthritis and primary dysmenorrhoea in adolescents and adults above 12 years old.

NIM was discovered in 1971 in the U.S. by George G.I. Moore at Riker Laboratories (later acquired by 3M Co.), but in 1980 NIM was licensed by Helsinn Healthcare SA (Switzerland) who proceeded to invest in extensive investigations on the drug (Rainsford, 2006). It was launched in Italy for the first time as Aulin® in 1985 (Consalvo et al., 2010) and is currently available in more than 50 countries worldwide, among others France, Portugal, Greece, Switzerland, Belgium, Mexico and Brazil. NIM has never been filed for Food and Drug Administration (FDA) evaluation in the United States, where it is not marketed (Traversa et al., 2003)

After the expiry of patent protection, a number of other companies have started production and marketing of NIM products.

Controversy regarding NIM toxicity persists due to the fact that clinical series reports and epidemiological trials continue to involve NIM in severe liver damage during the post-marketing studies (Bessone, 2010). Briefly, on August 1, 2003 the Committee for Proprietary Medicinal Products (CPMP) of the European Medicines Agency (EMA) reported that the benefit/risk profile of NIM containing medicinal products (e.g. Aulin, Mesulide, Nimed and associated product names) for systemic and topical use is favourable and that Marketing Authorisations should be maintained/granted. The CPMP recommended to restrict the use of NIM to the indications of treatment of acute pain, symptomatic treatment of painful osteoarthritis and primary dysmenorrhoea for the systemic formulations and symptomatic relief of pain associated with sprains and acute tendinitis for the topical formulation (EMEA, 2003).

The Irish Medicines Board (IMB) announced the suspension of NIM from the Irish market and reported it to the EU Committee for Human Medicinal Products (CHMP) for a review of its benefit/risk profile. The decision is due to the reporting of six cases of potentially related liver failures to the IMB by the National Liver Transplant Unit, St Vincent Hospital.

These cases occurred in the period from 1999 to 2006 (IMB, 2007). On December 3, 2007 Ireland's RTÉ aired an investigative programme highlighting the deadly side effects of NIM and how it has been linked to over 300 cases of liver disease throughout Europe.

On September 21, 2007 the EMA released a press release on their review on the liver-related safety of NIM. The EMA has concluded that the benefits of these medicines outweigh their risks, but that there is a need to limit the duration of use to ensure that the risk of patients developing liver problems is kept to a minimum. Therefore the EMA has limited the use of systemic formulations (tablets, solutions, suppositories) of NIM-containing medicinal products to 15 days because of reports of severe hepatic adverse reactions (EMA, 2007; Li et al., 2009).

Singapore Health Science Authority (HSA) suspended NIM containing drugs in June 2007 (Singapore News, 2007; HSA, 2007). Several reports have been made of adverse drug reactions in India (Khan & Rahman, 2004a, 2004b; Rahman & Khan, 2004). On Feb 12, 2011, Express India reported that the Union Ministry of Health and Family Welfare had finally decided to ban the pediatric use of the analgesic, NIM suspension. From 2011 onwards, it has been totally banned in India.

NIM chemico-physical properties could be summarised as: i) weak acid properties (pKa reported ranging between 5.9 and 6.56 (Singh et al., 1999; Singh et al., 2001; Dellis et al., 2007); ii) values of octanol-water partition coefficient (log P) of 2.38 (Singh et al., 2001); iii) practically insoluble in water (10 µg/mL) (Piel et al. 1997); iv) according to the Biopharmaceutical Classification System, BCS, (FDA, 2000), NIM can be classified as a class II drug (low solubility and high permeability), therefore, the drug dissolution may be a rate-limiting step in the drug adsorption process.

Previous studies were carried out for both in vitro (Butler et al., 2000; Rădulescu et al., 2010) and in vivo comparisons among NIM-containing tablets (Hutt et al. 2001; Ilic et al. 2009). However, in the former only a small number of commercial preparations were investigated under sink-condition by means of abnormal surfactant concentration (Butler et al. 2000), and the release rate seems to be critically influenced not by pH value or the concentration of endogenous surfactant, but by the combination of the two characteristics of the *in vitro* dissolution media (Rădulescu et al., 2010), while in the latter no *in vitro* and *in vivo* correlation (IVIVC) was investigated. Moreover, since due to different crystallization processes, crystallographic modification has been recently reported (Kapoor et al. 1998; Di Martino et al. 2007; Moneghini et al. 2007), even though only a single crystal structure has been identified (Dupont et al., 1995). Thus, information on the influence of the different nature and/or amount of excipients as well as of the adopted technological parameters on the *in vitro* drug release characteristics are reputed of interest.

4. Materials and methods

4.1 Dosage form selection

Ten multisource IR NIM tablet formulations (RF for reference formulation, MSF for the multiple-source product formulation, and BF1-BF8 for non-branded bioequivalent formulations) were obtained from the Italian market. They all nominally contain 100 mg of the active ingredient, but greatly differ with respect to the excipient composition. Table 2 summarizes the qualitative excipient composition of the various NIM tablets.

Auxiliary Substances	RF	MSF	BF1	BF2	BF3	BF4	BF5	BF6	BF7	BF8
Hydroxypropyl cellulose	X	X	X	X	X			X		
Lactose	X		X	X	X	X	X	X	X*	X
Cellulose, microcrystalline	X	X	X	X	X	X	X	X†	X	X
Castor oil, hydrogenate	X	X	X	X	X					X
Magnesium stearate	X	X	X	X	X	X	X	X	X	X
Sodium docusate	X	X	X	X	X		X			
Sodium starch glycolate	X	X	X	X	X			X	X	X
Maize starch						X	X			
Sodium dodecyl sulphate						X	X		X	
Glyceryl behenate						X‡	X			
PEG§										X
Talc									X	

*explicitly reported as Lactose monohydrate; †reported as microgranular; ‡referred as Compritol 888; §no more info are reported

Table 2. Qualitative excipient composition of the various NIM tablets.

4.2 Tablet appearance

Each tablet was visually examined for shape and any evidence of physical differences such as weight, thickness and dimension was recorded.

4.3 Calibration curve

Calibration curve for NIM reference standard (RS) was obtained by measuring the UV absorption (Perkin Elmer L25 spectrophotometer, λ_{max}: 392.6 nm) in dissolution medium (Simulated Intestinal Fluid, SIF, pH 6.8) prepared according to EP (Council of Europe, 2010a) except for the absence of pancreatin, in conformity with the aim of this study. This pH value was selected because of the NIM negligible dissolution in acidic conditions. Due to the low aqueous NIM solubility, NIM stock solution was prepared by accurate weight of the substance and subsequent dissolution in 5 mL of ethanol, submitting to ultrasound in a sonicator bath for five minutes, and then diluted to a final volume of 100 mL with SIF, corresponding to 50 µg/mL of NIM. Calibration samples were prepared from three separately weighed stock solutions to obtain sample solutions containing scalar concentrations of NIM. Samples were stored at +4 °C until analysis. The linearity of the calibration curves was confirmed over the range 1-20 µg/mL.

4.4 Solubility studies

Apparent solubility (S_{app}) referring to the dynamic solubility (Mosharraf & Nystrom, 2003) of both NIM RS and NIM tablets were determined by stirring an excess amount of the samples in 250 mL of SIF, on a multistirrer thermostatted at 37 ± 0.5 °C for a suitable time in order to achieve equilibrium (max 72 hours). Twenty tablets of the same commercial product were weighed and powdered (particle size ≤ 150 µm, by sieving). An amount corresponding to one-fourth of a tablet (equivalent to 25 mg of NIM) was weighed and suspended in 250 mL dissolution medium. In such a way the ratio among active agent, excipients and volume agrees with dissolution studies conditions (see below). The samples were filtered with a 0.45 µm nylon membrane filter (Whatman, Maidstone, UK) and the absorbance of the filtrate was measured by UV. Temperature (37 ± 0.5 °C) was carefully maintained constant during all the operations and the amount of drug dissolved was calculated using the calibration curve (see above). All solubility determinations were performed in triplicate.

4.5 Dissolution studies

For tablet dissolution tests, apparatus I (rotating basket method) (Council of Europe, 2011) was used employing 1000 mL of SIF at a temperature of 37 ± 0.5 °C and a rotational speed of 100 rpm. Sample solution (5 mL) was withdrawn at appropriated time intervals (5, 10, 15, 30, 45 and 60 min) and the drawn volume was replaced with the same amount of blank dissolution medium from a separate vessel, also held at a temperature of 37 ± 0.5 °C. The samples were filtered with a 0.45 µm nylon membrane filter (Whatman, Maidstone, UK) and the absorbance of the filtrate was measured by UV. The amount of NIM was calculated through the calibration curve. All the dissolution tests were conducted on twelve tablets for each formulation.

4.6 Mathematical dissolution models

The data obtained from dissolution studies were analyzed using various mathematical models (Table 3), as reported in DDSolver. It is a specialized, freely available software program developed by Zhang *et al.* with the main objective to provide a tool for facilitating the parameter calculations in dissolution data analysis using nonlinear optimization model-dependent approaches (Zhang et al., 2010). In the present chapter, the selection of the models for fitting dissolution data has been based on their theoretical applicability.

Dissolution model	Equation[a]
First-order[b,c]	$F = F_{max} \cdot (1 - e^{-k_1 \cdot t})$
Higuchi[d]	$F = k_H \cdot t^{0.5}$
Korsmeyer-Peppas[e]	$F = k_{KP} \cdot t^n$
Hixson-Crowell[f]	$F = 100 \cdot [1 - (1 - k_{HC} \cdot t)^3]$
Hopfenberg[g]	$F = 100 \cdot [1 - (1 - k_{HB} \cdot t)^n]$
Baker-Lonsdale[h]	$\frac{3}{2}\left[1 - \left(1 - \frac{F}{100}\right)^{\frac{2}{3}}\right] - \frac{F}{100} = k_{BL} \cdot t$
Makoid-Banakar[i]	$F = k_{MB} \cdot t^n \cdot e^{-k \cdot t}$
Peppas-Sahlin 1[l]	$F = k_1 \cdot t^m + k_2 \cdot t^{2m}$
Peppas-Sahlin 2[m]	$F = k_1 \cdot t^{0.5} + k_2 \cdot t$
Quadratic[n]	$F = 100 \cdot (k_1 \cdot t^2 + k_2 \cdot t)$
Weibull 1[o,p]	$F = 100 \cdot \left[1 - e^{-\frac{(t - T_i)^\beta}{\alpha}}\right]$

Weibull 2[o]	$F = 100 \cdot \left[1 - e^{-\frac{t^{\beta}}{\alpha}}\right]$
Weibull 3[c,o]	$F = F_{\max} \cdot \left[1 - e^{-\frac{t^{\beta}}{\alpha}}\right]$
Weibull 4[c,o,p]	$F = F_{\max} \cdot \left[1 - e^{-\frac{(t-T_i)^{\beta}}{\alpha}}\right]$
Logistic 1[q]	$F = 100 \cdot \frac{e^{\alpha} + \beta \cdot \log(t)}{1 + e^{\alpha} + \beta \cdot \log(t)}$
Logistic 2[c,q]	$F = F_{\max} \cdot \frac{e^{\alpha} + \beta \cdot \log(t)}{1 + e^{\alpha} + \beta \cdot \log(t)}$
Logistic 3[c,r]	$F = F_{\max} \cdot \frac{1}{1 + e^{-k \cdot (t-\gamma)}}$
Gompertz 1[s]	$F = 100 \cdot e^{-\alpha \cdot e^{\beta \cdot \log(t)}}$
Gompertz 2[c,s]	$F = F_{\max} \cdot e^{-\alpha \cdot e^{\beta \cdot \log(t)}}$
Gompertz 3[c,t]	$F = F_{\max} \cdot e^{-e^{-k \cdot (t-\gamma)}}$
Gompertz 4[c,u]	$F = F_{\max} \cdot e^{-\beta \cdot e^{-k \cdot t}}$
Probit 1[v]	$F = 100 \cdot \Phi[\alpha + \beta \cdot \log(t)]$
Probit 2[c,v]	$F = F_{\max} \cdot \Phi[\alpha + \beta \cdot \log(t)]$

Table 3. Applied dissolution methods.

[a]In all models. F is the concentration (µg/mL) of the drug release in time t.
[b]k_1 is the first-order release constant.
[c]F_{max} is the maximum fraction of the drug released at infinite time
[d]k_H is the Higuchi release constant
[e]k_{KP} is the release constant incorporating structural and geometric characteristics of the drug-dosage form; n is the diffusional exponent indicating the drug-release mechanism
[f]k_{HC} is the release constant in Hixson–Crowell model
[g]k_{HB} is the combined constant in Hopfenberg model, $k_{HB}=k_0/(C_0 \times a_0)$, where k_0 is the erosion rate constant, C_0 is the initial concentration of drug in the matrix, and a_0 is the initial radius for a sphere or cylinder or the half thickness for a slab; n is 1, 2, and 3 for a slab, cylinder, and sphere, respectively
[h]k_{BL} is the combined constant in Baker–Lonsdale model, $k_{BL}=[3 \times D \times C_s/(r_0^2 \times C_0)]$, where D is the diffusion coefficient, C_s is the saturation solubility, r_0 is the initial radius for a sphere or cylinder or the half-thickness for a slab, and C_0 is the initial drug loading in the matrix
[i]k_{MB}, n, and k are empirical parameters in Makoid–Banakar model (k_{MB}, n, k>0)
[l]k_1 is the constant related to the Fickian kinetics; k_2 is the constant related to Case-II relaxation kinetics; m is the diffusional exponent for a device of any geometric shape which inhibits controlled release
[m]k_1 is the constant denoting the relative contribution of $t^{0.5}$-dependent drug diffusion to drug release; k_2 is the constant denoting the relative contribution of t-dependent polymer relaxation to drug release
[n]k_1 is the constant in Quadratic model denoting the relative contribution of t^2-dependent drug release; k_2

is the constant in Quadratic model denoting the relative contribution of t-dependent drug release
[o]α is the scale parameter which defines the time scale of the process; β is the shape parameter which characterizes the curve as either exponential (β=1; case 1), sigmoid, S-shaped, with upward curvature followed by a turning point (β>1; case 2), or parabolic, with a higher initial slope and after that consistent with the exponential (β<1; case 3)
[p]T_i is the location parameter which represents the lag time before the onset of the dissolution or release process and in most cases will be near zero
[q]α is the scale factor in Logistic 1 and 2 models; β is the shape factor in Logistic 1 and 2 models
[r]k is the shape factor in Logistic 3 model; γ is the time at which $F = F_{max}/2$
[s]α is the scale factor in Gompertz 1 and 2 models; β is the shape factor in Gompertz 1 and 2 models
[t]k is the shape factor in Gompertz 3 model; γ is the time at which $F = F_{max}/\exp(1) \approx 0.368 \times F_{max}$
[u]β is the scale factor in Gompertz 4 model; k is the shape factor in Gompertz 4 model
[v]Φ is the standard normal distribution; α is the scale factor in Probit model; β is the shape factor in Probit model

4.7 Statistical analysis

Results were expressed as the mean ± SD of at least six independent measurements. ANOVA one-way performing the Bonferroni post-test (Instat software, version 3.0 GraphPAD Software Inc., San Diego, CA) were used for the statistical analysis of the results. Significance was defined as a p value less than 0.05 (* $p < 0.05$; ** $p < 0.01$; *** $p < 0.001$).

5. Results and discussion

Tablet weight and dimensions data obtained for the formulations studied are reported in Table 4.

PRODUCT	Weight (g ± SD)	Thickness (mm ± SD)	Diameter (mm ± SD)
RF	0.4022 ± 0.0032	0.59 ± 0.006	0.97 ± 0.02
MSF*	0.3995 ± 0.0037	0.58 ± 0.004	0.96 ± 0.01
BF1*	0.4018 ± 0.0033	0.57 ± 0.002	0.91 ± 0.01
BF2	0.4049 ± 0.0077	0.58 ± 0.005	0.96 ± 0.02
BF3	0.4017 ± 0.0130	0.57 ± 0.006	0.95 ± 0.03
BF4	0.4065 ± 0.0098	0.53 ± 0.002	1.02 ± 0.01
BF5	0.4061 ± 0.0073	0.58 ± 0.003	0.92 ± 0.02
BF6	0.7074 ± 0.0083	0.42 ± 0.003	1.33 ± 0.02
BF7†	0.7063 ± 0.0075	0.42 ± 0.001	1.32 ± 0.02
BF8	0.4044 ± 0.0068	0.46 ± 0.003	1.12 ± 0.03

*a fracture line appears along the tablets diameter; †visible lamination with different coloration along the thickness.

Table 4. Weight and shape size of tablets

In detail, all the tablets have the same shape and each tablet has a weight of about 400 mg, except BF6 and BF7 that are heavier reaching a weight of about 700 mg. As far as the visual inspection is concerned, BF1 and BF8 show a fracture line along the tablets diameter as well as a different appearance along thickness of BF7 tablets was observed, suggesting lamination due to compression steps (Carstensen et al., 1985).

From dissolution data analysis it is possible to note that, apart from BF8 representing the lower amount released (6.0 mg, corresponding to the 6% after 1 h), the % of release for the formulations was between 16.1% and 23.0% (Figure 1).

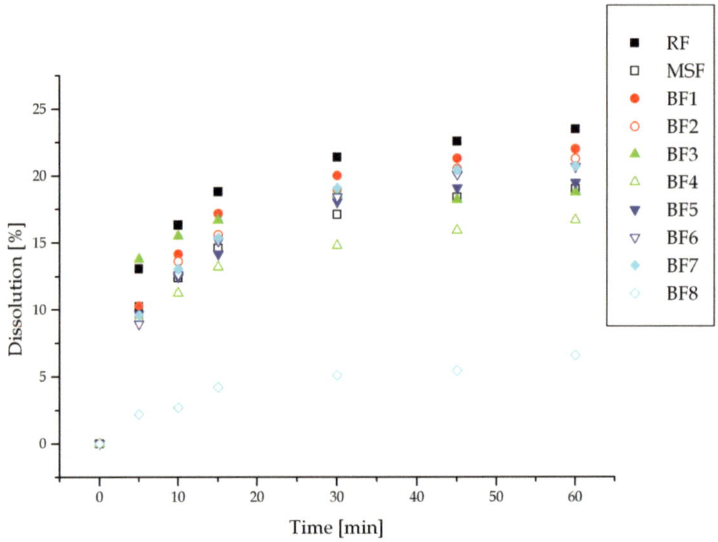

Fig. 1. Dissolution profiles of the various tablets at pH 6.8 (CV%<5).

Such differences, that our adopted experimental conditions in the absence of sink-conditions were able to blow up, were attributed to formulation differences and/or manufacturing procedures. For this reason, to better explain the dissolution profile, saturation concentrations obtained from solubility studies in the presence of the various auxiliary substances were also adopted. They are shown in Figure 2.

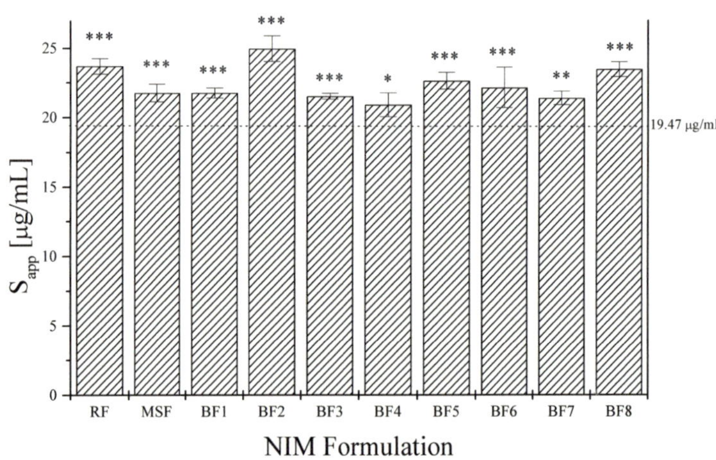

Fig. 2. Apparent solubility of NIM in the presence of tablet excipients (mean ± SD). The apparent solubility of NIM RS alone is indicated by the dotted line. Statistical significance with respect to NIM RS are also indicated.

NIM RS has the lowest S_{app} (19.47 µg/mL) while for BF2 an increment of S_{app} value near 30% (24.97 µg/mL) was obtained. With respect to NIM value, statistically significant increase in Sapp was obtained in all cases ($p < 0.001$, except than NIM vs. BF7 and NIM vs. BF4, for which $p < 0.01$ and $p < 0.05$ were observed, respectively).

These data suggested us to use S_{app} value of each formulation as normalization factor for each dissolution evaluation, instead of that of NIM solubility. Results are depicted in Figure 3, from which it appears that also in this case BF8 is not able to reach the 30% of dissolution.

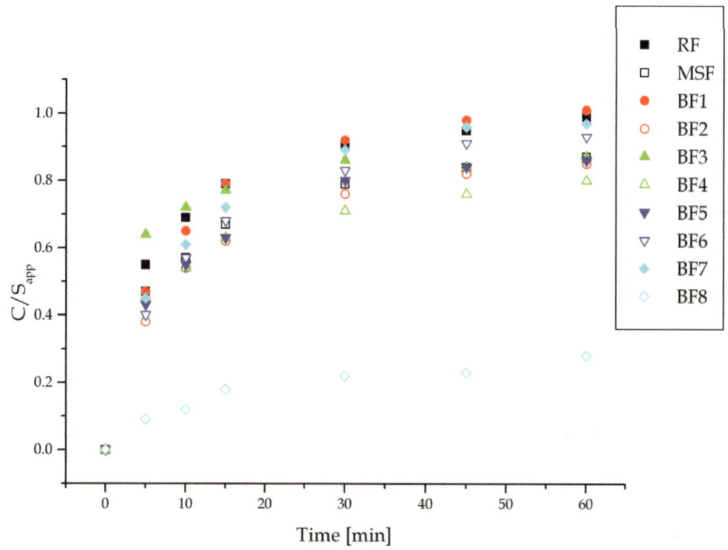

Fig. 3. Dissolution profiles of the various tablets at pH 6.8 as obtained with respect to apparent solubility (CV%<5).

As concerns BF4 its profile remains below all other curves. On the contrary, for BF1, after 1h is appreciable the achievement of 100%; such a result were not obtained by the other formulations, except than for RF.

The simplest model to represent a dissolution of a BCS II drug is a first-order model, with a dissolution rate proportional to the difference between the apparent solubility of drug and the drug concentration in the liquid phase. Such a model, along with others, has been applied with DDSolver Software and the obtained results are shown in Table 5.

The corresponding correlation coefficients, R^2, in most of the adopted equations gave results higher than 0.97, and in all these cases the worst result is obtained in the description of the dissolution of the BF8 formulation.

On the other hand, for Higuchi ($R^2<0.97$, except than for BF8), Baker-Lonsdale ($R^2<0.97$, except than for BF8), Quadratic ($R^2<0.90$), Logistic3 ($R^2<0.97$), Gompertz 3 and 4 ($R^2<0.95$) models, the mathematical description often did not appear to be entirely sufficient. Moreover, for both Hixson-Crowell and Hopfenberg models, the mathematical fitting cannot be considered acceptable ($R^2<0.61$).

Best-fit values	RF	MSF	BF1	BF2	BF3	BF4	BF5	BF6	BF7	BF8
Dissolution model										
First-order with F_{max}										
k_1	0.144	0.129	0.115	0.170	0.251	0.144	0.111	0.100	0.106	0.067
F_{max}	22.374	18.130	21.344	20.541	18.071	15.708	18.970	20.125	20.334	6.195
R^2	0.9855	0.9797	0.9942	0.9914	0.9860	0.9786	0.9846	0.9933	0.9921	0.9708
Higuchi										
k_H	3.626	2.925	3.376	3.218	3.113	2.573	2.989	3.115	3.176	0.881
R^2	0.9274	0.9427	0.9496	0.9597	0.8429	0.9315	0.9551	0.9647	0.9581	0.9854
Korsmeyer-Peppas										
k_{KP}	9.864	7.264	7.596	6.819	11.787	6.858	6.651	6.233	6.738	1.192
N	0.219	0.242	0.271	0.288	0.119	0.222	0.274	0.304	0.287	0.415
R^2	0.9931	0.9949	0.9839	0.9887	0.9939	0.9957	0.9902	0.9870	0.9863	0.9793
Hixson-Crowell										
k_{HC}	$1.96 \cdot 10^{-3}$	$1.53 \cdot 10^{-3}$	$1.80 \cdot 10^{-3}$	$1.71 \cdot 10^{-3}$	$1.60 \cdot 10^{-3}$	$1.32 \cdot 10^{-3}$	$1.58 \cdot 10^{-3}$	$1.66 \cdot 10^{-3}$	$1.69 \cdot 10^{-3}$	$4.45 \cdot 10^{-4}$
R^2	-0.0173	0.0746	0.1949	0.2647	-0.5867	-0.0293	0.2054	0.3204	0.2582	0.6021
Hopfenberg										
k_{HC}	$3.06 \cdot 10^{-5}$	$1.15 \cdot 10^{-5}$	$7.04 \cdot 10^{-5}$	$1.91 \cdot 10^{-5}$	$2.31 \cdot 10^{-5}$	$2.50 \cdot 10^{-5}$	$2.09 \cdot 10^{-5}$	$1.72 \cdot 10^{-5}$	$1.27 \cdot 10^{-5}$	$2.27 \cdot 10^{-5}$
n	204.251	418.380	811.300	284.294	218.499	165.644	237.060	304.395	418.635	59.470
R^2	0.0338	0.1126	0.2371	0.3025	-0.5351	0.0046	0.2417	0.3555	0.2961	0.6082
Baker-Lonsdale										
k_{BL}	$2.53 \cdot 10^{-4}$	$1.57 \cdot 10^{-4}$	$2.12 \cdot 10^{-4}$	$1.92 \cdot 10^{-4}$	$1.80 \cdot 10^{-4}$	$1.20 \cdot 10^{-4}$	$1.64 \cdot 10^{-4}$	$1.79 \cdot 10^{-4}$	$1.87 \cdot 10^{-4}$	$1.33 \cdot 10^{-5}$
R^2	0.7892	0.8286	0.8655	0.8919	0.5211	0.7882	0.8737	0.9084	0.8888	0.9673
Makoid-Banakar										
k_{MB}	7.743	5.831	5.020	4.754	9.821	5.794	4.758	4.134	4.410	0.984
n	0.350	0.360	0.491	0.478	0.221	0.313	0.451	0.520	0.511	0.513
k	0.006	0.005	0.009	0.008	0.004	0.004	0.007	0.009	0.009	0.004
R^2	0.9991	0.9994	0.9981	0.9989	0.9984	0.9986	0.9992	0.9993	1.0000	0.9811
Peppas-Sahlin 1										
k_1	8.128	6.052	5.287	4.935	10.950	6.091	4.873	4.302	4.572	0.995
k_2	-0.708	-0.478	-0.320	-0.288	-1.608	-0.548	-0.304	-0.225	-0.252	-0.033
m	0.418	0.426	0.528	0.523	0.310	0.381	0.506	0.555	0.550	0.547
R^2	0.9992	0.9994	0.9980	0.9990	0.9984	0.9987	0.9992	0.9992	1.0000	0.9813
Peppas-Sahlin 2										
k_1	6.639	5.075	5.671	5.209	6.605	4.605	4.948	4.908	5.168	1.087
k_2	-0.476	-0.344	-0.367	-0.318	-0.558	-0.325	-0.313	-0.287	-0.319	-0.033
R^2	0.9960	0.9973	0.9976	0.9988	0.9759	0.9931	0.9992	0.9981	0.9990	0.9809
Quadratic										
k_1	$-1.64 \cdot 10^{-4}$	$-1.26 \cdot 10^{-4}$	$-1.45 \cdot 10^{-4}$	$-1.33 \cdot 10^{-4}$	$-1.58 \cdot 10^{-4}$	$-1.13 \cdot 10^{-4}$	$-1.26 \cdot 10^{-4}$	$-1.27 \cdot 10^{-4}$	$-1.33 \cdot 10^{-4}$	$-2.78 \cdot 10^{-5}$
k_2	0.013	0.010	0.012	0.011	0.012	0.009	0.011	0.011	0.011	0.003
R^2	0.7173	0.7597	0.8227	0.8378	0.4934	0.7077	0.8284	0.8639	0.8539	0.9008
Weibull 1										
α	7.498	10.917	8.863	9.992	6.820	11.592	11.339	10.889	10.364	64.265
β	0.176	0.210	0.202	0.221	0.090	0.187	0.231	0.236	0.227	0.359
T_i	3.717	2.900	4.198	4.011	3.910	3.058	3.257	3.960	3.845	2.533
R^2	0.9987	0.9978	0.9967	0.9990	0.9967	0.9984	0.9952	0.9977	0.9957	0.9818
Weibull 2										
α	9.851	13.529	13.054	14.618	8.026	14.282	14.921	16.069	14.795	84.457
β	0.244	0.264	0.299	0.317	0.131	0.239	0.299	0.333	0.316	0.425
R^2	0.9937	0.9954	0.9851	0.9898	0.9940	0.9960	0.9910	0.9881	0.9874	0.9795
Weibull 3										
α	3.270	3.537	5.410	5.303	1.703	3.067	4.589	6.038	5.551	9.326
β	0.567	0.522	0.749	0.692	0.472	0.479	0.624	0.732	0.719	0.626
F_{max}	24.458	20.970	22.296	22.119	19.086	18.408	20.968	21.461	21.608	8.499
R^2	0.9996	0.9992	0.9994	0.9997	0.9981	0.9989	0.9982	0.9998	0.9995	0.9818

Weibull 4										
α	3.136	3.531	4.935	3.580	1.708	3.021	4.584	5.517	5.551	8.735
β	0.551	0.522	0.718	0.539	0.474	0.472	0.624	0.700	0.719	0.490
T_i	0.208	0.000	0.338	1.726	0.000	0.103	0.000	0.357	0.000	1.577
F_{max}	24.559	20.980	22.387	23.231	19.074	18.482	20.980	21.597	21.608	11.250
R^2	0.9996	0.9992	0.9994	0.9999	0.9981	0.9989	0.9982	0.9998	0.9995	0.9820
Logistic 1										
α	-2.261	-2.588	-2.563	-2.680	-2.026	-2.639	-2.696	-2.781	-2.693	-4.444
β	0.626	0.659	0.760	0.799	0.331	0.591	0.749	0.839	0.796	1.001
R^2	0.9942	0.9957	0.9861	0.9907	0.9942	0.9962	0.9916	0.9892	0.9884	0.9797
Logistic 2										
α	-1.342	-1.411	-2.006	-1.945	-0.497	-1.244	-1.709	-2.091	-1.968	-2.546
β	1.805	1.490	2.399	2.128	1.786	1.414	1.778	2.215	2.156	1.635
F_{max}	27.070	24.666	24.318	24.700	20.109	21.295	24.443	24.070	24.293	10.810
R^2	0.9996	0.9990	0.9993	0.9999	0.9978	0.9989	0.9976	0.9997	0.9988	0.9821
Logistic 3										
k	0.340	0.269	0.265	0.248	1.197	0.324	0.231	0.235	0.236	0.192
γ	5.271	6.083	6.837	7.154	3.923	5.324	7.072	7.637	7.358	10.074
F_{max}	21.639	17.707	20.766	19.927	17.549	15.229	18.552	19.506	19.803	5.775
R^2	0.9285	0.9190	0.9489	0.9423	0.9699	0.9179	0.9287	0.9480	0.9433	0.9344
Gompertz 1										
α	2.462	2.776	2.806	2.932	2.176	2.797	2.919	3.050	2.944	4.713
β	0.307	0.297	0.361	0.372	0.155	0.255	0.339	0.385	0.369	0.305
R^2	0.9959	0.9971	0.9898	0.9939	0.9946	0.9973	0.9939	0.9929	0.9918	0.9815
Gompertz 2										
α	1.903	1.936	2.913	2.708	1.119	1.761	2.284	2.912	2.714	3.479
β	1.223	0.864	1.615	1.353	1.455	0.857	1.041	1.374	1.351	0.628
F_{max}	29.151	29.053	26.049	27.274	20.482	24.445	28.420	26.859	26.975	19.954
R^2	0.9995	0.9988	0.9991	0.9999	0.9977	0.9989	0.9971	0.9995	0.9983	0.9823
Gompertz 3										
k	0.243	0.202	0.191	0.178	0.517	0.237	0.172	0.167	0.171	0.120
γ	3.569	3.899	4.530	4.731	2.523	3.537	4.515	5.058	4.804	7.011
F_{max}	21.88	17.800	20.905	20.082	17.685	15.369	18.650	19.657	19.930	5.907
R^2	0.9560	0.9467	0.9705	0.9651	0.9739	0.9466	0.9538	0.9688	0.9656	0.9492
Gompertz 4										
k	0.243	0.202	0.191	0.178	0.518	0.237	0.172	0.167	0.171	0.120
β	2.378	2.202	2.381	2.319	3.693	2.310	2.169	2.325	2.272	2.315
F_{max}	21.882	17.801	20.904	20.082	17.685	15.370	18.650	19.659	19.931	5.908
R^2	0.9560	0.9467	0.9705	0.9651	0.9739	0.9466	0.9538	0.9688	0.9656	0.9492
Probit 1										
α	-1.337	-1.502	-1.500	-1.560	-1.199	-1.521	-1.562	-1.612	-1.566	-2.318
β	0.356	0.361	0.427	0.444	0.185	0.318	0.412	0.464	0.442	0.452
R^2	0.9949	0.9964	0.9877	0.9922	0.9944	0.9968	0.9927	0.9909	0.9900	0.9808
Probit 2										
α	-0.830	-0.872	-1.256	-1.215	-0.279	-0.765	-1.065	-1.308	-1.234	-1.581
β	1.175	0.966	1.551	1.375	1.136	0.917	1.158	1.430	1.404	0.926
F_{max}	26.154	23.865	23.571	23.928	19.598	20.617	23.574	23.317	23.449	12.131
R^2	0.9996	0.9989	0.9993	0.9999	0.9978	0.9989	0.9975	0.9997	0.9988	0.9822

Table 5. Parameters and determination coefficients of various dissolution models.

Further investigation may be done by going to compare the S_{app} experimental data with those determined using some equations, which allows to calculate a value of F_{max} (Figure 4).

As it is possible to observe, no model is able to estimate properly the experimental S_{app} parameter of the various preparations, except than the Weibull functions. In detail, either under- or overestimations have been observed, with the model Gompertz 2 that provides a value always greater than the others. As for BF8, the non-sink conditions allow to show a significant extension of time to reach the maximum value of the dynamic solubility.

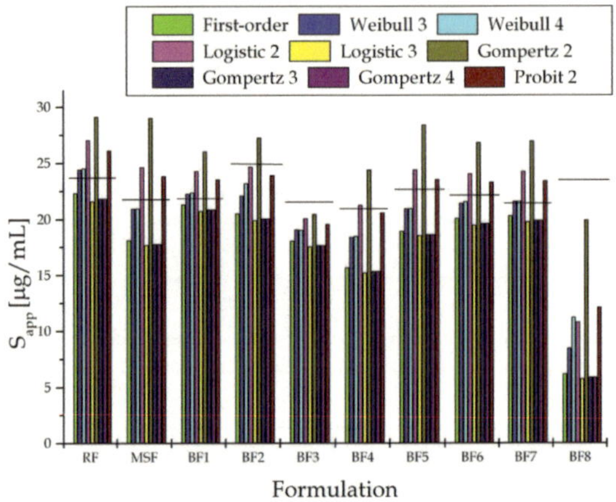

Fig. 4. Comparison of experimental S_{app} and calculated F_{max} derived from mathematical fitting.

6. Conclusion

A continuous know-how improvement of both formulation and manufacturing process parameters with respect to drug release modalities is a basic aspect of the quality framework for pharmaceutical products. Such features become of paramount relevance for generic manufacturers in the case of formulation of insoluble or poorly soluble drugs, where dissolution represents the most critical factor. In fact, both the excipients used as well as the manufacture parameters are of great importance to solid dosage form performance. The *in vivo* solubility behaviour is dependent on many factors and it cannot be fully obtained *in vitro*. Regardless the worth of "sink conditions" in the achievement of bio-relevant dissolution methods for poorly water-soluble drugs, an approach more suitable as developmental tool as well as for batch quality control in both pre-formulation and formulation stages is of great interest.

For such purposes, various commercial Immediate Release tablets containing a drug, namely NIM, differently banned, used and prescribed in the various European Countries have been chosen. NIM apparent solubilities and dissolution patterns as obtained in "non-sink conditions", i.e. in a system where the solute is present for more than 15% of its maximum solubility, have been studied. "Non-sink conditions" represented a very discriminating dissolution conditions, acting as a sort of magnifier lens for an in-depth evaluation of the dissolution phenomenology, useful since the preformulation stages.

Eventually, in such a situation of drug saturation during tablet dissolution the mathematical approaches far developed usually are not capable of describing the overall profile peculiarity.

For this reason, a more complex dissolution scheme based on the ash layer diffusion control by shrinking core model is under study.

7. Acknowledgment

The authors thank the MIUR for partial financial support.

8. References

Bessone, F. (2010). Non-steroidal anti-inflammatory drugs: What is the actual risk of liver damage? World Journal of Gastroenterology, Vol. 16, No. 45, (December 2010), pp. 5651-5661. P.ISSN 1007-9327 E.ISSN 2219-2840

Butler, D.; Bonadeo, D.; Maroni, A.; Foppoli, A.; Zema, L. & Giordano, F. (2000). Comparative in vitro evaluation of nimesulide-containing preparations on the Italian market. Bollettino Chimico Farmaceutico, Vol. 139, No. 6, (November-December 2000), pp. 237-241. ISSN 0006-6648

Carstensen, J.T.; Alcorn, G.J.; Hussain, S.A. & Zoglio, M.A. (1985). Triaxial compression of cappable formulations. *Journal of Pharmaceutical Sciences*, Vol. 74, No. 11, (November 1985), pp. 1239-1241. ISSN 0022-3549

Consalvo, M.; Ciarcia S.; Muhindo, A. & Coluzzi F. (2010). Nimesulide: 25 years later. *Minerva Medica*, Vol. 101, No. 4, (August 2010), pp. 285-293. P.ISSN 0026-4806 E.ISSN 1827-1669.

Council of Europe. (2010a). Recommendations on methods for dosage forms testing, In: *European Pharmacopoeia 7th Edition*, Vol. 1, pp. 665-667, Druckerei C. H. Beck, ISBN 978-92-871-9700-2, Nördlingen, Germany

Council of Europe. (2010b). Nimesulide, In: *European Pharmacopoeia 7th Edition*, Vol. 2, pp. 2577-2578, Druckerei C. H. Beck, ISBN 978-92-871-9700-2, Nördlingen, Germany

Council of Europe. (2011). Dissolution test for solid dosage forms, In: *European Pharmacopoeia 7th Edition*, Suppl. 3, pp. 3797-3803, Druckerei C. H. Beck, ISBN 978- 92-871-9656-3, Nördlingen, Germany

De Castro, W.V.; Pires, M.A.S.; Oliveira, M.A.; Vianna-Soares, C.D.; Nunan, E.A.; Pianetti, G.A.; Moreira-Campos, L.M.; De Castro, W.V.; Mertens-Talcott, S.U. & Derendorf, H. (2006). The influence of formulation on the dissolution profile of diclofenac sodium tablets. *Drug Development and Industrial Pharmacy*, Vol. 32, No. 9, (October 2006), pp. 1103-1109. P.ISSN 0363-9045 E.ISSN 1520-5762

Dellis, D.; Giaginis, C. & Tsantili-Kakoulidou, A. (2007). Physicochemical profile of nimesulide: exploring the interplay of lipophilicity, solubility and ionization. *Journal of Pharmaceutical and Biomedical Analysis*, Vol. 44, No. 1, (May 2007), pp. 57-62. ISSN 0731-7085

Di Martino, P.; Censi, R.; Barthélémy, C.; Gobetto, R.; Joiris, E.; Masic, A.; Odou, P. & Martelli, S. (2007). Characterization and compaction behaviour of nimesulide crystal forms. *International Journal of Pharmaceutics*, Vol. 42, No. 1-2, (September 2007), pp. 137-144. P.ISSN 0378-5173 E.ISSN 1873-3476

Dressman, J.B.; Reppas C. (2010). *Oral drug absorption. Prediction and assessment*, Informa Healthcare, ISBN 1420077341, New York (NY)

Dupont, L.; Pirotte B.; Masereel, B.; Delarge J. & Geczy, J. (1995). Nimesulide. Acta Crystallographica Section C, Vol. 51C, No. 3, (March 1995), pp. 507-509. ISSN 0108-2701

EMA. (2007). European Medicines Agency recommends restricted use of nimesulide-containing medicinal products. EMEA/432604/2007.

http://www.ema.europa.eu/docs/en_GB/document_library/Press_release/2009/11/WC500011199.pdf

EMEA. (2003). Committee for proprietary medicinal products 22-24 July 2003 Plenary Meeting Monthly Report. EMEA/CPMP/3754/03. http://www.ema.europa.eu/docs/en_GB/document_library/Committee_meeting_report/2009/10/WC500006477.pdf

FDA. (2000). Guidance for industry. Waiver of in vivo bioavailability and bioequivalence studies for immediate-release solid oral dosage forms based on a Biopharmaceutics Classification System. http://www.fda.gov/downloads/Drugs/GuidanceComplianceRegulatoryInformation/Guidances/ucm070246.pdf

Hlinak, A.J.; Kuriyan, K.; Morris, K.R.; Reklaitis, G.V. & Basu, P.K. (2006). Understanding critical material properties for solid dosage form design. *Journal of Pharmaceutical Innovation*, Vol. 1, No. 1, (September-October 2006), pp. 12-17. P.ISSN 1872-5120 E.ISSN: 1939-8042

HSA. (2007). HSA suspends sales of products containing nimesulide. http://www.hsa.gov.sg/publish/hsaportal/en/health_products_regulation/safety_information/product_safety_alerts/safety_alerts_2007/Nimesulide.html

Hutt, V.; Waitzinger, J. & Macchi, F. (2001). Comparative bioavailability study of two different nimesulide-containing preparations available on the Italian market. *Clinical Drug Investigation*, Vol. 21, No. 5 (May 2001), pp. 361-369. ISSN 1173-2563

Ilic, K.V.; Sefik-Bukilica, M.; Jankovic, S. & Vujasinovic-Stupar, N. (2009). Efficacy and safety of two generic copies of nimesulide in patients with low back pain or knee osteoarthritis. *Reumatismo*, Vol. 61, No. 1, (2009), pp. 27-33. ISSN 0048-7449

IMB. (2007). Notice Information: Human Medicines - Warning - 15/05/2007. Nimesulide Suspension. http://www.imb.ie/EN/Safety--Quality/Advisory-Warning--Recall-Notices/Human-Medicines/Nimesulide-Suspension.aspx

Jamzad, S. & Fassihi, R. (2006). Role of surfactant and pH on dissolution properties of fenofibrate and glipizide - A Technical Note. *AAPS PharmSciTech*, Vol. 7, No. 2, (April 2006), pp. E33. ISSN 1530-9932

Kapoor, A.; Majumdar, D.K. & Yadav, M.R. (1998). Crystal forms of nimesulide - A sulfonanilide (non-steroidal anti-inflammatory drug). *Indian Journal of Chemistry*, Vol. 37, No. 6, (1998), pp. 572-575. ISSN 0376-4699

Khan R.A. & Rahman, S.Z. (2004a). Nimesulide induced coronary artery insufficiency - A case report. *Journal Pharmacovigilance Drug Safety*, Vol. 1, (2004), pp. 11-13

Khan, R.A. & Rahman, S.Z. (2004b). A case report on nimesulide and its relation with angina. *Journal Pharmacovigilance Drug Safety*, Vol. 1, (2004), pp. 19-21

Li, F.; Chordia, M.D.; Huang, T. & Macdonald, T.L. (2009). In vitro nimesulide studies toward understanding idiosyncratic hepatotoxicity: diiminoquinone formation and conjugation. *Chemical Research in Toxicology*, Vol. 22, No. 1, (January 2009) pp. 72–80. P.ISSN 0893-228X E.ISSN 1520-5010

Macheras, P. & Iliadis A. (2006). *Modeling in Biopharmaceutics, Pharmacokinetics, and Pharmacodynamics. Homogeneous and Heterogeneous Approaches*, Springer, ISBN 0-387-28178-9, New York, NY

Martindale. (2009). Nimesulide, In: *Martindale The Complete Drug Reference 36th edition*, S.C. Sweetman, (Ed.), 95-96, Pharmaceutical Press, ISBN 978-0-85369-840-1, London, UK

Moneghini, M.; Perissutti, B.; Vecchione, F.; Kikic, I.; Alessi, P.; Cortesi, A. & Princivalle, F. (2007). Supercritical antisolvent precipitation of nimesulide: preliminary experiments. *Current Drug Delivery*, Vol. 4, No. 3, (July 2007), pp. 241-248. P.ISSN 1567-2018 E.ISSN 1875-5704

Mosharraf, M. & Nystrom, C. (2003). The apparent solubility of drugs in partially crystalline systems. *Drug Development and Industrial Pharmacy*, Vol. 29, No. 6, (July 2003), pp. 603-622. P.ISSN 0363-9045 E.ISSN 1520-5762

Piel, G.; Pirotte, B.; Delneuville, I.; Neven, P.; Llabres, G.; Delarge, J. & Delattre, L. (1997). Study of the influence of both cyclodextrins and L-lysine on the aqueous solubility of nimesulide; isolation and characterization of nimesulide-L-lysine-cyclodextrin complexes. *Journal of Pharmaceutical Sciences*, Vol. 86, No. 4, (April 1997), pp. 475-480. ISSN 0022-3549

Rădulescu, F.S.; Dumitrescu, I.-B.; Miron, D.S.; Lupuleasa, D.; Andries, A. & Drăgănescu, D. (2010) The in vitro release profiles of nimesulide from oral solid dosage forms, in compendial and modified physiological media. *Farmacia*, Vol. 58, No. 4, (2010), pp. 502-508. P.ISSN 0014-8237 E.ISSN 2065-0019

Rahman, S.Z. & Khan, R.A. (2004). Is nimesulide safe in a cardiovascular-Compromised patient? Indian Journal of Pharmacology, Vol. 36, No. 4, (2004), pp. 252-253. ISSN 0253-7613

Rainsford, K.D. (2006). Current status of the therapeutic uses and actions of the preferential cyclo-oxygenase-2 NSAID, nimesulide. *Inflammopharmacology, Vol.* 14, No. 3-4, (2006) pp. 120–137. ISSN 0925-4692

Siepmann, J. & Siepmann, F. (2008). Mathematical modeling of drug delivery. *International Journal of Pharmaceutics*, Vol. 364, No. 2, (November 2008), pp. 328-343. P.ISSN 0378-5173 E.ISSN 1873-3476

Siewert, M., Dressman, J.; Brown, C.K.; Shah, V.P.; FIP & AAPS. (2003). FIP/AAPS guidelines to dissolution/in vitro release testing of novel/special dosage forms. *AAPS PharmSciTech*, Vol. 4, No. 1, (2003), pp. E7. ISSN 1530-9932

Singapore News. (2007). Products with anti-inflammatory drug nimesulide suspended. http://www.channelnewsasia.com/stories/singaporelocalnews/view/282397/1/.html

Singh, S.; Sharda, N. & Mahajan, L. (1999) Spectrophotometric determination of pKa of nimesulide. *International Journal of Pharmaceutics*, Vol. 176, No. 2, (January 1999), pp. 261-264. ISSN 0378-5173

Singh, A.; Singh, P. & Kapoor VK. (2001). Nimesulide. In: *Analytical Profiles of Drug Substances and Excipients*, H.G. Brittain, (Ed.), pp. 198-249, Academic Press, ISBN 0-12-260828-3, Milford (NJ)

Sirisuth, N.; Augsburger, L.L. & Eddington, N.D. (2002). Development and validation of a non-linear IVIVC model for a diltiazem extended release formulation. *Biopharmaceutics & drug Disposition*, Vol. 23, No. 1, (January 2002), pp. 1-8. P.ISSN 42-2782 E.ISSN 1099-081X

Snider, D.A.; Addicks, W. & Owens, W. (2004). Polymorphism in generic drug product development. *Advanced Drug Delivery Reviews*, Vol. 56, No. 3, (February 2004), pp. 391-395. P.ISSN 0169-409X E.ISSN 1872-8294

Society of Japanese Pharmacopoeia. (2007). Dissolution test. In: *Japanese Pharmacopoeia 15th Edition*, pp. 116-120, Yakuji Nippo Ltd, ISBN 978-4-8408-0974-0, Tokyo, Japan

Tang, L.; Khan, S.U. & Muhammad, N.A. (2001). Evaluation and selection of bio-relevant dissolution media for a poorly water-soluble new chemical entity. *Pharmaceutical Development and Technology*, Vol. 6, No. 4, (November 2001), pp. 531-540. P.ISSN 1083-7450 E.ISSN 1097-9867

Traversa, G.; Bianchi, C.; Da Cas, R.; Abraha, I.; Menniti-Ippolito, F. & Venegoni M. (2003). Cohort study of hepatotoxicity associated with nimesulide and other non-steroidal anti-inflammatory drugs. *British Medical Journal*, Vol. 327, No. 7405, (July 2003), pp.18–22. P.ISSN 1759-2151 E.ISSN 1756-1833.

United States Convention. (2011a). Dissolution, In: The United States Pharmacopoeia 34 – The national Formulary 29, Vol. 1, pp. 278-284, United book Press, ISBN 1-889788-92-0, Baltimore, MD

United States Convention. (2011b). The dissolution procedure: development and validation, In: The United States Pharmacopoeia 34 – The national Formulary 29, Vol. 1, pp. 624-630, United book Press, ISBN 1-889788-92-0, Baltimore, MD

World Health Organization. (2011). Dissolution test for solid oral dosage forms, In: *International Pharmacopeia 4th Edition*, pp. 18-27, World Health Organization, ISBN 9241548134

Zhang, Y.; Huo, M.; Zhou, J.; Zou, A.; Li, W.; Yao, C. & Xie, S. (2010). DDSolver: an add-in program for modeling and comparison of drug dissolution profiles. *American Association of Pharmaceutical Scientists Journal*, Vol. 12, No. 3, (September 2010), pp. 263-271. ISSN 1550-7416

6

Good Manufacturing Practices (GMP) for Medicinal Products

Jaya Bir Karmacharya
Omnica Laboratories Private Limited
Nepal

1. Introduction

The term GMP was introduced to regulate manufacturing and packaging operations in the pharmaceutical company. Until the mid-1960s, operating procedures for the manufacture of drugs consisted of formulae and the basic methods of making products. Written procedures were often concise and often relied on the individual operator's skill and experience. As batches of medicines increased in number and size, the operating procedures were inadequate to produce consistent and reliable products. Much attention had focused on the purity of medicinal substances. Pharmacopoeias and codices specified formulae for mixtures and other preparation, but gave little detailed information on the methods of preparation. The factors affecting processing and packaging procedures were becoming more apparent and the need for appropriate guidelines was evident (Lund, 1994).

The Medicines Inspectorate of the Department of Health and Social Security of England, in consultation with other interested bodies compiled the guide to GMP also known as the Orange Guide. The first edition of the guide was published in 1971, before any formal inspections of drug manufacturers had been carried out under the Medicines Act. It was a relatively light volume of 20 pages, and was reissued as a third impression in 1972, with the addition of a 2-page appendix on sterile medicinal products. Because of the color of its cover, it became known as the Orange Guide. The guide was therefore written at a time when the nature, extent, and special problems of the manufacturer of drugs were not completely known. A second, more substantial edition (52 pages, including five appendices) was published in 1977. A third edition (110 pages, five appendices) was published in 1983 (Lund, 1994). Subsequently, the 2002 edition of Rules and Guidance for Pharmaceutical Manufacturers and Distributors, commonly known as the 'Orange Guide', was published with many changes and additions to the detailed European Community guidelines on GMP. The Medicines and Healthcare products Regulatory Agency (MHRA) has published new edition of the Orange Guide in 2007.

In United States, the first GMP regulations were issued in 1963 and described the GMP to be followed in the manufacture, packaging, and storage of finished pharmaceutical products. GMP regulations were developed by the US FDA and issued the United States CFR Chapter 21 in 1978. The regulations were similar in concept to the Orange Guide, but were enforceable by law whereas the UK guide was advisory. US congress passed the Federal Ani-tempering Act in 1983, making it a crime to tamper with packaged consumer products.

In the 1980s, US FDA began publishing series of guidance documents that have had a major effect on our interpretation of current GMP (cGMP). A "Guide to Inspection of Computerized Systems in Drug Processing" was published in 1983 and "Guideline on General Principles of Process Validation" was published in 1987. In 1992 the congress passed the General Drug Enforcement Act. In March 1997, the US FDA issued 21 CFR Part 11 which dealt with the use of electronic records and signatures. In 2000, US FDA introduced a guidance document on the incorporation of risk management into device development (Nally, 2007).

In August 2002, the US FDA announced a new initiative, Pharmaceutical cGMPs for the 21st Century—A Risk Based Approach. The September 2004 final report summarized the significant changes in the development and implementation of a new operational framework based on quality system and risk management approaches (Nally, 1998). Also in September 2004, the publication of the Process Analytical Technology (PAT) initiative guidance document supported innovation and efficiency in pharmaceutical manufacturing with a risk management foundation (USFDA, 2004).

The first World Health Organization (WHO) draft on GMP was prepared at the request of the twentieth World Health Assembly (resolution WHA 20.34) in 1967 by a group of consultants. The revised text was discussed by the WHO Expert Committee on Specifications for Pharmaceutical Preparations in 1968 and published as an annex to its twenty-second report. The text was further reproduced in 1971 in the Supplement to the second edition of The International Pharmacopoeia (WHOTRS823, 1992).

Text on GMP was accepted as an integral part of WHO certification scheme on the quality of pharmaceutical products moving in international market by WHA in 1969. The WHA, in resolution No.WHA28.65 accepted the revised version of both the GMPs and the certification scheme in 1975. The revised text is published in Thirty-second Report of WHO Expert Committee on Specifications for Pharmaceutical Preparations: WHO TRS 823 in 1992 (Sharma, 1995). In 2003, WHO TRS 908 had revised the content of GMP in its Annex 4: Good Manufacturing Practices for pharmaceutical products: main principles (WHO TRS 908, 2003). Recently WHO TRS 961 has published the updated contents on GMP in Annex 3: WHO good manufacturing practices: main principles for pharmaceutical products (WHO TRS 961, 2011).

2. Importance of GMP

In the United States the Center for Drug Evaluation and Research (CDER) promotes and protects public health by assuring that safe and effective drugs are available to Americans. There exits different types of risk with medicines (Figure 1), one of which is a preventable adverse event, which can be caused by different reasons. One of the reasons for this event can be a product quality defect. This risk can be avoided by effective implementation of GMP (US FDA CDER, 2001).

Friedrich Nietzsche once said, "If you know the *why* for living, you can endure any *how*." Everyone in our industry should know the story of how the GMP has come in practice. Most requirements were put in place as responses to tragic circumstances and to prevent future tragedies (Immel, 2005).

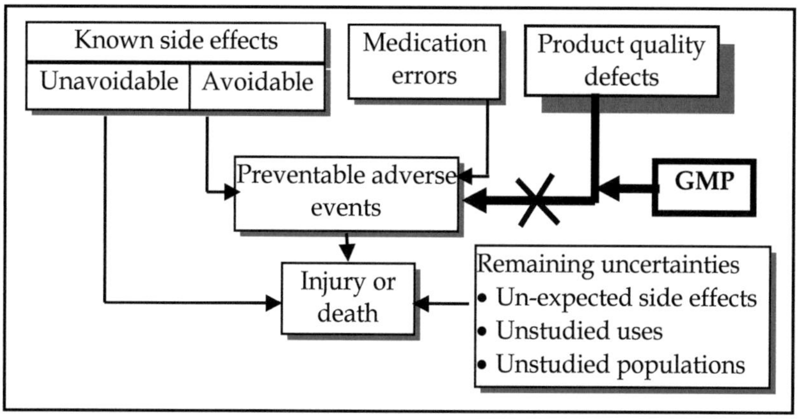

Fig. 1. Sources of Risk from Drug Products (Source: USFDA CDER 2001)

Sulfanilamide, a drug used to treat Streptococcal infections, had been shown to have dramatic curative effects and had been used safely for some time in tablet and powder form. In June 1937, however, a salesman for the S.E. Massengill Co., in Bristol, Tenn., reported a demand in the southern US states for the drug in liquid form. The company's chief chemist and pharmacist, Harold Cole Watkins, experimented and found that Sulfanilamide would dissolve in diethylene glycol. The company control laboratory tested the mixture for flavor, appearance, and fragrance and found it satisfactory. Immediately, the company compounded a quantity of Sulfanilamide elixir and sent shipments-all over the country (USA). The new formulation had not been tested for toxicity. At the time the food and drugs law did not require that safety studies be done on new drugs.

Because no pharmacological studies had been done on the new Sulfanilamide preparation, Watkins failed to note one characteristic of the solution. Diethylene glycol, a chemical normally used as antifreeze, is a deadly poison. The use of an oral Sulfanilamide elixir has caused the death of 107 people, many of them children before the problem was discovered. In response, US Congress passed the Federal Food, Drug and Cosmetic (FD&C) Act of 1938. For the first time, companies were required to prove that their products were safe before marketing them.

During 1960's Thalidomide was marketed in Europe as a sleeping pill and to treat morning sickness. When regulatory agencies gave permission to sell the drug for those indications, they knew nothing of its serious side effects. It turned out to be teratogenic: It caused serious deformities in developing fetuses. Children whose mothers took Thalidomide in the first trimester were born with severely deformed arms and legs. An estimated 10,000 cases of infant deformities in Europe were linked to Thalidomide use. Thalidomide galvanized public opinion. Two legislators, Kefauver and Harris, pushed more stringent legislation through US Congress that required companies to test not only to ensure that products were safe, but that they were efficacious for their intended uses (Immel, 2005).

Sharp, (1991) reported that at least 109 infants in Nigeria have died due to failure to follow GMP. This was caused due to the supply of mislabeled ethylene glycol as propylene glycol. This mislabeled material was then supplied to a pharmaceutical manufacturer. The manufacturer failed to perform adequate incoming quality control identification and potency tests and final product evaluation did not pick up the problem. This has resulted due to failure in following GMP norms in manufacturing drugs. The effective implementation of GMP would prevent this mistake.

There was an incident of the outbreak of diethylene glycol poisoning that occurred in Haiti from November 1995 to June 1996 due to contamination of glycerol with diethylene glycol used in the preparation of paracetamol syrup. The incident led to some 89 deaths of children from Kidney failure. This was notified by the WHO through its newsletter no.10th Oct. 1996. The cause of fetal incident once again became the same deadly poisonous chemical diethylene glycol which casued the death of 107 people way back in 1937. The outbreak in Haiti emphasizes the need for pharmaceutical manufacturers' world wide to be aware of possible contamination of glycerol and other raw materials with diethylene glycol and to use appropriate quality control measure to identify and prevent potential contamination. This also has strengthened the enforcement of GMP guidelines to ensure safety and efficacy of the pharmaceutical products.

Effective implementation of GMP would also provide the cost benefit to the manufacturers, by avoiding the cost of failures such as cost of waste, of rework, of recall, of consumer compensation, of company reputation, and of regulatory action suspending operations.

3. Good Manufacturing Practices (GMP) guidelines

GMP is a production and testing practice that helps to ensure a quality product. Many countries have legislated that pharmaceutical and medical device companies must follow GMP procedures, and have created their own GMP guidelines that correspond with their legislation. Basic concepts of all of these guidelines remain more or less similar to the ultimate goals of safeguarding the health of the patient as well as producing good quality medicine, medical devices or active pharmaceutical products

GMP guidelines are not prescriptive instructions on how to manufacture products. They are a series of general principles that must be observed during manufacturing. When a company is setting up its quality program and manufacturing process, there may be many ways it can fulfill GMP requirements. It is the company's responsibility to determine the most effective and efficient quality process. The formalization of GMP commenced in the 1960s and they are now in effect in over 100 countries ranging from Afghanistan to Zimbabwe. Although many countries have developed local requirements, many also rely on the World Health Organization recommended GMP (WHO GMP) for pharmaceutical products. Regional requirements have also appeared with application to several countries. Examples of these include the following.

a. Pharmaceutical Inspection Convention (PIC)—guide to GMP for pharmaceutical products—Australia, Austria, Belgium, Canada, Denmark, Finland, France, Hungary, Ireland, Italy, Latvia, Liechtenstein, Malaysia, The Netherlands, Norway, Poland, Portugal, Romania, Singapore, Slovak Republic, Spain, Sweden, Switzerland, and the United Kingdom.
b. Association of South-East Asia Nations (ASEAN)—GMP: general guidelines—Brunei Darussalaam, Cambodia, Indonesia, Lao PDR, Malaysia, Myanmar, Philippines, Singapore, Thailand, and Vietnam.

c. European Economic Community (EEC)—guide to GMP for medicinal products—Austria, Belgium, Denmark, Finland, France, Germany, Greece, Ireland, Italy, Luxembourg, the Netherlands, Portugal, Spain, Sweden, and the United Kingdom.

The above mentioned guidelines are similar in design and content and model more of a quality management approach or principle when compared with product testing and control more prevalent in the U.S. cGMP. Over the years, these regulations/guides have also been supplemented by descriptive guidelines providing additional information on specific topics. In general, GMP have been issued as guides to the achievement of consistent product quality, with interpretation and individual variations being accepted. GMP are enforced in the United States by the US FDA, under Section 501(B) of the 1938 Food, Drug, and Cosmetic Act (21 USCS § 351). The regulations use the phrase "current good manufacturing practices" (cGMP) to describe these guidelines.

The World Health Organization (WHO) version of GMP is used by pharmaceutical regulators and the pharmaceutical industry in over one hundred countries worldwide, primarily in the developing world including country like Nepal. The European Union's GMP (EU-GMP) enforces similar requirements to WHO GMP, as does the Food and Drug Administration's version in the US. Similar GMPs are used in other countries, with Australia, Canada, Japan, Singapore and others having highly developed/sophisticated GMP requirements. In the United Kingdom, the Medicines Act (1968) covers most aspects of GMP in what is commonly referred to as "The Orange Guide", which is officially known as Rules and Guidance for Pharmaceutical Manufacturers and Distributors.

In general, GMP inspections are performed by national regulatory agencies. GMP inspections are performed in the United Kingdom by the Medicines and Healthcare Products Regulatory Agency (MHRA); in the Republic of Korea (South Korea) by the Korea Food & Drug Administration (KFDA); in Australia by the Therapeutical Goods Administration (TGA); in South Africa by the Medicines Control Council (MCC); in Brazil by the Agência Nacional de Vigilância Sanitária (National Health Surveillance Agency Brazil) (ANVISA). In India GMP inspections are carried out by state Food and Drug Administration (FDA) and these FDA report to Central Drugs Standard Control Organization: in Nepal, GMP inspections are carried out by the Department of Drug Administration (DDA), and in Pakistan by the Ministry of Health. Nigeria has National Agency for Food and Drug Administration and Control (NAFDAC). Each of the inspectorates carry out routine GMP inspections to ensure that drug products are produced safely and correctly; additionally, many countries perform pre-approval inspections (PAI) for GMP compliance prior to the approval of a new drug for marketing (Wikipedia, 2012a).

4. Components of GMP

GMP requires that the manufacturing process is fully defined before being initiated and all the necessary facilities are provided. In practice, personnel must be adequately trained, suitable premises and equipment used, correct materials used, approved procedures adopted, suitable storage and transport facilities available, and appropriate records made. The essential components of GMP are summarized in Figure 2 (Lund, 1994).

The manufacturing premises of good design and regularly monitored is the most important component. There should be quality control of finished product, raw materials and packaging materials. The equipment of good design is to be considered and all the equipments are required to be maintained properly. There should be a correct choice of cleaning equipment. The staffs should be trained well and should be wearing protective clothing while on work. There should be written procedures for carrying out the operations.

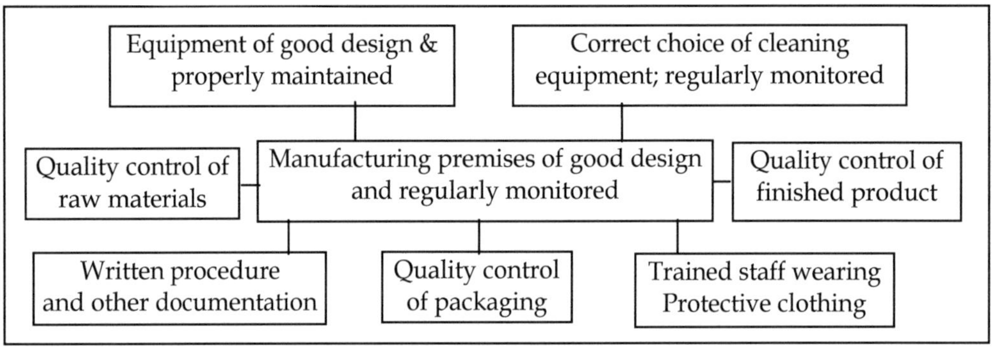

Fig. 2. Components of Good Manufacturing Practice (Source: Lund, 1994)

WHO Expert Committee on Specifications for Pharmaceutical Preparations had published the Forty-fifth Report of WHO TRS 961 in 2011. The committee reviewed the revision of the GMP text in the light of comments received from interested parties and brought out the basic guidelines on GMP in an Annex 3 under the title "WHO good manufacturing practice: main principles for pharmaceutical products."

Among other feedback which was discussed during the consultation on WHO guidelines for medicines quality assurance, quality control laboratories and transfer of technology on 27–31 July 2009, the need was identified to incorporate a new section on "Product quality review" under Chapter 1: "Quality assurance". In addition, several updates were suggested to further enhance the guidelines and include the concept of risk management, replacing "drugs" by the term "medicines" and newly introduce the concept of a "quality unit". Quality unit is an organizational unit independent of production which fulfils both quality assurance (QA) and quality control (QC) responsibilities. This can be in the form of separate QA and QC units or a single individual or group, depending upon the size and structure of the organization.

This has highlighted the different requirements of GMP as "Quality management in the medicines industry: philosophy and essential elements". The essential elements described in detail includes; Quality assurance, Good manufacturing practices for pharmaceutical products, Sanitation and hygiene, Qualification and validation, Complaints, Product recalls, Contract production and analysis, Self-inspection, quality audits and supplier's audits and approval, Personnel, Training, Personal hygiene, Premises, Equipment, Materials, Documentation, Good practices in production and Good practices in quality control (WHOTRS 961, 2011).

Volume 4 of "The rules governing medicinal products in the European Union" contains guidance for the interpretation of the principles and guidelines of good manufacturing practices for medicinal products for human and veterinary use. Its 1998 edition contains nine chapters describing Quality management, Personnel, Premises and Equipment,

Documentation, Production, Quality control, Contract manufacturing and analysis, Complaints and Product recall and Self Inspection as basic requirements of GMP with 14 annexes. Currently the guide is presented in three parts and supplemented with a series of annexes. Part I covers basic requirements for medicinal products, Part II covers basic requirements for active substances used as starting materials and Part III contains GMP related documents, which clarify the regulatory expectations (EudraLex, 2012).

Pharmaceutical inspection convention/Pharmaceutical Inspection Co-operation Scheme (PIC/S) had published PE 009-2 Guide to GMP for medicinal products in 2004. In order to further facilitate the removal of barriers to trade in medicinal products, to promote uniformity in licensing decisions and to ensure the maintaining of high standards of quality assurance in the development, manufacture and control of medicinal products throughout Europe, it was agreed to harmonize the rules of GMP applied under Pharmaceutical Inspection Convention (PIC) and the Pharmaceutical Inspection Co-operation Scheme (PIC/S) to those of the EU Guide to Good Manufacturing Practice for Medicinal Products and its Annexes. The guide contains nine chapters describing Quality management, Personnel, Premises and Equipment, Documentation, Production, Quality control, Contract manufacturing and analysis, Complaints and Product recall and Self Inspection with 18 annexes.

US FDA ensures the quality of drug products by carefully monitoring drug manufacturers' compliance with its cGMP regulations. Section 21 of the CFR contains most regulations pertaining to food and drugs. The regulations document the actions of drug sponsors that are required under Federal law. 21 CFR Part 210. cGMP in manufacturing processing, packing, or holding of drugs. 21 CFR Part 211. cGMP for finished pharmaceuticals. The CFR 21 part 211 dealing with cGMP for finished pharmaceuticals consists of Subparts A to K describing different components as General Provisions, Organization and Personnel, Building and Facilities, Equipment, Control of Components and Drug Product Containers and Closures, Production and Process Controls, Packaging and Labeling Control, Holding and Distribution, Laboratory Controls, Records and Reports and Returned and Salvaged Drug Products (Revised as of April 1, 2011).

The ASEAN GMP general guidelines have covered following elements such as Personnel, Premises, Sanitation, Equipment, Starting Materials, Production, Quality Control, Self Inspection, Handling of product complaint, product recall and returned drug products and Documentation, (ASEAN, 2000).

Indian schedule M for GMP and requirements of premises, plant and equipment for pharmaceutical products consists of Part I mentioning GMP for Premises and Materials. The Part I includes General requirements, Warehousing area, Production area, Ancillary area, Quality control area, Personnel, Health, clothing and sanitation of workers, Manufacturing operations and controls, Sanitation in the manufacturing premises, Raw materials, Equipment, Documentation and Records, Labels and other printed materials, Quality assurance, Self inspection and quality audit, Quality control system, Specification, Master formula records, Packing records, Batch packaging records, Batch processing records, Standard operating procedures (SOPs) and records, Reference samples, Reprocessing and recoveries, Distribution records, Validation and process validation, Product recalls, Complaints and adverse reactions and Site-master file. Part I-A to part I-E mentions about the specific requirements for manufacture of different products and Part I-F mentions about the specific requirements of premises, plant and materials for manufacture of active pharmaceutical ingredients (bulk drugs). Part II describes the Requirement of plant and equipments for various dosage forms (Schedule M).

Worldwide, there are now around 30 different official national and super national statements on GMP. These have been published variously as guides, codes and regulations and of the 30 or so of them, two stand out as being the most influential and most frequently referenced: The United States Current Good Manufacturing Practice (cGMP) Regulations and the European Commission's "Good Manufacturing Practices for Medicinal Products for Human and Veterinary Use". Thirdly the WHO version of GMP is used by the pharmaceutical regulators and the pharmaceutical industry in over 100 countries worldwide, primarily in the developing world (Nally, 2007).

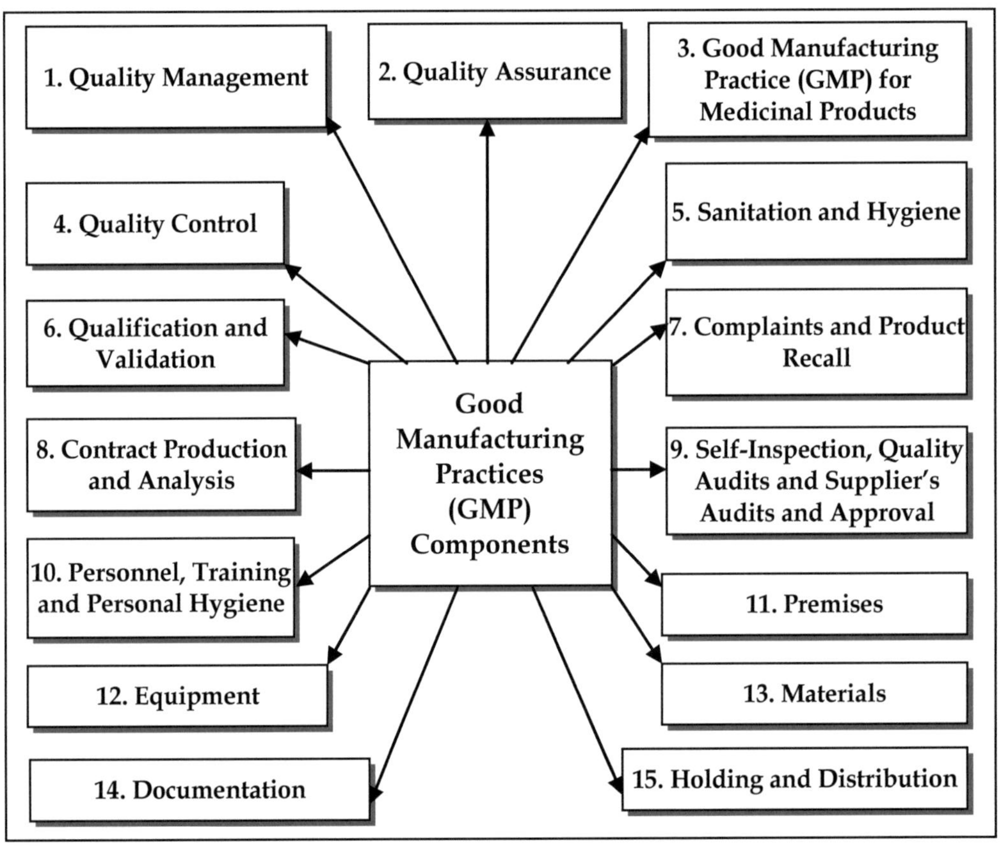

Fig. 3. Consolidated Components of Good Manufacturing Practices

While reviewing all the above documents, it is realized that most of the components identified for GMP aspects are similar in all the guidelines and publications. Based on the above discussion, the following components of GMP would cover all the requirements made by different authorities and also satisfy the WHO GMP guidelines for drug manufacturing: Quality management, Quality assurance, Good manufacturing practices for medicinal products, Quality control, Sanitation and hygiene, Qualification and validation, Complaints and product recalls, Contract production and analysis, Self-inspection, quality audits and supplier's audits and approval, Personnel training and personal hygiene, Premises, Equipment, Materials, Documentation and Holding and Distribution. These consolidated components shown in Figure 3 are dealt one by one independently with reference to above mentioned GMP statements.

4.1 Quality management

The holder of a Manufacturing Authorization must manufacture medicinal products so as to ensure that they are fit for their intended use, comply with the requirements of the Marketing Authorization and do not place patients at risk due to inadequate safety, quality or efficacy. The attainment of this quality objective is the responsibility of senior management and requires the participation and commitment by staff in many different departments and at all levels within the company, by the company's suppliers and by the distributors (EudraLex, 2012). In the pharmaceutical industry at large, quality management is usually defined as the aspect of management function that determines and implements the "quality policy", i.e. the overall intention and direction of an organization regarding quality, as formally expressed and authorized by top management (WHOTRS 961, 2011).

The basic elements of quality management are: an appropriate infrastructure or "quality system", encompassing the organizational structure, procedures, processes and resources; and systematic actions necessary to ensure adequate confidence that a product (or service) will satisfy given requirements for quality.

4.2 Quality Assurance (QA)

QA is a wide-ranging concept, which covers all matters, which individually or collectively influence the quality of a product. It is the sum total of the organized arrangements made with the objective of ensuring that pharmaceutical products are of the quality required for their intended use. QA, therefore, incorporates GMP and other factors such as product design and development.

The system of QA appropriate for the manufacture of pharmaceutical products should ensure that: (a) pharmaceutical products are designed and developed in a way that takes account of the requirements of GMP and other associated codes such as those of good laboratory practice (GLP) and good clinical practice (GCP); (b) production and control operations are clearly specified in a written form and GMP requirements are adopted; (c) managerial responsibilities are clearly specified in job descriptions; (d) arrangements are made for the manufacture, supply and use of the correct starting and packaging materials; (e) all necessary controls on starting materials, intermediate products, and bulk products and other in-process controls, calibrations, and validations are carried out; (f) the finished product is correctly processed and checked, according to the defined procedures; (g) pharmaceutical products are not sold or supplied before the authorized persons have certified that each production batch has been produced and controlled in accordance with the requirements of the marketing authorization and any other regulations relevant to the production, control and release of pharmaceutical products; (h) satisfactory arrangements exist to ensure, as far as possible, that the pharmaceutical products are stored by the manufacturer, distributed, and subsequently handled so that quality is maintained throughout their shelf-life; (i) here is a procedure for self-inspection and/or quality audit that regularly appraises the effectiveness and applicability of the QA system; (j) deviations are reported, investigated and recorded; (k) there is a system for approving changes that may have an impact on product quality; (l) regular evaluations of the quality of pharmaceutical products should be conducted with the objective of verifying the consistency of the process and ensuring its continuous improvement; and (m) there is a system for quality risk management (QRM).

4.2.1 Product quality review

Regular periodic or rolling quality reviews of all licensed medicinal products, including export-only products, should be conducted with the objective of verifying the consistency of the existing process, the appropriateness of current specifications for both starting materials and finished product to highlight any trends and to identify product and process improvements. Such reviews should normally be conducted and documented annually, taking into account previous reviews, and should include at least: (i) a review of starting materials including packaging materials used for the product, especially those from new sources; (ii) a review of critical in-process controls and finished product results; (iii) a review of all batches that failed to meet established specification(s) and their investigation; (iv) a review of all significant deviations or non-conformances, the related investigations, and the effectiveness of resultant corrective and preventative actions taken; (v) a review of all changes made to the processes or analytical methods; (vi) a review of dossier variations submitted, granted or refused; (vii) a review of the results of the stability monitoring programme and any adverse trends; (viii) a review of all quality-related returns, complaints and recalls and the investigations performed at the time; (ix) a review of adequacy of any other previous corrective actions on product process or equipment; (x) for new dossiers and variations to the dossiers, a review of post-marketing commitments; (xi) the qualification status of relevant equipment and utilities, e.g. heating, ventilation and air-conditioning (HVAC), water, or compressed gases; and (xii) a review of technical agreements to ensure that they are up to date (WHOTRS 961, 2011).

4.2.2 Quality Risk Management (QRM)

QRM is a systematic process for the assessment, control, communication and review of risks to the quality of the medicinal product. It can be applied both proactively and retrospectively. The quality risk management system should ensure that:

- the evaluation of the risk to quality is based on scientific knowledge, experience with the process and ultimately links to the protection of the patient; and
- the level of effort, formality and documentation of the QRM process is commensurate with the level of risk.

4.3 Good Manufacturing Practice (GMP) for medicinal products

GMP is that part of QA which ensures that products are consistently produced and controlled to the quality standards appropriate to their intended use and as required by the marketing authorizations or product specification. GMP is aimed primarily at diminishing the risks inherent in any pharmaceutical production. Such risks are essentially of two types: cross-contamination (in particular of unexpected contaminants) and mix ups (confusion) caused by, for example, false labels being put on containers.

The basic requirements of GMP are that: (a) all manufacturing processes are clearly defined, systematically reviewed in the light of experience, and shown to be capable of consistently manufacturing pharmaceutical products of the required quality that comply with their specifications; (b) qualification and validation are performed; (c) all necessary resources are provided; (d) instructions and procedures are written in clear and unambiguous language, specifically applicable to the facilities provided; (e) operators are trained to carry out procedures correctly; (f) records are made during manufacture to show that all the steps required by the defined procedures and instructions have in fact been taken and that the quantity and quality of the product are as expected; any significant deviations are fully recorded and investigated; (g) records covering manufacture and distribution, which enable the complete history of a batch to be traced, are retained in a comprehensible and accessible form; (h) the proper storage and distribution of the products minimizes any risk to their quality; (i) a system is available to recall any batch of product from sale or supply; and (j) complaints about marketed products are examined, the causes of quality defects investigated, and appropriate measures taken in respect of the defective products to prevent recurrence (WHOTRS 961, 2011).

4.4 Quality Control (QC)

QC is that part of GMP which is concerned with sampling, specifications and testing, and with the organization, documentation and release procedures which ensure that the necessary and relevant tests are actually carried out and that materials are not released for use, nor products released for sale or supply, until their quality has been judged to be satisfactory. QC is not confined to laboratory operations, but may be involved in many decisions concerning the quality of the product. QC as a whole will also have other duties, such as to establish, validate and implement all QC procedures, to evaluate, maintain, and store the reference standards for substances, to ensure the correct labeling of containers of materials and products, to ensure that the stability of the active pharmaceutical ingredients (APIs) and products is monitored, to participate in the investigation of complaints related to the quality of the product, and to participate in environmental monitoring. All these operations should be carried out in accordance with written procedures and, where necessary, recorded (WHOTRS 961, 2011).

4.5 Sanitation and hygiene

A high level of sanitation and hygiene should be practiced in every aspect of the manufacture of medicine products. The scope of sanitation and hygiene covers personnel, premises, equipment and apparatus, production materials and containers, products for cleaning and disinfection, and anything that could become a source of contamination to the product. Potential sources of contamination should be eliminated through an integrated comprehensive programme of sanitation and hygiene. Premises used in the manufacture, processing, packing, or holding of a drug product shall be maintained in a clean and sanitary condition, Any such building shall be free of infestation by rodents, birds, insects, and other vermin (other than laboratory animals). There shall be written procedures assigning responsibility for sanitation and describing in sufficient detail the cleaning schedules, methods, equipment, and materials to be used in cleaning the buildings and facilities; such written procedures shall be followed. Records should be maintained.

Substance	Suitable Concentration	Effect on Bacteria	Effect on Spores	Effect on Vegetative Fungi	Advantages	Disadvantages
Ethanol	70%	Good	Fair	Fair	Quick acting; evaporates rapidly, leaving no residues	Limited range of effect; flammable
Phenols	0.5–3%	Excellent	Good	Excellent	Broad range of effect; may be combined with surfactants	Corrosive on some surfaces (including skin)
Formaldehyde		Excellent	Good	Good	Broad range of effect; used for "gassing"	Premises not accessible during treatment; can be corrosive; short- and long-term human toxicity problems
Isopropanol	70–90%	Good	Good	Good	Quick acting; evaporates, leaving no residues	Not the most effective
Iodine and iodophors	75–150 ppm	Excellent	Good	Excellent	Quick acting; effective in low concentration	Can be corrosive; stains some surfaces
Chlorine compounds (hypochlorite, chloramines, etc.)	1–4%	Excellent	Good	Excellent	Broad range of effect	Corrosive
Quaternary ammonium compounds	1–5%	Good	Fair	Fair	Some cleaning effect; odorless	Limited effect; inactivated by soap detergents

Table 1. Disinfectants for Premises – Types and Applications (Source: Sharp, 2005)

The areas, surfaces, and equipment in and on which products are made must be kept clean. Dirt, and the microbes that it can harbor, must not get into or on products. Disinfectants can be inactivated by dirt. Dirt (particularly oily or greasy films and protein like matter) can also protect microorganisms against the action of disinfectants. So, before disinfection, it is important to first clean surfaces. Where gross amounts of dirt are present, it may be necessary to first remove most of it by scrubbing. Then surfaces may be cleaned by the application of a cleaning agent, followed by rinsing.

A wide range of substances are used as disinfectants. They may be single substances, like alcohols or phenols, and there are a number of commercially available mixtures. It is usually best not to make "do it yourself" mixtures. It could be dangerous, and some disinfectants can neutralize each other's activity. Disinfecting agents vary in the range of their activity and in the concentrations at which they are effective. All have their own special advantages and disadvantages. Some examples of disinfectants, with their range of effects, etc. are shown in Table 1. Disinfectants should always be used in accordance with instructions and at the right dilution (instructions as given either in the supplier's literature or in company procedures). Since some microorganisms can grow readily in dilute disinfectants, dilutions of disinfectants should not be stored unless they are sterilized. Otherwise, dilutions should be made freshly each time they are needed. It is advisable to use different disinfectants over a period of time, on an alternating, or rotating, basis to prevent the development of disinfectant-resistant strains of microorganisms.

4.5.1 Personal hygiene

All personnel, prior to and during employment, as appropriate, should undergo health examinations. Personnel conducting visual inspections should also undergo periodic eye examinations. All personnel should be trained in the practices of personal hygiene. Any person shown at any time to have an apparent illness or open lesions that may adversely affect the quality of products should not be allowed to handle starting materials, packaging materials, in-process materials or medicines products until the condition is no longer judged to be a risk. Direct contact should be avoided between the operator's hands and starting materials, primary packaging materials and intermediate or bulk product. To ensure protection of the product from contamination, personnel should wear clean body coverings appropriate to the duties they perform, including appropriate hair covering. To reduce the risk of infection through hand contact, the following should be instructed to all operators:

- Do not touch the product/objects that may come in contact with the product, with unprotected hands.
- Keep the hands well groomed with short, clean nails. Hands must be free of any lesions, wounds, cuts, boils, or any other sources of infection.
- Wrist watches, rings, or other jewelry should not be worn on the job.
- Hands should be washed before work and as often as the job requires (Figure 4).
- Protective gloves should be worn when working with open products and when handling objects that come in direct contact with the product.

Smoking, eating, drinking, chewing, and keeping plants, food, drink, smoking material and personal medicines should not be permitted in production, laboratory and storage areas. Personal hygiene procedures including the use of protective clothing should apply to all persons entering production areas, whether they are temporary or full-time employees or nonemployees, e.g. contractors' employees, visitors, senior managers and inspectors.

4.6 Qualification and validation

Qualification is an action of proving that any premises, systems and items of equipment work correctly and actually lead to the expected results. Validation is defined as the establishing of documented evidence which provides a high degree of assurance that a planned process will consistently perform according to the intended specified outcomes. Validation studies should reinforce GMP and be conducted in accordance with defined procedures. Results and conclusions should be recorded. When any new manufacturing formula or method of preparation is adopted, steps should be taken to demonstrate its

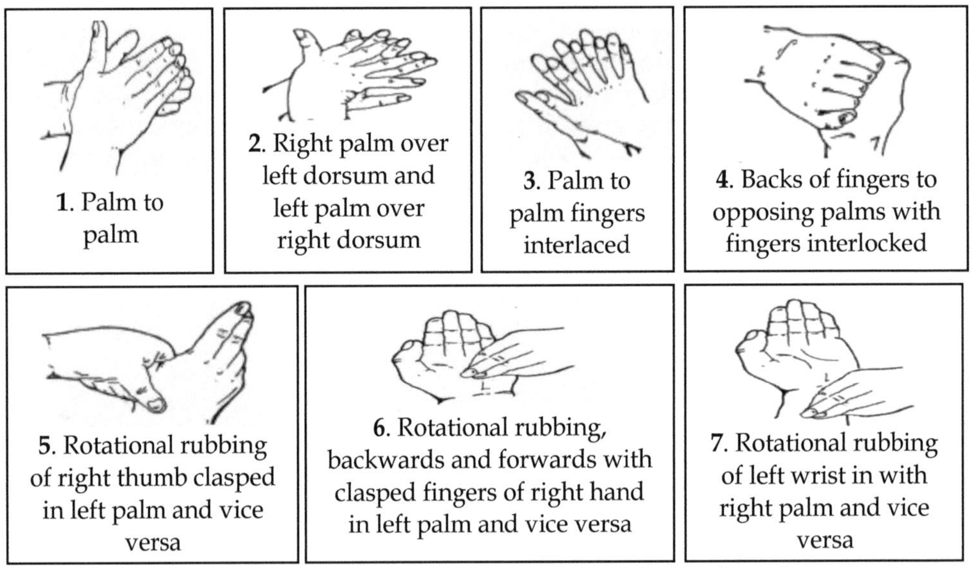

Pharma manufacturing personnel should be aware that hand washing is not as effective if rings, wrist watches, nail polish or false nails (including gel/acrylic nails) are worn and therefore there are **NOT PERMITTED** within the clean room area

Fig. 4. Seven Steps to Effective Hand Washing

suitability for routine processing. The defined process, using the materials and equipment specified, should be shown to yield a product consistently of the required quality. Significant amendments to the manufacturing process, including any change in equipment or materials, which may affect product quality and/or the reproducibility of the process, should be validated. Processes and procedures should undergo periodic critical revalidation to ensure that they remain capable of achieving the intended results (PIC/S, 2004). Every step of the process of manufacture of a medicinal product must be shown to perform as intended. Once the system or process has been validated, it is expected that it remains in control, provided no changes are made. In the event that modifications are made, or problems occur, or equipment is replaced or relocated, revalidation is performed. The validity of systems/equipment/tests/processes can be established by prospective, concurrent or retrospective studies.

Qualification and validation should establish and provide documentary evidence that: (a) the premises, supporting utilities, equipment and processes have been designed in accordance with the requirements for GMP (design qualification or DQ); (b) the premises, supporting utilities and equipment have been built and installed in compliance with their design specifications (installation qualification or IQ); (c) the premises, supporting utilities and equipment operate in accordance with their design specifications (operational qualification or OQ); and (d) a specific process will consistently produce a product meeting its predetermined specifications and quality attributes (process validation or PV, also called performance qualification or PQ).

4.6.1 Validation protocols and validation master plan

A protocol is a written set of instructions broader in scope than a Standard Operating Procedure (SOP). A protocol describes the details of a comprehensive planned study to investigate the consistent operation of new system/equipment, a new procedure, or the acceptability of a new process before it is implemented. The Validation Master Plan (VMP) is a high-level document which establishes an umbrella validation plan for the entire project, and is used as guidance by the project team for resource and technical planning (also referred to as master qualification plan). VMP describes which equipment, systems, methods and processes will be validated and when they will be validated. The document should provide the format required for each particular validation document (Installation Qualification, Operational Qualification and Performance Qualification for equipment and systems; Process Validation; Analytical Assay Validation), and indicate what information is to be contained within each document.

4.6.2 Analytical procedures and methods validation

Method validation is the process used to confirm that the analytical procedure employed for a specific test is suitable for its intended use. Results from method validation can be used to judge the quality, reliability and consistency of analytical results; it is an integral part of any good analytical practice. Analytical methods need to be validated or revalidated before their introduction into routine use; whenever the conditions change for which the method has been validated (e.g., an instrument with different characteristics or samples with a different matrix); and whenever the method is changed and the change is outside the original scope of the method (Huber, 2012).

The parameters for method validation have been defined in different working groups of national and international committees and are described in the literature. Unfortunately, some of the definitions vary between the different organizations. An attempt at harmonization was made for pharmaceutical applications through the ICH, where representatives from the industry and regulatory agencies from the United States, Europe and Japan defined parameters, requirements and, to some extent, methodology for analytical methods validation. The parameters, as defined by the ICH and by other organizations and authors, are summarized in Table 2.

Selectivity and Specificity (1,2) and	Precision (1,2) and reproducibility (3)
Accuracy (1,2) and Recovery	Linearity (1,2)
Range (1,2)	Limit of detection (1,2)
Limit of quantitation (1,2)	Robustness (2,3)
Ruggedness (2)	
(1) Included in ICH, (2) Included in USP, (3) Terminology included in ICH publication but not part of required parameters	

Table 2. Possible Analytical Parameters for Method Validation (Source: Huber, 2012)

4.7 Complaints and product recalls

QA and GMP are about preventing errors. However, in this imperfect universe there is no such thing as an infallibly perfect system, and an essential feature of any QA system is a plan for dealing with complaints, or reports of faulty products, if they do occur. A requirement to cover this occurs in all notable GMP guidelines. Complaints received from consumers, professionals, and the trade serves as a primary means of obtaining feedback about product quality after distribution. It is necessary, therefore, that each complaint or inquiry be evaluated by knowledgeable and responsible personnel (Nally, 2007).

The records of production, packaging, and distribution of drug and the retained samples provide the basis for assessing the validity and seriousness of the alleged deviations that precipitated the complaint. The complaint file itself also plays an important role in determining whether any other similar complaints have been received on the lot in question, or on any other lots of the same product. The evaluation of complaints serves several valuable purposes. First, there is the urgent need to confirm whether consumers are potentially at risk and to initiate any appropriate action. A second value is the review of the product and its production process to establish whether any modifications are required. Third is the need to rapidly respond to the customer, thereby attempting to maintain confidence in the product and company.

Manufacturers should have a written recall procedure, with nominated persons responsible for implementing it as necessary, within, or outside of, normal working hours. Distribution records should be maintained, which will facilitate effective recall, and the written procedure should include emergency and off-hours contacts and telephone numbers (Sharp, 2005).

The complaints and defect report procedure is intended to be operated in conjunction with a "COMPLAINT/DEFECT REPORT" record (Figure 5), a copy of which, as is indicated, should form part of the SOP. Copies of this report form should be provided to all persons in the organization who may possibly be the first recipients of a complaint. They should be trained in its use and in the crucial importance of taking all such reports very seriously. As the complaints and defect report SOP indicates, if the complaints (etc.) procedure leads to a conclusion to recall (or freeze), then the recall (or freeze) procedure must be implemented. It is vital that this SOP is kept up to date, particularly in regard to internal and external names, addresses, and phone numbers, and that it is regularly shown (by "dummy runs") to be operable at any time. (The need to urgently recall does not arise only between 08.00 hours to 17.00 hours, Monday through Friday.)

As explained above the extent of recall, if required to do so depends on the distribution channel and record system of the company. In case of developed countries with well developed system of distribution records starting form the manufacturer up to the end user level, the recall procedure would be possible up to the end user. In such countries, the effective recall can protect patients, in cases of the product defects which may have severe adverse effect on the patient from use of the product if it is not recalled. However, the scenario of such recall procedure is very much alarming in case of developing countries where the distribution records of products are not traceable up to the end user, which needs to be recalled. Majority of the cases the distribution records are maintained up to the wholesaler, and/or retailer's level. In this scenario for serious cases, the recall procedure simply fails to achieve its goal to protect the end user form the impact of the effect. This needs to be strengthened by developing stringent regulatory requirements to have proper distribution record available up to the patient level for effective recall at the time of need. Otherwise the system of effective recall remains as SOP only.

COMPLAINT/DEFECT REPORT

Page 1 of 1

1. Date Complaint/Report received ……………….. Time ………..
2. Received by ………………………………………
3. Received from:
   Name …………………………………..
   Address:
   Telephone number …………………..
   Fax number …………………………...
   e-mail …………………………………
4. Name/address/phone numbers, etc. of other contacts/persons/organizations:

5. Product(s) involved:
6. Batch/lot numbers:
7. Name of complaint/report (attach any written correspondence)

8. Have samples been returned for examination? (Give details)

9. Are samples available for collection/examination? (Give details)

10. Results of investigations/Tests (attach other sheets as necessary)

11. Conclusions, and decision on action to be taken

Signed ………………… Date………………

12. Letter(s) sent to ……………………Date ………………
13. Also considered necessary to inform: Done/Date:

14. Was decision taken to **FREEZE** (beyond own on-site stocks) or **Recall**?

IF "YES," RECALL (or FREEZE) SOP MUST BE IMPLEMENTED IMMEDIATELY

Signed ……………………………
Date …………………………..

Fig. 5. Complaint/Defect Report Record (Source: Sharp, 2005)

4.8 Contract production and analysis

The global industry is changing its shape through rationalization, mergers and acquisitions. Companies are increasingly considering the use of other manufacturers to produce or manufacture their products. Companies are also finding that they do not have the technology or expertise to manufacture certain new special dosage forms. In some cases, financial targets mean that companies are not using manufacturing as a core business process. This means that the importance of contract manufacturing and testing of products is also increasing. The main principle underlying contract production and analysis is very simple. The work has to be clearly defined, agreed and controlled to avoid misunderstandings. The simplest way to avoid such misunderstandings is to have a written contract, setting out the duties of all parties to the contract and the standards that must be met. The standards of performance refer not only to product quality standards but also many other non-GMP aspects, e.g. relating to financial matters. It must be clear to everyone who is the authorized person, having the responsibility and the final authority to release a batch for sale. The contract should also specify clearly what would happen to materials that are rejected.

4.8.1 The contract giver (the client/company)

The contract giver is responsible for assessing the competence of proposed contract accepters that they will be able to do the work. It must assess whether the companies that offer to do the work really have the capability to do it. This evaluation must also include an assessment as to whether they are able to operate in accordance with the GMP principles. Once the conclusion has been reached that the contract accepter has not only the technical competence but also the GMP competence and then the contract giver must provide a full package of technical information to the contract accepter. This means that all the information relevant to personnel, premises and equipment must be provided. If there are hazards associated with cross-contamination of other products these must be highlighted. Finally, the product made or tested under the contract must only be released by the authorized person in compliance with the marketing authorization. In some cases the authorized person may be a designated staff member of the contract accepter if this responsibility is delegated in writing by the contract giver and if such delegation is permitted by national regulations.

4.8.2 The contract accepter (contractor)

The contract accepter also has responsibilities. The company must be competent to do the work. It means that it has the necessary facilities, premises and equipment, both in type and in quantity, to undertake the work. It must have a manufacturing authorization to do this type of work. This means that its staff has the necessary qualifications, training and experience to be able to do the work. The contract accepter may not pass the work or any part of it on to a (third) subcontractor party without the approval of the contract giver. Finally, once a contract accepter has signed the contract, it must not then undertake new work which might adversely affect the quality of the existing products. An illustration of this would be to take on manufacture a penicillin product in the same facility, as other products of the contract giver.

4.9 Self-inspection, quality audits and supplier's audits/approval

The purpose of self-inspection is to evaluate the manufacturer's compliance with GMP in all aspects of production and quality control. The self-inspection programme should be designed to detect any shortcomings in the implementation of GMP and to recommend the necessary corrective actions. Self-inspections should be performed routinely, and may be, in addition, performed on special occasions, e.g. in the case of product recalls or repeated rejections, or when an inspection by the health authorities is announced. The team responsible for self-inspection should consist of personnel who can evaluate the implementation of GMP objectively. Management appoints a self-inspection team consisting of experts in their respective fields and familiar with GMP.

The frequency at which self-inspections are conducted may depend on company requirements but should preferably be at least once a year. A report should be made at the completion of a self-inspection. The report should include: (a) self-inspection results; (b) evaluation and conclusions; and (c) recommended corrective actions. All recommendations for corrective action should be implemented. The procedure for self-inspection should be documented, and there should be an effective follow-up programme. It may be useful to supplement self-inspections with a quality audit. A quality audit consists of an examination and assessment of all or part of a quality system with the specific purpose of improving it. A quality audit is usually conducted by outside or independent specialists or a team designated by the management for this purpose. Such audits may also be extended to suppliers and contractors.

The person responsible for QC should have responsibility together with other relevant departments for approving suppliers who can reliably supply starting and packaging materials that meet established specifications. Before suppliers are approved and included in the approved supplier's list or specifications, they should be evaluated. The evaluation should take into account a supplier's history and the nature of the materials to be supplied. If an audit is required, it should determine the supplier's ability to conform to GMP standards (WHOTRS 961, 2011).

The practice of supplier audit is difficult to conduct specially when the suppliers are in distance form the auditing company and/or the requirement of the auditing company are not of significant in values where is supplier is not interested with the party to do the business. This difficulty arises with the companies operating in developing countries with small business volume. With small business volume, the company's requirements are such that the process of conducting supplier audit shall be a costly affair in one end and the supplier shows not interest in the other end. In such cases, an alternative ways need to find out for supplier approval. In such case the suppliers are approved based on their history and list of customers of the suppliers. Another approach may be to form a group of all small companies together so that the quantities required in common are pulled together to create interest on the supplier for the business. All the companies in together can have an audit for approval of the supplier. In such cases of difficulty in supplier approval, all the initial supplies made are subjected for 100% sampling and test before approval of the material supplied.

4.10 Personnel, training and personal hygiene

The quality of a product ultimately depends on the quality of those producing it....

- Sir Dereck Dunlop (1971)

The establishment and maintenance of a satisfactory system of quality assurance and the correct manufacture and control of pharmaceutical products and active ingredients rely upon people. For this reason there must be sufficient qualified personnel to carry out all the tasks for which the manufacturer is responsible. Individual responsibilities should be clearly defined and understood by the persons concerned and recorded as written job descriptions (WHOTRS 961, 2011). Personnel should be aware of the principles of GMP that affect them and receive initial and continuing training, including hygiene instructions, relevant to their need (Sharp, 2005). In order to effectively monitor and control virtually all GMP documents/activities in a facility, the quality professional should have a very high level of knowledge, skills, and experience. Figure 6 represents a comprehensive list of the knowledge and skills needed for high level quality professional in the 21st century (Nally, 2007).

It is the people (the "men" — the human species, not the gender —or the personnel) that are the most important factor in the assurance of quality. This is true of all levels within an organization, from company president and managing director to the most-junior employee. It may well be possible (if not altogether desirable) for high-quality, well-trained, dedicated personnel to compensate for a lack or deficiency in the other elements. Nothing, not even the finest premises, equipment, materials, or procedures can compensate for the quality hazard represented by low-standard, ill-trained, or poorly motivated staff. Self-responsible, well-motivated staff will produce more goods, with a greater assurance of the quality of those goods, than will poorly motivated staff. Conversely, in the special context of medicines manufacture, poorly motivated staff can represent a hazard to themselves, to the public, and to company profits (Sharp, 2005).

4.10.1 Training system

Because the quality of the product is directly affected by actions that personnel take in their jobs, there must be assurance that they are properly trained. This assurance is built by having a training system that is robust, compliant, and sustainable and is able to produce individuals who are qualified (Nally, 2007). Elements that are needed in a strong training system include the following: an accurate description of the job or role; specific training requirements for each job or role; training plan to accomplish the training; training materials that are applicable to each type of training; qualified trainers to perform the training; evaluations to measure the effectiveness of the training; and a documentation and record keeping system for storage and retrieval of training records and materials.

Job Description: A job description should define the job and role of the individual. It should be fairly high level and include major job functions, not tasks the individual performs. The function may be divided into duties and responsibilities, competencies that an individual may have, and prerequisites needed (e.g., must be a college graduate, must have five years of experience, etc.). The manager is expected "to define appropriate qualifications for each position to help ensure individuals are assigned appropriate responsibilities."

Training Requirement: When a job description has been created and approved by both human resources and the functional area, training requirements can then be defined. The knowledge and skills the individual needs to successfully perform the job should be identified. The desired skills and knowledge are compared against the individual's skills and knowledge when entering the position; gaps are identified. The training requirements will be derived from the identified gaps. Training requirements must be updated on a periodic basis. Training requirements should be established for all levels within the organization.

Business Knowledge/Understanding • Policies/Standards/Regulations • Manufactured Products • Pharm/Bio Industry Knowledge (Rx, OTC) - local • Global • General Business (Mfg., Logistics, TS, Eng.) • HR, Finance, Marketing/Sales, IS	**Manufacturing** • Formulation & Manufacturing Procedures • Statistical Process Controls • Process Capability • Equipment & Processing Parameters • Environmental Monitoring
Leadership & Management Skills • Facilitation and Training • Positive Regard and Motivation • Performance Assessment/Feedback/Coaching • Team Building • Networking	**Chemistry/Microbiology** • Good Laboratory Practices • Latest Instrumentation & Automation • LIMS or Lab Management system • Methods Development • Methods Validation
Communication Skills • Oral • Written • Presentation • Influencing • Negotiation and Conflict Management • Language	**Audit/Assessment (Auditor) Skills** • Pharmaceutical/Biological Operations • Packaging Materials Operations • Bulk Pharmaceutical Chemical (BPC) Op. • ISO 9000 • Process/System Approach
Process Skills • Time Management • Quality Planning • Proposal Preparation • Project Management & Planning • Process Management • Change Management • Problem Solving/Decision making • Management Tools • Risk Analysis & Management	**Suppliers/Contractors/Third Parties** • Quality Assurance of Suppliers • Quality Assurance of Third Parties • Partnership Management
Quality Design & Prevention • Basic Quality Tools • Process Capability and Statistical QC • Process/System Design • Design of Experiments (DOE) • Failure Mode Effect Analysis (FMEA) • Value Engineering/Analysis & Re-Engineering • Benchmarking	**Quality Systems** • Policies/Procedures • Annual Product Review (APR) • Complaints • Failure Investigations/Materials Decisions • Product Release • Change Control • Components, Materials/Warehousing/Dist. • Calibration & Maintenance • Management Notification • Training • Recall • Technology Transfer
Validation • Facilities/Critical Plant Systems (IQ/OQ/PQ) • Production Equipment (IQ/OQ/PQ) • Manufacturing Process Validation • Retrospective Process Validation (data review) • Equipment Cleaning Validation • Computer System Validation	**Customer Awareness/Understanding** • Complaint Handling • Product Audits/Competitive Comparisons • Customer Visits/Interviews • Market/Customer Surveys • Next Operation as Customer (NOAC) • Six Sigma Approach

Fig. 6. Knowledge and Skill Requirements for Today's Quality Professional (Source: Nally, 2007)

Training Plan: To ensure that the individual receives the "right" training at the "right" time, an individual training plan should be created and executed for each individual. The individual's curriculum should include procedural (knowledge) training, usually SOPs, and competency-based skills training (on-the-job training or OJT). Both these types of training should be standardized as much as possible with the same training material used for all trainees. The individual's curriculum will include different levels of training. These can be divided into three levels. The first level is an overview or general training conducted by the site HR or corporate training group as part of a new hire or induction training. The second level is held within the functional area. The third level, most specific to the employee, is one-on-one training (Figure 7). The training plan should include an approximate training time. The site may have an annual or semi-annual training plan that defines what GMP training should be given to functional areas at the site and when.

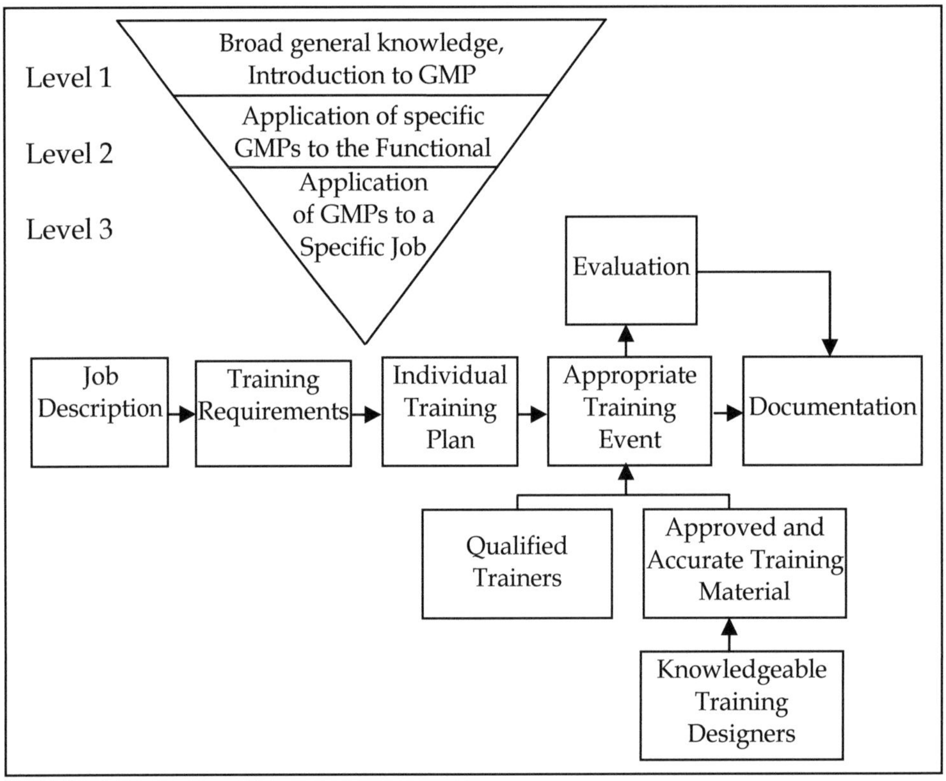

Fig. 7. Training System (Source: Nally, 2007)

Training Materials: Training materials should be designed and developed for most training. Whether the training is given once or many times, the information should be the same. The training material should be clear and well organized. Training materials should contain stated objectives. In addition to the content being trained, the reason behind the training should be explained and stressed. If training GMPs, the impact of the particular training on the production of the product should be explained.

Qualified Trainers: GMP training to be given by qualified personnel, the company should have a procedure and process for qualifying trainers. Minimum requirements for trainers may include some formal education (e.g., Train-the-Trainer course) or experience in presenting training, subject matter expertise in the subject they will be training, understanding of GMPs in terms of how it impacts the specific training they are responsible for, and the knowledge about how to train adults. Trainers should be selected for their ability to help individuals learn. If they are on-the-job trainer, they should be able to demonstrate the skills and also clearly explain how to perform the skill.

Evaluation, Documentation/Record Keeping: Job skills and GMP training should be evaluated. For GMP training, evaluation tools such as questionnaires, case studies, discussions, and other tools may be used. For job skills, a performance-based evaluation is used. The usual method is to have an observer watch the individual in training and complete a checklist. The individual should be able to demonstrate the correct practice without the coaching or help from another individual. The performance checklist is usually signed by the trainee and by a member of management. This document is retained. Evaluations should be performed after the training. The training system and training processes should be documented, possibly in an SOP, describing how the training system works and the type of training included in the training system. Training records should be retained in a documentation system. There should also be a method to ensure that training curricula and training requirements are up-to-date in the event that an individual transfers to another job within the company. Any changes made to curricula should be documented and approved. Training documentation should be readily retrievable (Nally, 2007).

There should be two types of training records:

1. The personal file of each member of staff should contain a record of the training received, indicated by module reference number (see Figure 8).
2. Departmental training records should be maintained, indicating in tabular form the training received by each member of staff (see Figure 9).

ABC Company

Personal Training Record

Name: .... Date Joined Company.....................

Job Title:

1. ....
2. ....
3. ....

Training Record (module ref. and title)	Date

Fig. 8. Personal Training Record (Source: Sharp, 2005)

Name	GI/1	GI/2	GMP/1	GMP/2	GMP/3	GMP/4	GMP/5	STT/1	STT/2

Fig. 9. Company Training Record (Source: Sharp, 2005)

The concept of personal hygiene is described in the subheading of Sanitation and hygiene.

4.11 Premises

Premises must be located, designed, constructed, adapted, and maintained to suit the operations to be carried out. The layout and design of premises must aim to minimize the risk of errors and permit effective cleaning and maintenance in order to avoid cross-contamination, build-up of dust or dirt, and, in general, any adverse effect on the quality of products. Although the most important single factor in the assurance of the quality of medicinal products is the quality of the people who manufacture them, the premises in which they are manufactured will also have an important bearing on the quality of those products (Sharp, 2005). Pertinent consideration should be made prior to the selection of location for construction of pharmaceutical premises or alteration of existing facilities to ensure that the surrounding neighborhood is free form unsanitary environmental condition.

The choices of materials of construction for manufacturing facilities are numerous. Some examples are presented subsequently.

a. Walls. Walls in manufacturing areas, corridors, and packaging areas should be of plaster finish on high-quality concrete blocks or gypsum board. The finish should be smooth, usually with enamel or epoxy paint. They should be washable and able to resist repeated applications of cleaning and disinfecting agents. Internally, there should be no recesses that cannot be cleaned, and a minimum of projecting ledges, shelves, fixtures and fittings.

b. Floors. Floor covering should be selected for durability as well as for cleanability and resistance to the chemicals with which it is likely to come into contact. Terrazzo provides a hard-wearing finish; both tiles and poured-in-place finishes are available. The latter is preferable for manufacturing areas; if tiles are used, care must be taken to ensure effective sealing between the tiles, which, otherwise, could become a harboring area of dirt and microorganisms. Welded vinyl sheeting provides an even, easy to clean surface. Epoxy flooring provides a durable and readily cleanable surface. However, the subsurface finish is extremely important. Where drains or drainage gullies are installed, they should be easily cleanable and trapped to prevent reflux.

c. Ceilings. Suspended ceilings may be provided in office areas, laboratories, toilets, and cafeterias. They usually consist of lay-in acoustical panels of non brittle, non friable, non asbestos and non combustible material. Manufacturing areas require a smooth finish, often of seamless plaster or gypsum board. All ceiling fixtures such as light fittings, air outlets and returns should be designed to assure ease of cleaning and to minimize the potential for accumulation of dust.

d. Services. In the building design, provisions must be made for drains, water, steam, electricity, and other services to allow for ease of maintenance. Access should, ideally, be possible without disruption of activity within the actual rooms provided with the services.

Doors and window-frames should all have a smooth, hard, impervious finish, and should close tightly. Window and door frames should be fitted flush, at least on sides facing inward to processing areas. Doors, except emergency exits, should not open directly from production areas to the outside world. Any emergency exit doors should be kept shut and sealed, and designed so as to be openable only when emergency demands. Despite the space-saving advantages, sliding doors should be avoided because of the difficulty of maintaining the sliding gear in a clean condition.

The layout design of the facility must minimize the possibility of mix-ups or contamination. Sufficient space must be provided to allow adequate separation of adjacent equipment and operations. An example of this includes the spatial separation of packaging lines so that packaging components, bulk product, and finished product cannot intermix between lines and that dust or spillage from one line cannot result in the contamination of adjacent equipment. For example, a common practice is to introduce a physical barrier between the packaging lines. The layout of the manufacturing and support operations must account for efficient material, personnel, and equipment flow patterns. Adequate access control is required to restrict entrance to manufacturing areas. The most efficient and compliant flow pattern is the one that provides for unidirectional flow.

Temperature and humidity need to be controlled primarily for the comfort of operators. The gowning requirements to minimize the potential for microbial contamination from operators are rather stringent and can easily cause personal discomfort, which could, in turn, adversely impact on the aseptic processing. Conditions in the order of 68°F /20°C (65°F/18°C -70°F/21°C) and 45% (40%-50%) relative humidity have been found to be suitable. Independent of gowning requirements, relative humidity ranges must be carefully selected. Continuous relative humidity levels below 15% can cause static electricity discharge and health concerns and levels above 60% can be the source of microbial growth and corrosion (Signore & Jacobs, 2005).

4.11.1 Layout concepts

A very basic block design showing a simple single-storey linear flow layout is given in Figure 10. The internal building requirements vary according to the nature of the operations carried out or type of product produced within the various departments, sections, or rooms (Sharp, 2000). Within the facility there will be various flow-patterns. These flows will be principally of materials and products, and of personnel. Materials will be received, held pending test, released for use, held in store, dispensed for manufacture, and processed into products that are then packaged, tested, and held in quarantine pending release, and then stored pending distribution.

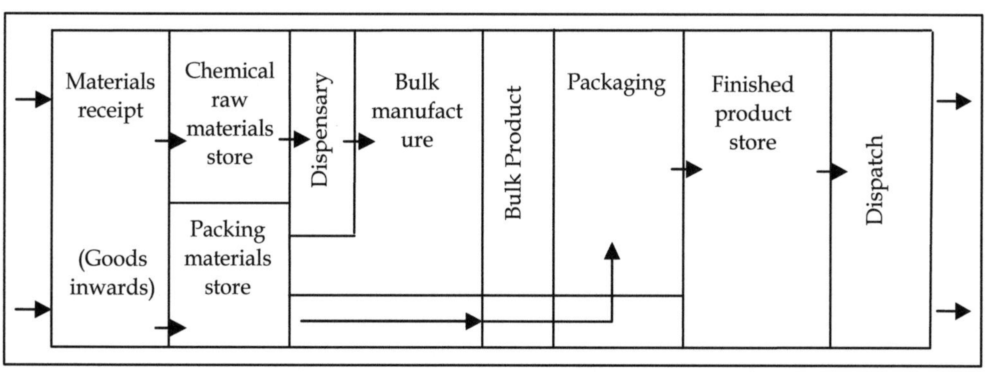

Fig. 10. Simple Single-Story Linear Flow Pattern for Pharmaceutical Manufacturing. Sampling Quarantine and Release Stages not shown. Not a scale (Source: Sharp, 2000)

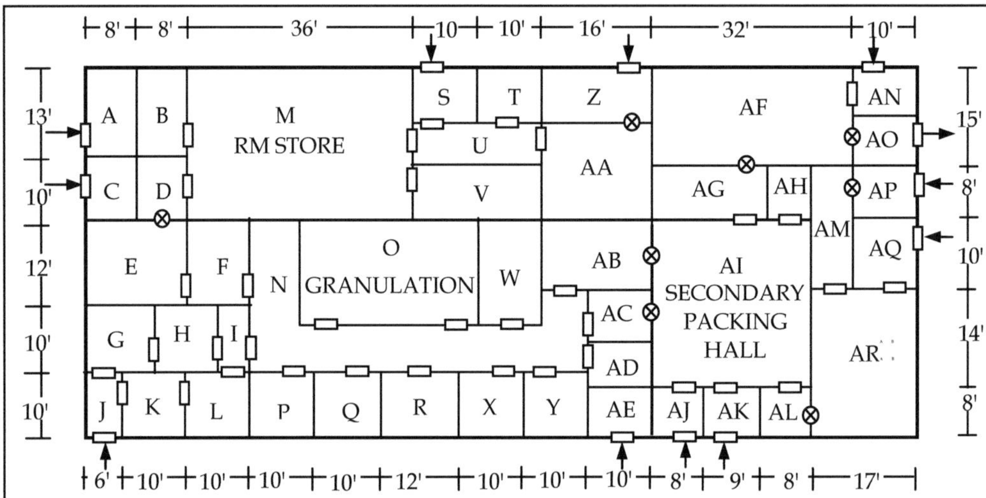

A=Return goods store
B=Special items store
C=Rejected material store
D=Material air lock for dispensing room
E=Dispensing room
F=Raw material (RM)/ Primary packaging material quarantine
G=Gents change room 1
H=Gents change room 2
I=Air lock for manufacturing area entry
J=Air lock for change room entry
K=Ladies change room 1
L=Ladies change room 2
M=Raw material store
N=7 ft. wide corridor
O=Granulation room
P=Production office
Q=Intermediate quarantine 1
R=Compression room

S=Change room for RM store
T=Sampling room
U=Store lobby
V=Primary packaging material store
W=Coating room
X=Intermediate quarantine 2
Y=Washing room
Z=Raw material receiving room
AA=Raw material quarantine room
AB=Blister packaging room
AC=Strip packaging room
AD=In-process control room
AE=Electrical panel room
AF=Finished goods (FG) store
AG=Finished goods quarantine
AH=Over printing room
AI=Secondary packing hall
AJ=Gents change to secondary packing hall
AK=Ladies change to secondary packing hall

AL=Material air lock to secondary packing hall
AM=Secondary packing material quarantine
AN=Change room to FG store
AO=Material air lock for FG dispatch
AP=Material Air lock for secondary packing materials
AQ=Change room to secondary packing material store
AR=Secondary packing material store

□ = Door
⊗ = Hatch for material transfer

Stores area (A-D, M, S-V, Z, AA, AF-AH, AM-AR) = 3534 sq. ft.
Production area (E-L, N-R, W-Y, AB-AE) = 2816 sq. ft.
Packing area (AI-AL) = 800 sq ft
Total area (A-AR)= 7150 sq. ft.

Fig. 11. Single-Story Linear Flow Pattern for a Tablet Manufacturing Unit (Detail Design) QC Area is not shown. Not a Scale

A horizontal layout plan for manufacturing tablet dosage form with detail drawing is shown in Figure 11. The layout is considered as the smallest possible design of 7150 sq. ft. area covering all requirements of manufacturing and packaging including stores area for a tablet manufacturing unit. The design does not cover QC and other supporting areas such as canteen, engineering and/or administration rooms.

Most of the required pipe works are taken from inside the wall in concealed manner. Exposed pipelines should not touch walls but be suspended from or be supported by brackets, sufficiently separated to allow through cleaning. The pipe works at exposed surfaces are required to be clearly marked with direction flow of the utilities used. In general all the exposed pipelined inside the processing area is made of SS 304 grade with exception of SS 316L for those used in supply of purified water. Different colour codes are used for identification of the utility pipe lines (Table 3).

Utility used	Pipe colour code	Colour of letter for legend
Pressurized steam	Red	Black
Compressed air	Orange	Black
Vacuum	Yellow	Black
Nitrogen	Grey	Black
Oxygen	Light Blue	Black
LPG	Dark Green	Black
Carbon dioxide	Violet	Black
Distilled water (water for injection)	White	Black
Deionized water	Light Green	Black
Well water/ water for fire fighting	Black	White

Table 3. Identification of Pipelines (Source: ASEAN, 2000)

A manufacturing facility, built and finished as designed, still requires various other inputs, in addition to people, equipment, and materials, before the manufacture of products can begin. These can be referred to collectively as "plant services, systems, and utilities." Heating, ventilation, and air-conditioning (HVAC), Lighting, Water for pharmaceutical use (WPU), Electricity and Gases/Compressed air are considered as the major plant services, systems and utilities requirements for a pharmaceutical unit.

4.11.2 Heating, Ventilation and Air-Conditioning (HVAC)

"Natural" ventilation (via doors and windows) is not acceptable in medicine manufacturing area because of the risk of product contamination from the outside world (particulate matter, dust, dirt, microorganisms, insects, etc.). Control of humidity is also important for a number of products, particularly effervescent products. Windows from production areas to the outside world should thus normally remain closed, and preferably not be openable. External doors should be air locked, or only openable in an emergency. Therefore, some form of forced; conditioned, usually filtered, air supply is required with proper heating, ventilation and air-conditioning (HVAC) system (WHOTRS 937, 2006).

HVAC play an important role in ensuring the manufacture of quality medicinal products. A well designed HVAC system will also provide comfortable conditions for operators. HVAC system design influences architectural layouts with regard to items such as airlock positions, doorways and lobbies. The architectural components have an effect on room pressure differential cascades and cross-contamination control. The prevention of contamination and cross-contamination is an essential design consideration of the HVAC system. In view of these critical aspects, the design of the HVAC system should be considered at the concept design stage of a pharmaceutical manufacturing plant.

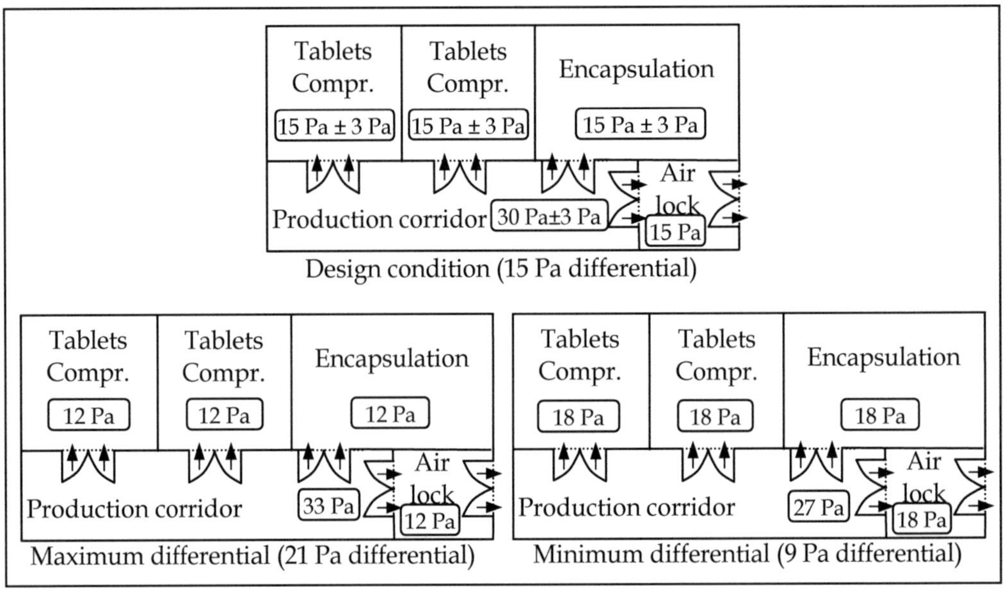

Fig. 12. Examples of Pressure Cascade (Source: WHOTRS 937, 2006)

While designing the HVAC system following parameters are required to be considered for operation of oral solid dosage (OSD) formulations avoiding cross contamination. The operating room should be of Class 100000 condition. The dispensing room used for weighing raw materials and sampling room used for raw material sampling for testing should be provided with reverse laminar air flow system with Class 100 condition. The most widely accepted pressure differential for achieving containment between two adjacent zones is 15 Pa, but pressure differentials of between 5 Pa and 20 Pa may be acceptable (WHO TRS 937, 2006). The door in the room should always open towards the high pressure area (Figure 12). The air changes per hour in the operating room that is the times the volume of air supplied per hour in comparison to the volume of room should be at least 20 per hour. In general room temperature and humidity maintained at 22±3°C and 50±5% respectably have been found to be suitable for personal comfort.

The HVAC system may be designed either with 100% fresh air system or with 85-90% reticulated air system. In case of recirculation system the supply air stream is to be provided with high-efficiency particulate air (HEPA) filters to remove contaminants, and thus prevent cross-contamination. Recirculated air should not be used if there are no HEPA filters installed in the system, unless the air handling system is serving a single product facility. In case of 100% fresh air system the degree of filtration on the supply air and exhaust air should be determined depend on the level of cleanliness required; exhaust air contaminants and local environmental regulations. The required degree of air cleanliness in most OSD manufacturing facilities can normally be achieved without use of HEPA filters. In locations with different climatic conditions, difference between a systems operating on 100% fresh air versus a system utilizing recirculated air with HEPA filtration should be considered in the context of cost of installation as against operating cost.

4.11.3 Lighting

Lighting levels should be adequate to permit operators to do their work properly, accurately, and attentively. Lighting of production and packaging areas should be sufficiently bright to enable good vision (Table 4). Although daylight is preferable from a number of aspects, it needs to be noted that a number of pharmaceutical products and materials are affected by UV light. The design and layout of a modern pharmaceutical factory also usually make artificial lighting inevitable. It should be installed so as not to create uncleanable dust traps, e.g., preferably flush-fitted to the ceiling, or with smooth easily accessible and cleanable surfaces. To avoid photo degradation, a suitable light using sodium vapor lamp is to be provided with dispensing/sampling booth for weighing/sampling of highly light sensitive materials.

Illumination intensity (in Lux)	Specific Area
20	- narrow corridor, aisle
50	- warehouse for big size containers, corridor for personal traffic
100	- corridor for traffic of personnel and forklift, break room, locker rooms, rest rooms, utility rooms, staircase lobby
200	- workshop, warehouse
300	- laboratory
500	- offices with reading activities, production room, first aid room
750	- draft room
1000	- visual inspection
1 foot candle = 1 lumen/ feet^2 = 10.764 lux (ft.c) lm/ ft^2	

Table 4. The Recommended Illumination in Premises (Source: ASEAN, 2000)

4.11.4 Water for Pharmaceutical Use (WPU)

Water is the most widely used substance in the production, processing and formulation of pharmaceutical products. It has unique chemical properties due to its polarity and hydrogen bonds. This means it is able to dissolve, absorb, adsorb or suspend many different compounds. These include contaminants that may represent hazards in themselves or that may be able to react with intended product substances, resulting in hazards to health (WHOTRS 929, 2005).

Different grades of water quality are required depending on the route of administration of the pharmaceutical products. Control of the quality of water throughout the production, storage and distribution processes, including microbiological and chemical quality, is a major concern. Unlike other product and process ingredients, water is usually drawn from a system on demand, and is not subject to testing and batch or lot release before use. Assurance of quality to meet the on-demand expectation is, therefore, essential. Additionally, certain microbiological tests may require periods of incubation and, therefore, the results are likely to lag behind the water use. Control of the microbiological quality of WPU is a high priority. Some types of microorganism may proliferate in water treatment components and in the storage and distribution systems. It is very important to minimize microbial contamination by routine sanitization and taking appropriate measures to prevent microbial proliferation (WHOTRS 929, 2005).

Pharmaceutical water production, storage and distribution systems should be designed, installed, commissioned, validated and maintained to ensure the reliable production of water of an appropriate quality. Where chemical sanitization of the water systems is part of the biocontamination control programme, a validated procedure should be followed to ensure that the sanitizing agent has been effectively removed. Steam sanitization is considered as one of the best alternative for WPU system. Water may be originally obtained from a number of sources. Water from wells or bore-holes, given suitable treatment, has been used to manufacture pharmaceuticals. In many countries, the most usual source is normal mains, or town, water of potable (drinkable) quality. For pharmaceutical purposes, it may be considered that there are four basic grades of water:

Drinking Water is unmodified except for limited treatment of the water derived from a natural or stored source. Examples of natural sources include springs, wells, rivers, lakes and the sea. The condition of the source water will dictate the treatment required to render it safe for human consumption (drinking). It is common for drinking-water to be derived from a public water supply that may be a combination of more than one of the natural sources listed above. Typical processes employed at a user plant or by a water supply authority include: filtration, softening, disinfection or sanitization (e.g. by sodium hypochlorite (chlorine) injection), iron (ferrous) removal, precipitation, and reduction of specific inorganic/organic materials.

Purified Water (PW) should be prepared from a potable water source as a minimum-quality feed-water, should meet the pharmacopoeial specifications for chemical and microbiological purity, and should be protected from recontamination and microbial proliferation. There are no prescribed methods for the production of PW in the pharmacopoeias. Any appropriate qualified purification technique or sequence of techniques may be used to prepare PW. Typically ion exchange, ultra filtration and/or reverse osmosis processes are used. Electodionization or Distillation can also be used. Ambient-temperature PW systems are especially susceptible to microbiological contamination, particularly when equipment is static during periods of no or low demand for water. It is essential to consider the following mechanisms for the efficient control of contamination.

- The headspace in the storage vessel is an area of risk where water droplets and air can come into contact at temperatures that encourage the proliferation of microbiological organisms. The water distribution loop should be configured to ensure that the headspace of the storage vessel is effectively wetted by a flow of water. The use of spray ball or distributor devices to wet the surfaces should be considered.
- Nozzles within the storage vessels should be configured to avoid dead zones where microbiological contamination might be harboured.
- Vent filters are fitted to storage vessels to allow the internal level of liquid to fluctuate. The filters should be bacteria-retentive, hydrophobic and ideally be configured to allow in situ testing of integrity. Offline testing is also acceptable.
- Where pressure-relief valves and bursting discs are provided on storage vessels to protect them from over-pressurization, these devices should be of a sanitary design.
- Maintenance of continuous turbulent flow circulation within water distribution systems reduces the propensity for the formation of biofilms.

- For ambient temperature systems, pipework should be isolated from adjacent hot pipes. Deadlegs in the pipework installation greater than 1.5 times the branch diameter should be avoided.
- Pressure gauges should be separated from the system by membranes.
- Hygienic pattern diaphragm valves should be used.
- Pipework should be laid to falls to allow drainage.
- The growth of microorganisms can be inhibited by: ultraviolet radiation sources in pipe work; maintaining the system heated (guidance temperature 70–80 °C); sanitizing the system periodically using hot water (guidance temperature >70 °C); sterilizing or sanitizing the system periodically using superheated hot water or clean steam; and routine chemical sanitization using ozone or other suitable chemical agents. When chemical sanitization is used, it is essential to prove that the agent has been removed prior to using the water. Ozone can be effectively removed by using ultraviolet radiation.

4.11.5 Electricity

In general the electricity supply is made through concealed wiring with five wires (three phase wires, one neutral wire and one ground wire) for three-phase connections and three wires (one phase wire, one neutral wire and one ground wire) for single-phase connections using suitable size wires. Conductors of a three-phase system are usually identified by a color code, to allow for balanced loading and to assure the correct phase rotation for induction motors. Colors used may adhere to International Standard IEC 60446, older standards or to no standard at all and may vary even within a single installation. For example, in the U.S. and Canada, different color codes are used for grounded (earthed) and ungrounded systems (Wikipedia. (2012b). In case of India, Pakistan and Nepal, generally red, yellow and blue color wires are used for three phases L1, L2 and L3 connections, black for neutral and green for ground connections.

Continuity of electricity supply is essential for a number of systems or processes (air supply and extraction, particularly for sterile manufacture; fermentation plants; incubators; stability chambers) and thus backup systems should be available in the event of mains failure. Ideally, there should be automatic changeover and reset from mains to emergency generator supply. Certain equipment (computers, microprocessor control systems, some analytical instruments) may need voltage stabilization in order to operate reliably (Sharp, 2005).

4.11.6 Gases/compressed air

Various gases may be used for a variety of purposes, for example, inert gases used as a protective "blanket" or to displace air in an ampoule head-space, as propellants in aerosol products, as sterilants (e.g., ethylene oxide), as a source of flame in glass ampoule sealing. Any gas that may come into contact with a product (or product contact surfaces), or that is used in the manufacture of a product, must be treated as if it were a raw material and must therefore be subject to standard quality control procedures to ensure that it conforms to predetermined quality standards. A number of gases are used in laboratory test procedures. If these are not of the required or specified quality, then the reliability of the test results may suffer. Gas pipelines, from cylinders or from bulk gas storage, should be clearly marked as to contents. It should not be possible to switch pipelines and connections and thus to supply the wrong gas. Dedicated, pin-indexed valves and connections, as (one hopes) used in hospital gas supply lines, should be employed where possible.

Gases (including compressed air) may need to be filtered when supplied to production areas generally. Gases (including compressed air), when supplied to sterile products manufacturing areas (and other controlled environments), will certainly need to be filtered (as close to the point of use as possible) to ensure that they conform to the particulate and microbial standards for the area (Sharp, 2005). In general the compressed air coming in contact with OSD products is recommend to be oil and moisture free with particulate matter filtered through initial coarse and terminal 1μ filters.

4.12 Equipment

Manufacturing equipment should be capable of producing products, materials, and intermediates that are intended and that conform to the required or specified quality characteristics. Furthermore, the equipment must be designed and built so that it is possible (and relatively easily possible) to clean it thoroughly. Surfaces that come into contact with products should have smooth, polished finishes, with no recesses, crevices, difficult corners, uneven joints, dead-legs, projections, or rough welds to harbor contamination or make cleaning difficult. Equipment must also be capable of withstanding repeated, thorough cleaning. Traces of previous product, at levels that might be acceptable in other industries, are totally unacceptable in the manufacture of medicines.

As far as the properties of the materials of construction of the equipment are concerned, there are two major concerns:

1. The possibility of contamination, or degradation, of the product by the material from which the equipment is constructed
2. The action of the product, or material in-process, on the material from which the equipment is constructed

Contamination of product can arise from shedding or leaching of contaminants from the equipment into the product or from reaction between the product and the material of the equipment. It is worth remembering that there are two aspects of the potential release of product contaminants by equipment: they could be toxic to patients, even in very small amounts, and they could cause product decomposition. As an example of the latter – penicillin can be inactivated by trace heavy metals.

Fixed equipment should be installed, piped in, and supplied with services in a manner that creates a minimum of recesses, corners, or areas that are difficult for cleaning. The equipment should be designed and located to suit the processes and products for which it is to be used. It must be shown to be capable of carrying out the processes for which it is used (that is, it should be properly commissioned, or "qualified") and of being operated to the necessary hygienic standards. It should be maintained so as to be fit to perform its functions, and it should be easily and conveniently cleanable, both inside and out. Parts that come into contact with materials being processed should be non reactive or absorptive with respect to those materials. Equipment should be kept and stored in a clean condition and checked for cleanliness before each use.

Between batches (or "campaigns") all manufacturing equipment must be thoroughly cleaned and (as necessary) disinfected or sterilized. There should be written procedures for doing this, which must be followed exactly. The cleaning program consists of two parts—the validation of the processes and detergents/sanitization agents and the day-to-day use of the validated processes and qualified detergents and sanitizers. Many cleaning processes are automated. These falls into two classes: clean in place (CIP) and clean out of place (COP). The CIP systems have their equipment provided with hard-piped services with cleaning solutions. The cleaning process is automated and usually is documented through a printout of the automation system. The COP systems consist of bringing the equipment to a cleaning station or placing the equipment in an automated washer.

Effectiveness of cleaning is a function of a number of factors, including time, temperature, and rate of turbulent flow of the cleaning solution; the concentration of chemical cleaning agents in the cleaning solution; and the surface finish (smoothness or roughness) of the surfaces to be cleaned. All these factors interact. For example, all other things being equal, it will take a longer time to completely clean a relatively rough internal surface as compared to a high-polish, smooth one. Higher temperatures will need lower times and flow rates, and so on. Cleaning solutions commonly employed contain caustic agents and detergents, and it must be remembered that, before cleaning is complete, it is necessary to ensure removal of the cleaning agents themselves. That is, there must be a rinsing stage, using (for aqueous products) water of a quality appropriate to, and compatible with, the products to be manufactured in the equipment.

4.13 Materials

A flow diagram illustrating the ordering, receipt, sampling, approval (or rejection), and dispensing of starting materials is shown in Figure 13. The purchasing department orders the material on the basis of a starting material specification provided to them by the QC. Purchasing department sends the order to an approved supplier, which is a company that has been approved, jointly by the QA, QC and production to supply the material in question. To continue with the flow-diagram, at the time of placing the order, the purchasing department sends a copy of the purchase order to the goods inwards (or receiving) department, where it is (accessibly) retained, pending the receipt of the goods.

On receipt, the goods are carefully examined by a responsible member of the goods inwards department for general condition, and to check for any signs of external damage, soiling, or dampness. At the same time, the labeled identity of the delivered material is checked and compared with the goods inwards copy of the purchase order, and with any supplier's delivery, or advice note, to confirm that the material delivered is, as far as its labeling is concerned, the material that was ordered. A check is also made at this time on all the identity labels on the containers in a multi container delivery. Different suppliers' batches within one delivery are to be segregated, one from another, with a different internal lot number for each entered on the QUARANTINE label, which is applied to each container. If all the containers in the delivery appear to be correct and in good condition, the goods inwards department then place on each container a QUARANTINE label (see Figure 14), with the entries for "Code Number," "Name of Material," "Lot Number," and "Date Received" are completed.

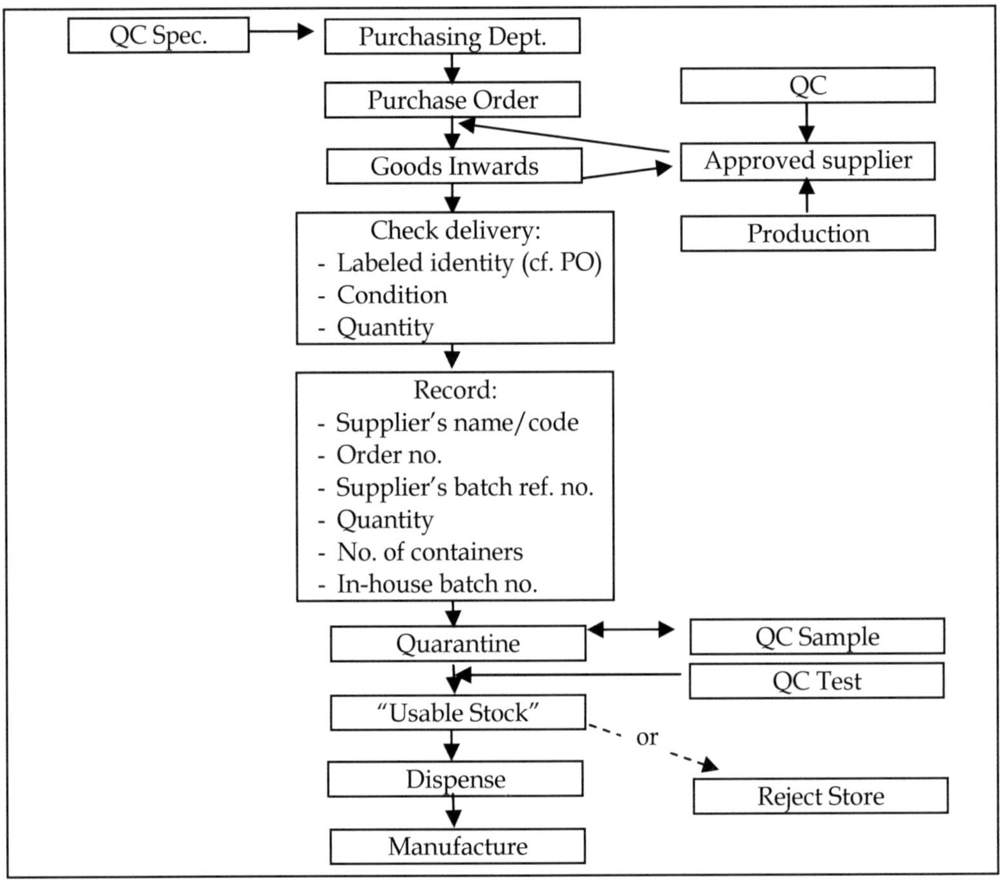

Fig. 13. Components/Starting Materials Flow Chart (Source: Sharp, 2005)

Notes:

a. It is useful to have the QUARANTINE label, and the RELEASED and REJECTED labels printed in different colors, for example, for QUARANTINE, black print on a yellow background, for RELEASED green print on a white background, and for REJECTED red print on a white background.
b. In the examples shown, the intention is that, when the QC decision is made, the RELEASED (or REJECTED) label should be applied just over the lower QUARANTINE panel. This may seem an infringement of the golden rule about not applying new labels over old ones, but here (if the, say, RELEASED label falls off, or is removed) the labeled status of the material reverts to QUARANTINE, i.e., it is fail-safe. The benefit of the labeling system illustrated is the elimination of any possible error in transcribing the information originally entered on the QUARANTINE label.
c. It is important that at least the QUARANTINE label is in a house style, with company name or logo, to avoid confusion with any other identity and status labels (e.g., those applied by vendors) that may already be on the container.

Goods inwards then completes a materials receiving report (Figure 15) in four copies, retaining one copy and sending the other three to QC. They then make the appropriate

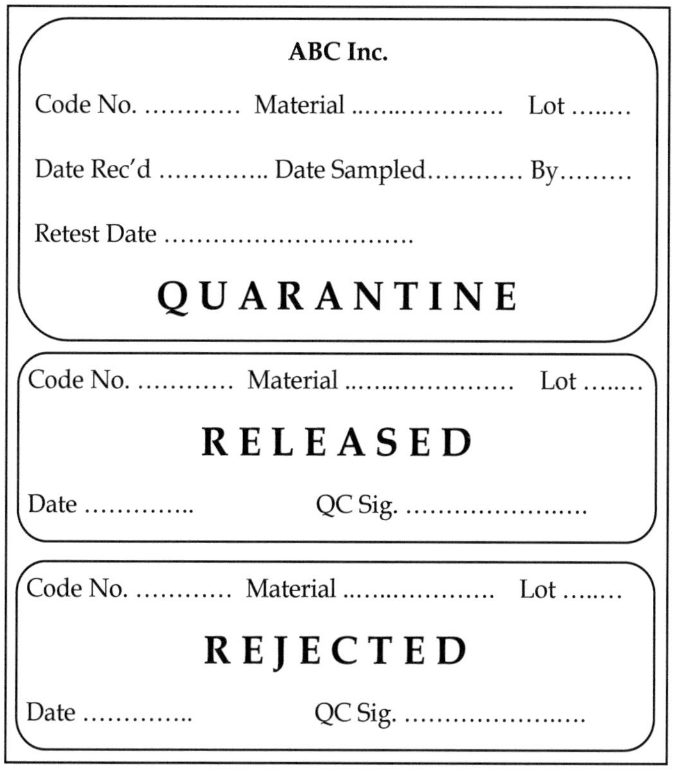

Fig. 14. Quarantine, Releases and Rejected Labels (Source: Sharp, 2005)

entries (except for entries in the last two columns) in a departmental running record – a "Materials Delivery Record" (Figure 16). This can be a printed sheet or card, or manually drawn up in a record book (or a computer record).

Receipt of the copies of the materials receiving report alerts the QC that the material has been delivered, and is required to be sampled. Following sampling ("date sampled__" and "by__" on the QUARANTINE label completed by the sampler) and testing against the agreed specification, the QC decision is entered on the copies of materials receiving report, one copy being sent to the purchasing department (for information), one to materials inventory control (so, if material is released, it may be allocated to manufacturing batches), and one retained on QC file, with the full analytical report. An authorized member of the QC then places a RELEASED (or REJECTED as appropriate) label, over the QUARANTINE portion, with the necessary details entered. S/he also enters a date at "retest date__" on the original label, to indicate when the material is due for reexamination.

On receipt of the QC decision, goods inwards either moves the released goods into the usable stock area of the stores, or the rejected material to a secure reject store. The two last columns of the material delivery record are then completed ("date approved by QC" and "location").

GOODS INWARDS - MATERIALS RECEIVING REPORT

Material…………………………………… Code No. …………

INSTRUCTIONS:

1. Complete a separate Receiving Report for each delivery, and for each supplier's batch number within a delivery
2. Retain one copy in Goods Inwards file, and send three copies to Quality Control.
3. **Quality Control:** On completion of testing, mark this report, where indicated. "RELEASED," "REJECTED," "HOLD" as appropriate, and send a copy to:
   Purchasing Department
   Materials Inventory Control
   Retain one copy on Quality Control files

Date goods received …………………..
Supplier ………………………………………
Supplier's batch no. …………………..
Quantity received …………………..
Number of containers …………………..
Purchase order no. …………………..
Assigned lot no. …………………..

General condition/cleanliness of delivery
……………………………………………

Delivery examined by (signed) …………………… Date ……….
Remarks/Comments

QUALITY CONTROL DECISION

Fig. 15. Goods Inwards -Materials Receiving Report (Source: Sharp, 2000)

Date of Delivery	Material	Code No.	Lot No.	Quantity	No. of Containers	Supplier No.	Delivery Note	Supplier's Batch No. (s)	Supplier's Name for Materials	Date Approved by QC	Location

Fig. 16. Materials Delivery Report (Source: Sharp, 2005)

4.13.1 Packaging materials

The purchase, receipt, sampling, release, and control of printed packaging materials and primary packaging materials (that is packaging materials that come into direct contact with the product, as compared with secondary packaging materials, which do not) need to be accorded the same level of attention as given to starting materials. Documents, records, and procedures analogous to those outlined above should be employed. All the regulatory requirements are in agreement that components or (starting materials) and containers, etc. should be stored and handled in a manner that will prevent contamination. Some specifically require storage off the floor and suitable spacing "to permit cleaning and inspection." Some guide adds that one of the objectives of storage "in an orderly fashion" is to "permit batch segregation and stock rotation" [FEFO, "first expiry, first out" or FIFO "first in, first out"]. Storage off the floor guards against damage from flooding and liquid spillages. It also permits wet-cleaning of floors, without the risk of wetting the materials. A well-laid-out, orderly store not only permits segregation of different types, lots, and batches of material (hence, aiding against contamination and mix up) and rotation of stock, it also enables more (labor-, management-, and cost-) efficient running of the store.

4.13.2 Sampling of materials for testing

It is also important that the containers in which the materials are received should be cleaned before the goods are placed in quarantine. A record should be made of all goods received (Materials Delivery Record). The GMP requirements agree that received materials (both components or starting materials and packaging materials) should be held in a quarantined state until they have been sampled, tested for compliance with specification, and formally released for use (or rejected and removed from stock). Quarantine status can be established and maintained by status labeling, by secure physical segregation (for example in separate quarantine store, apart form the usable materials store) or by manual or electronic stock control systems. A combination of all three provides the greatest security against inadvertent use of material that has not been approved for use.

The process of sampling can itself pose risks of contamination. For this reason, containers may need to be cleaned prior to sampling—a vacuum system is very effective for a large container. Small containers may be wiped down with an appropriate solvent or distilled water. Containers should be opened for sampling in an acceptable environment that will not expose the material to further risk of contamination. This sampling area may be a designated room near or adjacent to the warehouse with the provision of reverse laminar flow sampling booth maintaining class 100 condition to avoid cross contamination to or by the material being sampled.

The release of components, containers, and closures for use cannot be for an indefinite time. During storage, degradation may occur, moisture may be absorbed, or materials may simply become contaminated during the storage process. Re-evaluation time scales should be developed from historical data, where possible. Except for particularly sensitive materials, a onetime period, often one year, has been established by many manufacturers. Either the product release label or the system should clearly indicate when materials are to be re-evaluated. This re-evaluation will not usually require full testing, but only examination of those parameters known to be subject to change. For infrequently used materials, re-evaluation coincides with just prior to the use of the material.

4.14 Documentation

Good documentation is an essential part of the QA system and, as such, should exist for all aspects of GMP. Its aims are to define the specifications and procedures for all materials and methods of manufacture and control; to ensure that all personnel concerned with manufacture know what to do and when to do it; to ensure that authorized persons have all the information necessary to decide whether or not to release a batch of a medicine for sale, to ensure the existence of documented evidence, traceability, and to provide records and an audit trail that will permit investigation. It ensures the availability of the data needed for validation, review and statistical analysis. The design and use of documents depend upon the manufacturer (WHO TRS 961, 2011).

The various types of documents used should be fully defined in the manufacturer's quality management system (QMS). Documentation may exist in a variety of forms, including paper-based, electronic or photographic media. The main objective of the system of documentation utilized must be to establish, control, monitor and record all activities which directly or indirectly impact on all aspects of the quality of medicinal products. The QMS should include sufficient instructional detail to facilitate a common understanding of the requirements, in addition to providing for sufficient recording of the various processes and evaluation of any observations, so that ongoing application of the requirements may be demonstrated (EudraLex, 2012).

There are two primary types of documentation used to manage and record GMP compliance: instructions (directions, requirements) and records/reports. Appropriate good documentation practice should be applied with respect to the type of document. Suitable controls should be implemented to ensure the accuracy, integrity, availability and legibility of documents. Instruction documents should be free from errors and available in writing (EudraLex, 2012).

'If it's not written down, then it didn't happen!' The basic rules in any GMP regulations specify that the pharmaceutical manufacturer must maintain proper documentation and records. Documentation helps to build up a detailed picture of what a manufacturing function has done in the past and what it is doing now and, thus, it provides a basis for planning what it is going to do in the future. Regulatory inspectors, during their inspections of manufacturing sites, often spend much time examining a company's documents and records. Effective documentation enhances the visibility of the quality assurance system. Issue and use of documents should be under formal control. They should be available to all who need them, and *not* available to those who do not. They should be kept up-to-date, but all revisions should be formal and authorized, not haphazard. The documentation system, overall, should be subject to review. It is vital that systems exist for the removal from active use of outdated or superseded documents. (Sharp, 2005)

In the manufacture of anything as important to human health and well-being as medicinal products, every activity must be preplanned and formally defined in advance. Nothing can be left to chance. There is no room for "playing it by ear" or "by the seat of the pants." Manufacture of consistent quality drug products demands consistent, predetermined, *defined* activity.

The objectives are, in short:

1. To state clearly, in advance and in writing, what is to be done
2. To do it – in accordance with those instructions
3. To record what was done and the results of doing it

The reasons for all this documentation are:

1. To ensure there is no doubt about what has to be done, by having formally approved written instructions for each job, and then following them

2. To define standards for materials, equipment, premises, services, and products
3. To confirm, as work proceeds, that each step has been carried out, and carried out *correctly*, using the correct materials and equipment
4. In the longer term, to keep, for later reference, records of what *has* been done, for example, manufacturing and test records, installation, commissioning, servicing, and maintenance records
5. To enable investigation of complaints, defect reports, and any other problems, and to permit observation of any drifts away from defined quality standards
6. To help decide on, and take, any necessary corrective action (including action to prevent reoccurrence) in the event of any complaint or defect report

Document owners are required to ensure that all aspects of documentation and records management specified in form of SOPs. All associates have the responsibility of ensuring that all GMP activities are performed according to the official SOPs; any deviations in procedure are reported to their supervisor and are adequately documented.

There are various types of procedures that a GMP facility can follow. Given below is a list of the most common types of documents, along with a brief description of each.

Site Master File: A document describing the GMP related activities of the manufacturer.

Quality Manual: A global company document that describes, in paragraph form, the regulations and/or parts of the regulations that the company is required to follow.

Policies: Documents that describe in general terms, and not with step-by-step instructions, how specific GMP aspects (such as security, documentation, health, and responsibilities) will be implemented.

Standard Operating Procedures (SOPs): Step-by-step instructions for performing operational tasks or activities.

Batch Records: These documents are typically used and completed by the manufacturing department. Batch records provide step-by-step instructions for production-related tasks and activities, besides including areas on the batch record itself for documenting such tasks.

Test Methods: These documents are typically used and completed by the quality control (QC) department. Test methods provide step-by-step instructions for testing supplies, materials, products, and other production-related tasks and activities, e.g., environmental monitoring of the GMP facility.

Logbooks: Bound collection of forms used to document activities. Typically, logbooks are used for documenting the operation, maintenance, and calibration of a piece of equipment. Logbooks are also used to record critical activities, e.g., monitoring of clean rooms, solution preparation, recording of deviation, change controls and its corrective action assignment.

4.14.1 Hierarchical document system

A company's controlled GMP document system should be established in a hierarchical manner starting with the general regulations and working downward to more specific documents such as batch records (Figure 17).

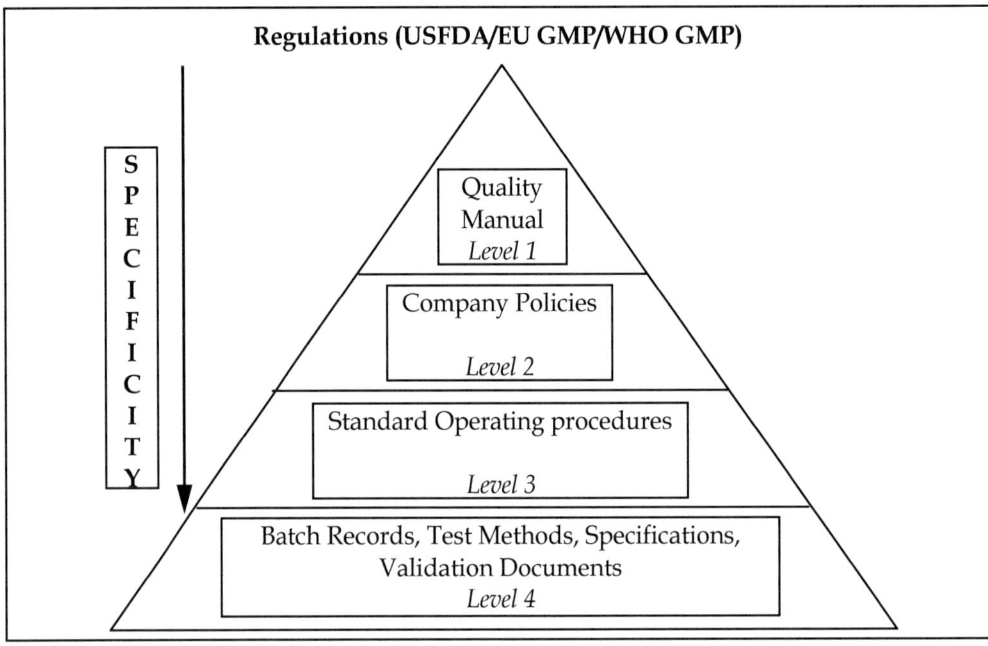

Fig. 17. Document Hierarchical System (Source: Patel & Chotai, 2011)

The regulations that a company is responsible for following (e.g., USFDA/EU GMP/ICH/WHO GMP/Schedule M, etc.) should be at the top of the document pyramid and should govern the directives of the sublevels. The level immediately beneath the regulations, level 1 document (e.g., the Quality Manual), should break the regulations into parts specific to those that the company is required to follow. These documents should establish overall principles and guidelines for how the company plans on developing, documenting, and implementing a GMP-compliant quality system.

The next level, level 2, of documents in the hierarchical document pyramid should further break down the parts of the regulations into specific subjects or topics. These documents (e.g., Company Polices) should establish guidelines with which all subordinate level procedures must comply to ensure consistency across departments. SOPs should be the next level in the document hierarchy after company policy documents. These types of documents should provide specific step-by-step instructions for performing the operational tasks or activities that were talked about in the previous levels. Level 3 documents (i.e., SOPs) should be department specific or function specific. The last level of documents in a document hierarchical structure is level 4 documents. These documents are the most specific in nature, (e.g., batch record, test methods, validation procedures). They apply to a specific department, product, equipment, or process. Level 4 documents provide step-by-step instructions for production-related tasks and activities as well as provide a means for documenting such tasks using, for example, data sheets, forms, or batch records.

The document hierarchy pyramid is one way of organizing a company's documents. More/less levels may be added/subtracted to meet the company's specific needs. Another way the required GMP documentation may be categorized as;

Instructions (directions, or requirements) type:

Specifications: Documents that list the requirements that a supply, material, or product must meet before being released for use or sale. The QC department will compare their test results to specifications to determine if they pass the test.

Manufacturing Formulae, Processing, Packaging and Testing Instructions: Provide detail all the starting materials, equipment and computerized systems (if any) to be used and specify all processing, packaging, sampling and testing instructions. In process controls and process analytical technologies to be employed should be specified where relevant, together with acceptance criteria.

Procedures: (Otherwise known as Standard Operating Procedures, or SOPs), give directions for performing certain operations.

Protocols: Give instructions for performing and recording certain discreet operations.

Technical Agreements: Are agreed between contract givers and acceptors for outsourced activities.

Record/Report type:

Records: Provide evidence of various actions taken to demonstrate compliance with instructions, e.g. activities, events, investigations, and in the case of manufactured batches a history of each batch of product, including its distribution. Records include the raw data which is used to generate other records. For electronic records regulated users should define which data are to be used as raw data. At least, all data on which quality decisions are based should be defined as raw data

Certificates of Analysis: Provide a summary of testing results on samples of products or materials1 together with the evaluation for compliance to a stated specification.

Reports: Document the conduct of particular exercises, projects or investigations, together with results, conclusions and recommendations (EudraLex, 2012).

4.14.2 Manufacturing formula and processing instructions

Approved, written Manufacturing Formula and Processing Instructions should exist for each product and batch size to be manufactured.

The Manufacturing Formula should include:

a. The name of the product, with a product reference code relating to its specification;
b. A description of the pharmaceutical form, strength of the product and batch size;
c. A list of all starting materials to be used, with the amount of each, described; mention should be made of any substance that may disappear in the course of processing;

d. A statement of the expected final yield with the acceptable limits, and of relevant intermediate yields, where applicable

The Processing Instructions should include:

a. A statement of the processing location and the principal equipment to be used;
b. The methods, or reference to the methods, to be used for preparing the critical equipment (e.g. cleaning, assembling, calibrating, sterilizing);
c. Checks that the equipment and work station are clear of previous products, documents or materials not required for the planned process, and that equipment is clean and suitable for use;
d. Detailed stepwise processing instructions [e.g. checks on materials, pre-treatments, sequence for adding materials, critical process parameters (time, temp etc)];
e. The instructions for any in-process controls with their limits;
f. Where necessary, the requirements for bulk storage of the products; including the container, labeling and special storage conditions where applicable;
g. Any special precautions to be observed.

Approved Packaging Instructions for each product, pack size and type should exist. These should include, or have a reference to, the following:

a. Name of the product; including the batch number of bulk and finished product
b. Description of its pharmaceutical form, and strength where applicable;
c. The pack size expressed in terms of the number, weight or volume of the product in the final container;
d. A complete list of all the packaging materials required, including quantities, sizes and types, with the code or reference number relating to the specifications of each packaging material;
e. Where appropriate, an example or reproduction of the relevant printed packaging materials, and specimens indicating where to apply batch number references, and shelf life of the product;
f. Checks that the equipment and work station are clear of previous products, documents or materials not required for the planned packaging operations (line clearance), and that equipment is clean and suitable for use.
g. Special precautions to be observed, including a careful examination of the area and equipment in order to ascertain the line clearance before operations begin;
h. A description of the packaging operation, including any significant subsidiary operations, and equipment to be used;
i. Details of in-process controls with instructions for sampling and acceptance limits.

4.14.3 Batch processing record

A Batch Processing Record should be kept for each batch processed. It should be based on the relevant parts of the currently approved Manufacturing Formula and Processing Instructions, and should contain the following information:

a. The name and batch number of the product;
b. Dates and times of commencement, of significant intermediate stages and of completion of production;

c. Identification (initials) of the operator(s) who performed each significant step of the process and, where appropriate, the name of any person who checked these operations;
d. The batch number and/or analytical control number as well as the quantities of each starting material actually weighed (including the batch number and amount of any recovered or reprocessed material added);
e. Any relevant processing operation or event and major equipment used;
f. A record of the in-process controls and the initials of the person(s) carrying them out, and the results obtained;
g. The product yield obtained at different and pertinent stages of manufacture;
h. Notes on special problems including details, with signed authorisation for any deviation from the Manufacturing Formula and Processing Instructions;
i. Approval by the person responsible for the processing operations.

4.14.4 Batch packaging record

A Batch Packaging Record should be kept for each batch or part batch processed. It should be based on the relevant parts of the Packaging Instructions. The batch packaging record should contain the following information:

a. The name and batch number of the product,
b. The date(s) and times of the packaging operations;
c. Identification (initials) of the operator(s) who performed each significant step of the process and, where appropriate, the name of any person who checked these operations;
d. Records of checks for identity and conformity with the packaging instructions, including the results of in-process controls;
e. Details of the packaging operations carried out, including references to equipment and the packaging lines used;
f. Whenever possible, samples of printed packaging materials used, including specimens of the batch coding, expiry dating and any additional overprinting;
g. Notes on any special problems or unusual events including details, with signed authorization for any deviation from the Packaging Instructions;
h. The quantities and reference number or identification of all printed packaging materials and bulk product issued, used, destroyed or returned to stock and the quantities of obtained product, in order to provide for an adequate reconciliation. Where there are there are robust electronic controls in place during packaging there may be justification for not including this information
i. Approval by the person responsible for the packaging operations

4.15 Holding and distribution

It cannot, indeed must not, be considered that concern for the quality of the products of the pharmaceutical industry may cease at the point where the product is filled, sealed, labeled, and approved or released by QC. True QA should extend right up to the point where the product is delivered to the ultimate consumer – the patient. Certainly, there will come a point where the influence that the manufacturer is able to exert will significantly decline. For example, the manufacturer can do little more than advise the dispensing pharmacist on the correct handling and storage of his drug products. Thereafter, the influence of the manufacturer becomes distinctly tenuous. Despite warnings and advice to patients given in enclosure leaflets, it does seem that many patients neither handle nor take their medicines properly. That said, it is incumbent upon pharmaceutical manufacturers to ensure that having manufactured, packaged and labeled their products, the quality (i.e., "fitness") of these product remains unimpaired for as far along the supply chain as they are able to exert influence. Manufacturers who distribute via external wholesale dealers should thus ensure that any such wholesale dealer is, indeed, in possession of an authorization to do so.

Whatever their size and type, stores or warehouses all have a few things in common – they receive and take in goods or materials, they hold them (hopefully, safely and securely) for a while, and then they send them out again. Put very simply, even naively, its just a matter of goods in, goods hold, goods out. It may all seem simple, but it is worth pausing to think of how important it really is. Pharmaceutical products can do a lot of good – if they are of the right quality and are used properly. If they are incorrect, damaged, soiled, contaminated, wrongly labeled, have the wrong instructions for use, or have deteriorated, they could fail to have their desired good effects, and could be a danger to the health (or even the life) of the ultimate consumer or patient.

The goods in phase provides an opportunity of checking that purchased materials or bought-in products, or finished products delivered from an internal packaging line, are correct and in good condition. The goods inwards (or receiving) office will normally have a copy of the original purchase order, and the supplying company will usually send with the goods some form of delivery (or advice) note. The order, the delivery note, and the labeling on the goods should all be compared with each other to ensure that everything ties up. At the same time, the delivered goods should be checked for quantity, cleanliness, condition, and for any signs of damage or deterioration. If anything appears to be wrong, it should be reported by the goods-inwards staff immediately, so a decision can be made about accepting the delivery or sending the goods back. There also needs also to be a check on the batch number(s) of the delivery, to see if they match up with the batch numbers on the supplier's delivery (or advice) note. When a delivery of a particular product or material consists of more than one supplier's batch number, the different suppliers' batches should be kept apart from each other, as far as recording, handling, and storing – and any sampling and testing that may be required – are concerned.

It is usual to make a distinction between "returns" and "recalled products." Returns are products returned from the market to a manufacturer's warehouse, which are not specifically known to be seriously defective, but which have been sent back by a wholesale or retail customer because of overstocking, superficial damage, or some such similar reason. Recalled products are products that have been withdrawn from the market, at the request of the manufacturer, or the authorities, because of a known or suspected defect.

4.15.1 Goods holding

The goods hold stage is where it is necessary to ensure that the goods remain in good condition, and do not become harmed or damaged through incorrect or unsuitable storage conditions or bad handling. That is, it is important to ensure that quality goods are not reduced to rubbish. All goods must be stored in a clean, neat, orderly way, in conditions that will not affect their quality or cause them to deteriorate in any way. It is not just an issue of looking good. Untidy, scruffy stores are more difficult to run and control. They increase the possibility of mix-up and confusion – mix-up of different types of goods, mix-up of different batches (or lots), mix-up of goods of different status. It is very difficult to have effective stock rotation unless goods are stored in an orderly fashion.

4.15.2 Goods out — distribution of products

Goods out might well be the last chance of checking and ensuring that everything is in order before the goods leave a manufacturer's hands, to the next step in the distribution chain, on their way to the consumer. It cannot be overstressed that people in stores and warehouses play a vital part in the QA of pharmaceutical products. They must be properly trained and fully aware of the significance of the job they are doing. Particular care is necessary in the picking and assembly of orders for dispatch. It is vitally important to ensure that the items picked are as specified in the customer's order. But it goes further than that. This is perhaps the last chance to check that everything is OK. It is not only important to ensure that the right amounts of the right products, of the right strengths and sizes, are being picked for dispatch. It is also important that a watchful eye is kept open to check that the products being picked are in good condition, that they have been approved for distribution, and that they have not passed their expiry date (or shelf life).

It is necessary to make, and keep, a record of each order that is dispatched, which shows:

- Date of dispatch of goods
- Customer's name and address
- Quantity, name, batch number, and expiry date of each product dispatched

Distribution records must be constructed and procedures established to facilitate recall of defective product. A requisite of the system is approval and specific release of each lot of drug by the QC function before distribution can occur. This control of finished goods for shipment allows only those drugs into commerce that have been shown by testing to conform to appropriate requirements. The manufacturer must maintain records of all distribution transactions involving in process or finished goods. All records should be indexed by either the manufacturing batch lot number of the packaging control number as a means of accountability until the shipment passes from the direct control of the manufacturer. This type of indexing permits an efficient determination of the receiver of a lot to be recalled since only one shipment record need be examined. Depending on the marketing procedures of the individual company, distribution records may list shipments to consignees for packaging or labeling, or to an independent distributor, a wholesaler, a retail pharmacist, a physician, or possibly the ultimate consumer. All distribution records should be maintained for a minimum 3-year period after the distribution process for any control number has been completed. If expiration dating is used for a product, distribution records must be maintained at least for one year past the expiration date of the product.

5. Conclusion

GMP is a production and testing practice that helps to ensure in built quality product. Many countries have legislated that pharmaceutical companies must follow GMP procedures, and have created their own GMP guidelines that correspond with their legislation. Basic concepts of all of these guidelines remain more or less similar to the ultimate goals of safeguarding the health of the patient as well as producing good quality medicines.

The holder of a manufacturing authorization must manufacture quality medicines so as to ensure the products fit for the intended use, comply with the requirement of marketing authorization and place patients in safe with adequacy, quality and efficacy of the product. Quality objective can be achieved only through careful planning and implementation of QA system and practical implementation of GMP. The effective implementation of GMP requires extensive care and knowledge about the different components of GMP that should be incorporated form the inception of the manufacturing building and product development till the production. *The compliance to QA/GMP does not happen by accident.* The GMP compliance can be achieved as the result of careful planning and installation of quality system. The manufacturers remain responsible for product quality till the shelf life of the product. The effective implementation of GMP requires top level commitment and support from all level of employees of the organization and different external bodies such as government regulatory agencies, material suppliers, distributor, wholesalers, retailers, medical practitioners and the end users of the medicines.

6. References

ASEAN. (2000). *ASEAN Operational Manual for Implementation of GMP,* (Edition 2000), Indonesian National GMP Team ASEAN

Chaloner-Larsson, G., Anderson, R., Filho, M.A.F.C., & Herrera, J.F.G. (1997). Part 2: Validation In: *A WHO guide to good manufacturing practice (GMP) requirements,* World Health Organization, Geneva

21CFR211. (2011). PART 211; CURRENT GOOD MANUFACTURING PRACTICE FOR FINISHED PHARMACEUTICALS, *TITLE 21--FOOD AND DRUGS, CHAPTER I--FOOD AND DRUG ADMINISTRATION, DEPARTMENT OF HEALTH AND HUMAN SERVICES SUBCHAPTER C--DRUGS: GENERAL,* [Code of Federal Regulations, Title 21, Volume 4, Revised as of April 1, 2011], 21.03.2012, <http://www.accessdata.fda.gov/scripts/cdrh/cfdocs/cfcfr/CFRSearch.cfm?CFRPart=211&showFR=1>

EudraLex. (2012). EudraLex - Volume 4 Good manufacturing practice (GMP) Guidelines, 23.03.2012, <http://ec.europa.eu/health/documents/eudralex/vol-4/index_en.htm>

Huber, L. (2012). *Validation of Analytical Methods and Procedures,* 25.03.2012, <http://www.labcompliance.com/tutorial/methods/default.aspx >

Immel, B. K. (2005). A Brief History of the GMPs, *Regulatory Compliance Newsletter, The GMP Labeling System,* (25.03.2012), http://www.gmplabeling.com/news_letters/news1105.pdf

Lund, W. (1994). Good manufacturing practices. *The Pharmaceutical Codex: Principle and Practice of Pharmaceutics.* London: The Pharmaceutical Press. Twelfth Edition, PP. 362-397.

Nally, J. D. (Ed.) (2007). *Good Manufacturing Practices for Pharmaceuticals,* Sixth Edition, Informa Healthcare USA, Inc., ISBN 10: 0-8593-3972-3 & ISBN 13: 978-0-8493-3972-1, New York

Nally, J., & Kieffer, RG. (1998). *GMP Compliance, Productivity and Quality*. Ch. 13. Interpharm, PP 465–466

Patel KT, & Chotai NP. (2011). Documentation and records: Harmonized GMP requirements. *Journal of Young Pharmacists* [serial online] 2011 [cited 2012 May 1]; 3:138-50. Available from: <http://www.jyoungpharm.in/text.asp?2011/3/2/138/80303>

PIC/S Secretariat (Ed.) (2004). GUIDE TO GOOD MANUFACTURING PRACTICE FOR MEDICINAL PRODUCTS, *PHARMACEUTICAL INSPECTION CONVENTION/ PHARMACEUTICAL INSPECTION CO-OPERATION SCHEME PE 009-2 1 July 2004*, Geneva

Schedule M. GOOD MANUFACTURING PRACTICES AND REQUIREMENTS OF PREMISES, PLANT AND EQUIPMENT FOR PHARMACEUTICAL PRODUCTS, 25.03.2012, http://www.cdsco.nic.in/html/GMP/ScheduleM(GMP).pdf

Sharp, J. (1991). Wider aspects of GMP. *Good Manufacturing Practice: Philosophy and Applications*. Illinois: Interpharm Press, PP. 71-79.

Sharp, J. (2000). *Quality in the Manufacture of Medicines and other Healthcare Products*, Pharmaceutical Press, ISBN 0- 85369-431-1, London

Sharp, J. (2005). *Good Pharmaceutical Manufacturing Practice Rationale and Compliance*, CRC Press, ISBN 0-8493-1994-3, Washington, D.C.

Signore, A. A., & Jacobs, T. (Eds.) (2005). *Good Design Practices for GMP Pharmaceutical Facilities*, Taylor & Francis Group, ISBN 10: 0-8247-5463-8 & ISBN 13: 978-0-247-5463-1, Boca Raton

US FDA. (2001). Improving Public Health Through Human Drugs, *CDER 2001 Report to the Nation, Food and Drug Administration, Center for Drug Evaluation and Research*

US FDA. (2004). Guidance for Industry, Quality Systems Approach to Pharmaceutical Current Good Manufacturing Practice Regulations, *Food and Drug Administration, Center for Drug Evaluation and Research (CDER), Center for Biologics Evaluation and Research (CBER), Center for Veterinary Medicine, Office of Regulatory Affairs (ORA)*, Rockville, MD, http://www.fda.gov/cvm/guidance/published.html

WHOTRS823. (1992). *WHO expert committee on specifications for pharmaceutical preparations: thirty-second report. WHO Technical Report Series: 823*, ISBN 92 4140823 6, ISSN 0512-3054, Geneva

WHOTR929. (2005). Annex 3 WHO Good Manufacturing Practices: water for pharmaceutical use, In; *WHO expert committee on specifications for pharmaceutical preparations Thirty-ninth report WHO Technical Report Series 929*, PP. 40-58, ISBN 92 4 120929 1, ISSN 0512-3054, Geneva

WHOTR937. (2006). Annex 2 Supplementary guidelines on good manufacturing practices for heating, ventilation and air-conditioning systems for non-sterile pharmaceutical dosage forms, In; *WHO expert committee on specifications for pharmaceutical preparations Fortieth report WHO Technical Report Series 937*, PP. 45-84, Geneva

WHOTRS961. (2011). Annex 3 WHO good manufacturing practices: main principles for pharmaceutical products, In; *WHO expert committee on specifications for pharmaceutical preparations Forty-fifth report WHO Technical Report Series 961*, PP. 94-147, ISBN 978 92 4 120961 8, ISSN 0512-3054, Geneva

Wikipedia. (2012a). Good manufacturing practice From Wikipedia, the free encyclopedia, 25.03.2012, http://en.wikipedia.org/wiki/Good_Manufacturing_Practice

Wikipedia, (2012b). Three-phase electric power from Wikipedia, the free encyclopedia, 01.05.2012, http://en.wikipedia.org/wiki/Three-phase_electric_power